"A winner . . . Deftly explores the relationship between the former NBA superstars that started at arm's length [and] became a lasting friendship."
—*USA Today*

"A riveting and pag̲_____ y captures the defining moments _____ new and previously untold stories _____ why 'the Game' will always belong to _____ —Bill Walton

"An exhilarating ride down one of the most competitive rivalries ever."
—Pat Riley

"At long last the great book on Bird and Magic—their own account, told from behind the scenes, inside huddles, confidential phone conversations, backseats of cars, and most importantly, from their inner hearts . . . Brilliantly told with the help of prize-winning writer Jackie MacMullan."
—Sally Jenkins, co-author, with Lance Armstrong, of *It's Not About the Bike*

"Bird and Johnson's account of how much they grew to care about each other while maintaining their ferocity is especially uplifting . . . If ever there was a two-man Dream Team, they were it."
—*New York Times Book Review*

"*When The Game Was Ours* is the ultimate insiders' account of the rivalry, the friendship, the tension and the bond between Bird and Magic that launched the modern NBA. A real treat for all hoops fans."
—Tom Verducci, co-author with Joe Torre, of *The Yankee Years*

"You know that game where you pick a certain number of characters for your favorite dinner party of all time? I just spent a couple of nights with Larry and Magic in the lyrical *When the Game Was Ours*, and they should be in the mix. They're funny, frank, anecdotal and just plain interesting. This book is terrific."
—Leigh Montville, author of *Ted Williams* and *The Big Bam*

"A terrific read."
—*Sports Illustrated*

WHEN THE GAME

LARRY BIRD &

HarperCollins*Publishers*
Boston   New York

WAS OURS

EARVIN "MAGIC" JOHNSON

with
JACKIE
MacMULLAN

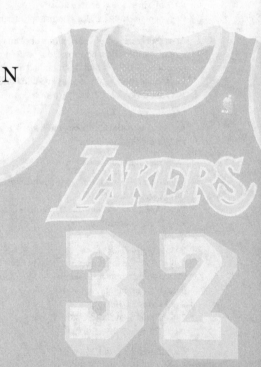

For our fans
—LARRY BIRD AND EARVIN "MAGIC" JOHNSON

To my parents, Margarethe and Fred MacMullan,
who taught me anything was possible
—JACKIE MACMULLAN

First Mariner Books edition 2010
Copyright © 2009 by Magic Johnson Enterprises and Larry Bird

Mariner Books
An Imprint of HarperCollins Publishers, registered in the United States of America
and/or other jurisdictions.

www.marinerbooks.com

Library of Congress Cataloging-in-Publication Data
Bird, Larry, date.
When the game was ours / Larry Bird and Earvin Magic Johnson Jr.
with Jackie MacMullan.
p. cm.
ISBN 978-0-547-22547-0
1. Bird, Larry, date 2. Johnson, Earvin, date 3. Basketball players—United
States—Biography. 4. Basketball—United States—History. I. Johnson, Earvin,
date II. MacMullan, Jackie. III. Title.
GV884.A1B47 2009
796.3230922—dc22 [B]   2009020839
ISBN 978-0-547-39458-9 (pbk.)

Book design by Brian Moore

Printed in the United States of America

23 24 25 26 27 LBC 19 18 17 16 15

INTRODUCTION

from LARRY

WHEN I WAS YOUNG, the only thing I cared about was beating my brothers. Mark and Mike were older than me and that meant they were bigger, stronger, and better — in basketball, baseball, everything.

They pushed me. They drove me. I wanted to beat them more than anything, more than anyone.

But I hadn't met Magic yet. Once I did, he was the one I *had* to beat. What I had with Magic went beyond brothers.

I never let on how much he dominated my thoughts during my playing days. I couldn't. But once we agreed to do this book, I knew it was finally time to let people in on my relationship with the person who motivated me like no other.

Our careers, right from the start, were headed down the same path. We played each other for the college national championship, and then went to the pros in exactly the same year. He was West Coast, I was East Coast, and both of us were playing for the two best NBA franchises of all time. You couldn't have made it up any better.

I didn't like how it went in the beginning. It was always Bird and Magic instead of the Celtics and Lakers, and that didn't seem right to me. We didn't even guard each other.

I did have incredible respect for Magic — more than anyone else I ever competed against. From the first time I saw him, I could see he approached the game the same way I did.

It's all about the competition, and that's what both of us shared. That's what we both thrived on. My teammates used to rip Magic all the time. They made fun of his smile, his "Showtime" routine. But when you got right down to it and asked them what they honestly thought, even they had to admit, "He's the best."

I didn't spend a whole lot of time comparing myself to him. We were two totally different players, with a few similarities. We both loved to pass the ball and keep our teammates involved. Neither one of us cared about scoring 50 points, although we both could have done that just about any time we wanted when we were at our best.

I'd watch highlights of Magic after a game and I'd say, "How did he do that?" He controlled the tempo of the game like nobody else I've ever seen. There were times when we played the Lakers and I'd be the only guy back on one of their 3-on-1 breaks. Even though I'm not that quick, I used to be able to read the point guard in those situations and have an idea of which way he was leaning. Not with Magic. I never had any idea what he was going to do with that ball.

We didn't like each other that much. It was too hard. We were trying to beat each other year after year, and people kept comparing us. I wanted what he had, so I didn't want to get to know him, because I knew I'd probably like him and then I'd lose my edge.

People think it all started with the NCAA championship in 1979. It didn't. We were teammates the summer before that in an international competition, and we made some incredible plays together. Too bad nobody saw them. The coach didn't play us, so we had to figure out other ways besides playing in the games to prove we belonged among the best college players. Trust me, you'll see when you read this — we figured out ways to get noticed.

In this book, we'll give you the inside story of our days leading up to the NCAA national championship, not what I call the "fish stories" that are out there. Through the years countless people who were on the fringe of our Indiana State team have been quoted about what I was doing or what I was thinking back then. I'm always amused by that, because I barely know them, which is why they never get the story right. People who have the least to do with the success of a team often have the most to say about it.

That's one of the reasons Magic and I decided to do this book together. For once, you can hear from *us* what we were feeling when we played against each other for the NCAA championship and those NBA championships. It's been an interesting ride, believe me.

It hasn't always been a smooth one either. When you are as competitive as the two of us are, there's going to be bad feelings along the way. I had them, and after doing this project, I've learned Magic had some too.

After years of battling each other, people couldn't think of one of us without the other. We were Frazier and Ali. When I retired, people asked me about him all the time. They'd say, "Is Magic okay? Have you seen him?" Even more than my own teammates. Nine times out of ten it was, "So what's Magic doing?" and one time out of ten it was, "What's McHale up to these days?"

It's hard to explain what it's like to be linked to someone like that. We didn't choose for it to be that way, it just happened. And now we're stuck with each other.

Once, a few years ago, I was driving down the road in my car and I got a call from a television reporter in Indianapolis. He asked me, "Have you heard the news?" I said, "What are you talking about?" He said, "Well, it isn't confirmed yet, but we've got a report that Magic Johnson died."

I almost went off the road. I got this pit in my stomach, and I really felt like I was going to lose it. I hung up and called Jill Leone, my agent, right away. She got on the phone with Lon Rosen, Magic's agent, and he told her it was a bad rumor, that Magic was fine. I called that TV guy back and said, "Don't you ever do that to me again."

People have been writing about Magic and me for years. Some of it they got right. Some of it they didn't. This is our story, from the two people who lived it.

When the Celtics and the Lakers played in the 2008 Finals, it brought back a lot of great memories for me. Those were the greatest times of my life, those battles with Magic and the Lakers. They were all I thought about. Nothing was sweeter than beating LA.

We fought like hell for the same thing for over 12 years, and through it all, the respect was always there. For the rest of our lives, we're connected.

I used to mind.

I don't anymore.

LARRY BIRD
Indianapolis, March 2009

from MAGIC

MY HIGH SCHOOL COACH George Fox used to tell me to never take my talent for granted.

"You're special, Earvin," Fox used to say. "But you can't stop working hard. Just remember — there's someone out there who is just as talented as you are, and he's working just as hard. Maybe even harder."

When Coach Fox told me those things, I'd nod my head, but in my mind I was thinking, "I'd like to meet this guy, because I haven't seen him." Truthfully? I wasn't sure anybody like that existed.

That changed the day in 1978 when I walked into a gym in Lexington, Kentucky, and met Larry Bird for the first time. Then I knew he was the guy Coach Fox was talking about.

Larry was a different kind of cat. He didn't say much, and he kept to himself. But, oh, could he play. I had never seen a player with his size pass the ball the way he did. Right away, we had chemistry. We played on the second team with a bunch of college All-Stars, and we just embarrassed the starters.

I knew I'd see him again, and I did — everywhere! When I got to the NBA and played for the Lakers, I watched as many Celtics games as I could so I could keep track of what he was doing. He became my measuring stick. The first time we played head-to-head in the Finals, in 1984, Larry got the best of me. It took me years to get over it. Actually, I'm not sure I'm over it yet.

I was surprised to hear Larry describe watching me win the NBA championship in my rookie season. He admitted he was jealous, which really shocked me, because he never ever showed it back then. Of course, as you'll learn when you start reading this book, I had my own bouts of jealousy when it came to Larry.

When I go out and speak to people, I tell them I wish their kids had a chance to see Larry Bird play, because he did it the right way. He played a team game, but it was his will to win, his toughness, his spirit, and his knowledge of the game that I admired the most.

I'm tied to Larry — forever. That's just how it is. I wanted the two of us to walk into the Hall of Fame together, but we didn't get a chance to do that, so this book is the next best thing. It gives us a chance to tell our story and share with you the evolution of our friendship.

Some of it will surprise you. I knew while we were playing I was doggedly scrutinizing Larry's every move, but I had no idea until we started talking for this book that he was following me just as closely.

I can't get away from Larry. I bet he can't get away from me either. I run into fans all the time and the first thing they want to know is, "Have you seen him? Have you talked to Larry?" No one ever asks me about Kareem or James Worthy or Byron or Coop. It's always Larry. We've gotten used to that.

When I go around the country, I always get a nice reception, especially in Boston. The people tell their children, "You missed it. Larry and this guy here put on a show. We used to hate this guy, but we respected him."

Every time I walk into the new Boston Garden, I have tons of memories. I swear they still have the same guys putting down that parquet floor that they had when I played. It takes me back to the day. The BEAT LA T-shirts, the vendors outside, the cold showers, the fire alarms in the middle of the night when we stayed at the Boston hotels. There has never been a better rivalry.

What we try to do in this book is put you right in the thick of it — like in 1984, just after the Celtics have won the championship. I'm stuck in a Boston hotel room, looking down at all those Celtics fans going crazy in the street. And you won't believe where Larry is!

Sometimes I'll pop in some of the old Celtics-Lakers games. I never get tired of watching them. On each team there are five bodies moving in sync with each other. Usually we scored 60 points by halftime. It was basketball poetry. When I'm watching those games, I can't help but notice the intensity on Larry's face, and on my own face. We never took a single play off. We couldn't afford to because, if we did, the other guy would exploit it. Can you imagine what it's like to have a player of Larry Bird's caliber pushing you night after night? It wore me out.

It took some time for us to get to know each other. It's hard to develop a relationship with someone who wants exactly the same thing that you want. We were different, that's for sure. I was very emotional on the court, while often Larry never even changed expression. Inside, I knew, his heart was pounding just as fast as mine, but there were countless times I'd look at him and wonder, "What's he thinking?"

Now — finally — I know.

I always wanted to work with Larry on a project like this. The love and respect I have for him is genuine. I've never met anyone else like him.

That's because there's only one Larry Bird.

I'm proud to call him my friend.

EARVIN "MAGIC" JOHNSON
Los Angeles, March 2009

1

* * *

APRIL 9, 1978

Lexington, Kentucky

T HE ERRANT SHOT came off the glass at a sharp angle, but Larry Bird, charting the flight of the ball, pulled down the rebound and advanced without hesitation, swiveling his head as he examined his options.

Earvin Johnson, Jr. had already begun to head down the court the moment the ball was in flight. He'd been playing with Bird for only six days on a team of college All-Stars in this international round-robin competition, yet already Johnson had determined that Bird was the most resourceful rebounder they had.

Bird filled the center lane, and Magic streaked down the right side, calling for the ball, but the forward looked away, as if he had pressing matters elsewhere. For one brief instant, Magic was disappointed. "I guess he's not going to give it to me," he murmured.

And that's when it came: a behind-the-back missile that landed directly on Magic's right palm. It remained there just long enough for Johnson to disarm defender Andrei Lapatov with a crossover dribble, then sling it back over his shoulder with a no-look feed to Bird.

Indiana State's star barely aligned the seams before his touch pass was back to Magic, leaving no time for the overmatched Soviet player to react. As Johnson banked in the lay-up, the crowd at Rupp Arena in Lexington, Kentucky, roared with delight.

Magic turned and charged toward Bird to offer him his signature high-five. Bird slapped the teenager's hand, and the two jogged back down the floor, side by side, one skipping, clapping, and celebrating as he went, the other, head down, expressionless, as if nothing remarkable had occurred.

The intertwined basketball journey of Earvin "Magic" Johnson and Larry "Joe" Bird had officially begun — as teammates.

Johnson had never met Bird before the tournament. He was stunned at how well the forward passed the ball, and when Bird fed him the no-look pass, Magic told himself, "I'm not going to let this guy upstage me."

"It was an incredible three seconds of basketball," Magic said. "It was boom, boom, boom! I'm thinking, 'Man, I love playing with this guy!' And believe me, the crowd loved it too."

Some thirty years after that collaborative transition basket, executed against the Soviet Union's national team when Magic was just 18 years old and Bird only 21, both remember the play with startling clarity.

"The defender was stumbling to keep up with us," Bird recalled. "We were coming at him so fast that his head was going around and around, and he ended up in a circle. I was sort of laughing, because the poor kid didn't have a clue."

He wasn't the only one. No one thought to chronicle the footage of Bird and Magic's wizardry in the open floor. There were no breathless descriptions of the artful passers in the morning papers. In 1978, though both had displayed a developing basketball pedigree, they were not widely recognized as elite players. At that juncture, neither had won an NBA championship, a league MVP, or, for that matter, an NCAA title. The irony of Bird and Magic commencing their storied relationship as teammates did not register because their parallel careers had not yet evolved into one of the compelling rivalries in basketball history.

"They were certainly good," noted Michael O'Koren, their tournament teammate, "but they weren't Magic and Larry — not yet."

Instead, Johnson and Bird were second-stringers on an amateur basketball team participating in an international round-robin competition called the World Invitational Tournament, or WIT, attempting in vain to prove to the coach, Joe B. Hall, they were worthy of prime-time minutes.

Although Bird and Magic occasionally shared knowing glances when the two of them outwitted the starters in practice, Bird revealed little of himself to Johnson. He was a young man of few words — until he went back home to French Lick, Indiana, and tracked down his brother, Mark Bird.

"I've just seen the best player in college basketball," Larry gushed. "It's Magic Johnson."

The World Invitational Tournament was a whirlwind, made-for-television event that assembled a group of top college players and held three games in five days against the Soviets, Cuba, and Yugoslavia at rotating venues: the Omni in Atlanta, Carmichael Auditorium on the campus of North Carolina, and Rupp Arena in Lexington.

Bird had just completed his junior season at Indiana State as a first-team All-America selection who would be drafted by the Boston Celtics within the next three months. Magic had just finished his first year at Michigan State, a third-team All-America pick who had dazzled the Big Ten with his array of no-look feeds, alley-oops, and backdoor bounce passes.

Yet, on the World Invitational team, also known as the Converse Cup, Johnson and Bird were afterthoughts. The headliners were Joe B. Hall and his Kentucky Wildcats, who had beaten Duke 94–88 the previous week to capture the NCAA championship. Coach Hall placed five of his guys on the WIT roster: swingman Jack "Goose" Givens, who had poured in 41 points in the title game against Duke; Rick Robey, their rugged big man; point guard Kyle Macy; lefty forward James Lee; and guard Jay Shidler.

Givens, Macy, and Robey garnered most of the minutes in the

tournament even though the second team, anchored by Johnson and Bird, dominated them in practice. Privately, both players fumed as they sat and watched inferior players gobble up their minutes.

"There were the Kentucky players, and the rest of us were fillers," Bird said. "Hall wanted to go around the country and show off his guys."

Bird and Magic spent a total of eight days together during the WIT. They engaged in no more than four or five conversations, even though they ate together, practiced together, and rode the bus together. While Magic hobnobbed with Arkansas star Sidney Moncrief, blasting his boom box and jiving to the beat of the Ohio Players, Bird remained largely to himself, surveying the Kentucky scenery out the bus window while Magic's music — and personality — overtook the team.

"Magic was nonstop chatter," said Rutgers star James Bailey. "And Larry said zero. It was 'Good morning,' and don't expect a lot more."

The World Invitational Tournament was the concoction of television executive Eddie Einhorn. While professional basketball in the 1970s produced dismal ratings, the colleges, provided the matchups had some national appeal, were proving to be a market with potential.

Einhorn had already successfully televised exhibition games against Russians and felt that a competition with some international flavor would prove to be successful. Thus, the WIT was born.

Einhorn enlisted the help of Brandeis athletic director Nick Rodis and Providence College basketball coach Dave Gavitt, prominent members of the Amateur Basketball Association of the United States (later renamed USA Basketball), to fill out the roster around the Kentucky players.

"At that time, I really didn't even know who Magic and Larry were," Einhorn admitted. "I would venture to say most other people didn't either."

Gavitt was painfully aware of the abilities of Michigan State's imposing point guard. Just weeks earlier, Magic and his Spartans had steamrolled Gavitt's Providence Friars in the opening round of the 1978 NCAA Mideast Regional in Indianapolis. Magic scored 14 points and dished out 7 assists, but his ability to push tempo and provide his teammates with high-percentage shots (Michigan State hit 61 percent of its field goals) was what caught Gavitt's eye. Johnson saw the game differently than the other players, almost as if he were watching the action unfold in slow motion.

Bird's Indiana State team posted a 23–9 mark that spring but was left out of the NCAA field, relegated instead to the less prestigious NIT tournament. Gavitt had never seen him play and knew little about him. Since Indiana State was not being featured on network television, many basketball fans assumed Bird was African American.

Boston Globe writer Bob Ryan hadn't seen Larry yet either, but was already well versed in Bird lore. Ryan was in Indianapolis to cover Providence but informed Gavitt he also was driving to Terre Haute to check out the Sycamores and this mysterious hidden gem, whom Celtics scouts assured him was a legitimate NBA prospect.

Ryan embarked on his pilgrimage with *Providence Journal* sportswriters Mike Madden and Jayson Stark, who were openly skeptical of Bird's credentials. He was playing at a small school in a small conference, which, they surmised, accounted for his prolific offensive numbers.

The writers barely had time to remove their jackets before the right-handed Bird snared a rebound and started up the left side of the floor dribbling left-handed. Just shy of midcourt, he fired an underhand rocket pass to his guard *off the dribble* for a lay-up.

"From that moment on, I was hooked," said Ryan.

Indiana State went on to win by a point on a jumper by Bird. Ryan was so animated talking about his performance on the way back to Indianapolis, he was driving 75 miles per hour when the state police pulled him over.

"Sorry," Ryan told the trooper. "I'm just excited because I'm coming back from the ISU game."

"Oh, yeah?" said the cop, ripping up the ticket. "Who won?"

The next morning the scribes were back court-side in Indianapolis to witness another legend in the making: a 6-foot-8 (and growing) floor general who dominated play without a consistent jump shot. Magic was a whirling dervish of energy and enthusiasm. Even though he was just a freshman, he barked orders to his older teammates and after every successful play slapped hands, whooped, and celebrated with his teammates. The Friars players took offense at his histrionics, particularly in light of the lopsided score (77–63).

"Some people thought he was a hot dog," Gavitt said. "I never did. He played like he loved the game. There was a lot of high-fives and fist-pumping, which you didn't see a whole lot of back then.

"I suppose it was annoying if you were on the other team. I asked his coach, Jud Heathcote, about it, and he said, 'Dave, he's like that every day in practice. Not some days — every day.'"

After Gavitt met with the press and gave proper credit to Michigan State and their remarkable blossoming star, he bumped into Bob Ryan in the hallway.

"So, how did your 'hidden gem' do in Terre Haute?" he asked.

"Dave," Ryan answered, "I just saw one of the game's next great players."

When it came time to flush out the World Invitational team roster, Gavitt recalled Ryan's endorsement and added both Magic and Bird to his list.

Bird was ecstatic about being chosen, until he learned the identity of the coach. Joe B. Hall recruited Bird out of Springs Valley High School in French Lick, Indiana, but after watching him, Hall determined that Bird was "too slow" to play Division 1 basketball. A wounded Bird vowed to prove him wrong someday and was disappointed that he never had the opportunity to play against Kentucky in college.

"I wanted a crack at that guy," Bird said.

The odds of that happening were slim. Kentucky was one of the more prestigious programs in the country. Their conference, the Southeastern, was known primarily as a football hotbed, with heavyweights Alabama, Auburn, Florida, and Georgia among its members. The Wildcats, under the tutelage of Adolph Rupp, had established themselves as one of the top basketball powers in the country in the late 1940s, winning four NCAA championships in ten years. Indiana State simply didn't measure up, and neither did Michigan State — at least not until students named Earvin and Larry arrived on their respective campuses and instantly altered the basketball landscape.

Michigan State competed in the glamorous Big Ten Conference, but largely in the shadow of state rival Michigan, which stole the spotlight through the years with stars like George Lee, Cazzie Russell, Rudy Tomjanovich, Phil Hubbard, and Rickey Green, all of whom would go on to enjoy successful NBA careers.

While the Spartans produced their own crop of NBA alumni (Bob Brannum, Johnny Green, Al Ferrari, Ralph Simpson), the program experienced only moderate success. Their cachet paled in comparison to their Ann Arbor neighbors, and they were reminded of it regularly.

"We were the stepsons," explained Heathcote. "We always told our players, every game counts just once on the schedule except for Michigan games — they counted one and a half."

One of the few highlights in Michigan State history before Magic's arrival was the success of former coach Pete Newell, who guided the Spartans from 1950 to 1954, then migrated west to the University of California at Berkeley, where he won an NCAA championship in 1959.

That same year, Michigan State posted a 19–4 record of its own, but that proved to be the program's high-water mark in the ensuing 18 seasons, when the team's overall record was a forgettable 204–233.

But then, in the fall of 1977, along came Magic. At the time the enthusiasm level in MSU's home gymnasium, Jenison Field House, was, to put it politely, restrained. When word leaked that Johnson, a hometown hero who was born and raised in Lansing, had inked with State even after being heavily recruited by dozens of top programs across the country (including Michigan), every available season ticket package was snapped up within hours. That fall Earvin Johnson appeared alongside Gregory Kelser and team captain Bob Chapman on the cover of the team's press guide, the first MSU basketball freshman to be bestowed with that honor.

There was no such fanfare when Larry "Joe" Bird unpacked his duffle bag and reported to class on the Indiana State campus in September 1975. Although there had been unconfirmed rumors of him dominating AAU tournaments and embarrassing accomplished college stars, Bird's circuitous route to Terre Haute — a brief and failed attempt to matriculate at Indiana University and a two-week stay at Northwood Institute — left ISU fans either wary or ignorant of his talents.

Not unlike Michigan State, Indiana State had grown accustomed to being a second-class sports program, dwarfed in its own region not just by Indiana University but also by Notre Dame and Purdue. The Sycamores toiled in the unheralded Missouri Valley Conference, which was dismissed as a junior varsity league when held up against the goliath Big Ten, of which Indiana and Purdue were members.

Indiana State's first basketball team was fielded at the turn of the twentieth century. In 1946 the school was known as Indiana State Teachers College, and the administration hired an earnest young man by the name of John Wooden to coach basketball and baseball and serve as the school's athletic director. Wooden's basketball teams went 47–14 in two seasons and were invited to the National Association of Intercollegiate Basketball tournament in 1947.

Wooden refused the invitation because of the tournament's policy of not allowing African American athletes to participate. A member of Wooden's team, Clarence Walker, was black.

In 1948 Wooden left what would be renamed Indiana State University to inject some life into a lackluster UCLA program. He proceeded to win ten national championships, was crowned "the Wizard of Westwood," and remains the standard by which all college coaches are measured. Indiana State, meanwhile, faded into relative obscurity.

"I never saw anything wrong with Indiana State, but Indiana was *the* school when I was growing up," Bird said. "If you got recruited by IU, you had really made it."

Both Bird and Magic qualified under those guidelines, since each appeared on Indiana coach Bob Knight's radar as high school seniors.

Johnson still rates Knight's visit to his high school as one of the greatest thrills of his young life. Knight, who had just led Indiana to an undefeated season and a national championship, was one of the most revered — and feared — men in basketball, an unrelenting disciplinarian who demanded instant respect.

When Johnson learned Knight was coming to Everett High School to meet with him, he woke up an hour earlier that morning, unlocked the school gym, and shot an extra 100 free throws — just in case coach Knight asked.

"He was 'the Man' back then," Magic said.

Knight told Magic's high school coach, George Fox, that he would meet with Johnson when school ended. Half an hour before the bell rang, Fox was walking down the hall and was stunned to see Knight leaning against the wall near Magic's classroom.

"Coach, you're early," Fox said.

"I always am," Knight said. "When I recruit a player, I like to see him with his peers, check out his attitude with the other students."

The coach's clandestine observations of Johnson revealed a confident, outgoing kid who was clearly adored by his classmates and who patrolled the hallways of the school as the undisputed leader of the student body.

When Magic sat down with Knight and Fox in Everett's cafeteria, the swagger that Knight had witnessed in the corridor quickly vanished. Johnson felt his shoulders tighten. He was nervous. The man he'd seen on television pacing the Indiana sidelines was ferocious, intimidating. But when Magic tentatively extended his hand, Knight received it warmly.

The Indiana coach proved to be a jocular host of the recruiting session and within minutes set both Fox and Johnson at ease with his anecdotes describing his passion for the game.

"He had a great smile," Johnson said. "I don't think I had ever seen him smile before."

Knight laid out what he expected of all players who came to Bloomington: they were required to go to class and expected to graduate. He would not guarantee playing time or special treatment. "If you come," Knight told Magic, "you will be treated like everyone else. You will be expected to earn your spot. I don't give anybody anything. You have to prove to me you deserve it."

The message was appealing to Johnson, who had been courted incessantly for months by schools that promised him corner lockers, starting jobs, and a few other perks (clothes, cash, cars) that were in direct violation of NCAA guidelines. It was refreshing to have someone challenge him to back up his play.

Knight's tone was conciliatory until he sharply asked: "So, Earvin, where the hell are you going to school?"

Both Magic and Fox were taken aback by the sudden change of tone. Coach Knight was done fooling around. There were countless kids who were dying to play for the Hoosiers. If Magic Johnson wasn't one of them, then Knight didn't want to waste his time.

Johnson was silent for a moment, then conceded, "I'm not sure. I don't know about Indiana. If you started getting in my face, I'm not sure how I'd react to that."

Knight cocked his head for a moment, then stood up. The interview was over. Knight shook Fox's hand and left Lansing.

"That was it," Magic said. "I never spoke to or heard from him again.

"To tell you the truth, I regret not taking a visit. He was a tremendous coach. And just imagine if Larry had stayed and I had gone there. The two of us would have played in college together. Now that would have been something."

Unlike Magic, who was recruited heavily from his junior season on, many of Bird's suitors did not arrive until his senior year of high school. He quickly narrowed his list to Kentucky, ISU, and IU, although that did not deter other programs from pursuing him.

Louisville coach Denny Crum diligently tracked Bird even though Bird refused to visit the school. He liked Crum, though, and when he discovered the Louisville coach shooting baskets in his high school gym one afternoon, he stopped to talk with him.

"Larry, we'd like for you to come on a recruiting visit," Crum said. "We really think you'll like it."

"I don't want to," Bird answered plainly.

"Look," Crum said, "I'll play a game of H-O-R-S-E with you. If I beat you, you've got to come for a visit."

Bird agreed to the terms — and almost instantly regretted his decision. Crum was a former UCLA guard under Wooden who had maintained his soft perimeter stroke. He matched Bird basket for basket for over 15 minutes, and the kid started to realize he had been hoodwinked.

It ended like most shooting competitions Bird would compete in through the years: with his arms raised in victory. He finally eliminated Crum with a 20-foot bomb, and when Crum's last gasp rolled off the rim, Bird cheered triumphantly before noticing the agonized look on the coach's face.

"It wasn't until then that I realized he was serious about the bet," Bird said.

He shook Crum's hand, patted his shoulder, and said, "At least I don't have to go see your school."

In truth, Bird couldn't imagine leaving his native state of Indiana — with the exception of one place. Kentucky, which happened to be Louisville's chief rival, was steeped in history, and Bird and his father had watched the Wildcats demolish some poor overmatched opponent on television once.

"Now that's a first-rate program," Joe Bird had said.

When Joe B. Hall contacted Bird, Larry brought along his parents for his official visit. All three Birds sat wide-eyed in the stands of Rupp Arena and listened to the explosion of sound when the basketball team sprinted onto the court. It was easy to be swept up in the energy and the tradition that was synonymous with Kentucky basketball. When Larry glanced over at his father, he could see that Joe Bird was suitably impressed.

Larry was too. His father still preferred Indiana State, and his mother was fascinated with Indiana, but Bird briefly daydreamed about what it would be like to wear Kentucky blue. The university was only 135 miles from his home. The campus was beautiful, and the athletic facilities were top-notch. Yet before he ever had a chance to give the Wildcats serious consideration, Gary Holland, his high school coach in his senior year, intercepted Bird in the hallway and informed him that Hall had concerns about him being able to get his shot off in the Southeastern Conference.

"In other words, he quit recruiting me," Bird said.

Although Bird's outer reaction to the news was muted, he was upset and angry. He never forgave Hall for giving up on him before he had a chance to prove himself.

"I don't know if I would have gone there," Bird said. "I liked it. They ended up taking Rick Robey instead of me. He was 6-foot-11, and they got who they wanted and went off and won a national championship. So I guess they were fine with their decision."

With his choices narrowed to the two Indiana schools, Bird was swayed by the same no-nonsense talk Knight would deliver to Magic two years later: no shortcuts, no guarantees, and no special treatment. He was speaking the boy's language — as well as his mother's. Georgia Bird won out. Her son Larry chose IU.

Since the Birds didn't have a family car, Larry's uncle, Amos Kerns, tossed Bird's lone bag into the back seat of his Ford and drove him 49 miles north to Bloomington when school began. Kerns stayed for a while, then stretched his arms and told his nephew, "Good luck, man. I'll be up to see you."

Suddenly, Bird was alone. He was not well traveled, having been content for most of his young life to stay within the confines of his county and play ball and hang with his friends. When he glanced around his dorm room, which he shared with fellow basketball recruit Jim Wisman, a wave of uneasiness overtook him. Although

Wisman was by no means wealthy, when he unpacked his clothes and personal effects, Bird realized, "Man, I don't have nothing."

As he walked the grounds of the Indiana campus, he couldn't help but notice the well-dressed students who looked nothing like his pals back in French Lick. Mindful that basketball always raised his comfort level, Bird showed up each night at Assembly Hall with Wisman and another IU freshman, Wayne Radford, with hopes of getting into the games with the varsity players. The newcomers rarely did. The regulars played game after game without including them.

Bird and Wisman (who would later become noteworthy as the player Knight pulled off the court by his jersey on national television during one of his famous tirades in 1976) finally switched venues to the outdoor courts on campus. When word got out that there was some pretty good basketball being played there, IU varsity players Bobby Wilkes and Scott May began showing up and playing 2-on-2 with them. May, already an All-American, rained jumper after jumper over Bird, beating the young forward repeatedly with his outside touch. It was both frustrating and humiliating.

Bird studied him carefully and realized that May had a knack of creating space for himself by leaning in as if to launch the shot, then stepping back ever so slightly when he finally did. He never shot beyond 16 or 17 feet and was meticulously mindful of his range.

"He couldn't beat people off the dribble, so he was a spot shooter," Bird said. "I started thinking, 'If I can add that kind of shooting with the movement and the drives and the rebounding and the other stuff I'm doing, I might be pretty good.'"

Although IU star Kent Benson pointedly ignored him during the pickup games at Assembly Hall, Bird hardly felt like an outcast. His school work was difficult, but he knew once the basketball season started he'd have tutors available to assist him. The classes were large, in some cases over 100 students, but Bird minimized his initial sense of feeling overwhelmed by sitting in the front.

"For the most part, everything was cool," he said. "I just didn't have any money. At night, if the guys wanted to go get something to eat, I had no money to do it. I couldn't buy a pair of pants or a shirt. Jimmy was pretty nice. He let me wear whatever I wanted of his. But it started to get to me, just never having any money."

Two weeks into school, Bird started to rethink his strategy. Maybe he should withdraw from IU, get a job, then try again when he had some financial security. He didn't share his concerns with any of his new friends on campus or his parents back home. The few times he called, Georgia could sense he was homesick, but she encouraged him to study hard and stick with it. Bird's interaction with Knight was minimal, particularly since the team's workouts had not yet officially begun. He occasionally bumped into Knight at the gym, but the coach was an intimidating figure, and Bird was not one to initiate a conversation.

Bird might have made it if not for the night he broke his toe during a pickup game on the outdoor courts after another player landed on his foot.

The injury was painful and left Bird limping all over campus. He got up 40 minutes earlier in the morning so he'd make it to his first class on time, but was consistently late getting to the next one.

"I'm sitting there saying to myself, 'I'm hurt, I can't work, I'm going to be in trouble for being late to class, I don't have any money, and they won't let me play in any of the games,'" Bird said. "'Time to go home.'"

After 24 days on campus, Bird packed up his duffle bag, closed his dormitory room door, and hitchhiked back to French Lick. He did not tell anyone of his plans — not even the coach who had recruited him.

When Larry walked into his house, his mother, who had just finished her waitress shift, was washing dishes at the sink.

"What are you doing home?" asked Georgia Bird.

"I'm done. I'm not going back," her son answered. "I'm going to work."

Georgia Bird's voice cracked. She was a strong, proud woman, but this news crushed her. "I thought you were going to be the first one to graduate college," she said. "This was a great opportunity for you. Don't you understand? I'm so disappointed."

"Mom," Bird said, "I don't have any money. I can't do the stuff everyone else is doing."

"You never had any money before, and you've always managed," she snapped.

"But this is different," Bird said. "I can't make this work until I get a job and earn some pay."

"You were going to be the first one," Georgia Bird said bitterly as she turned her back on her son.

Bird's mother said nothing more. She did not speak to Larry for nearly a month and a half. Bird moved in with his grandmother Lizzie Kerns and avoided Georgia completely. By then his parents were divorced, and while Joe Bird was not happy with his son's decision either, he advised him, "If you are leaving school to work, then you better get on that job — now."

Ten days after he left the IU campus, Bird borrowed Amos Kerns's car, corralled his childhood friend Beezer Carnes, and drove back to Bloomington to officially withdraw from class. He did not stop in to speak with Knight, Jim Wisman, or the other guys who would have been his teammates. He simply left as quietly as he came.

"I have no clue when Coach Knight even realized I was gone," Bird said. "I never heard from him. They had a great team. I'm sure he was thinking, 'The hell with Bird.' I can't say I blame him."

Word of Bird's departure from Bloomington spread quickly in the small towns of French Lick and West Baden. He had not just disappointed his family; the letdown reverberated throughout the entire community. He was pressured into briefly enrolling in Northwood Institute, but after two weeks of practicing with their team and finding the competition underwhelming, Bird withdrew from there as well.

He took a job working for the town of French Lick cutting trees, painting street signs, sweeping the roads, collecting garbage, and unplugging the sewers. He later worked for a company delivering mobile homes.

Through it all, he continued to play basketball in pickup games, summer leagues, and AAU tournaments. Although he was no longer part of the mainstream of college basketball, recruiters kept calling. Bill Hodges, the persistent Indiana State assistant, was among the suitors. Hodges repeatedly showed up, unannounced, at Bird's home, the local laundromat, and the Villager, one of the restaurants where Georgia Bird waited on tables.

One night both Hodges and Indiana State head coach Bob King appeared at one of Bird's AAU games in Mitchell, Indiana. The opponent was an Indiana All-Star team that included future Celtics guard Jerry Sichting. Bird had put up 1,300 bales of hay that week and barely made it to the game on time. He left the fields and changed into his uniform in the car while his brother drove him 25 miles to Mitchell. When Bird arrived, King immediately guessed the source of the scratches up and down Bird's arms.

"Have you been putting up hay?" King asked.

"Yes, sir," Bird replied.

"I bet your arms are pretty tired," King said.

"I can barely lift them," Bird admitted.

King was noncommittal about his interest in Bird before the game, but after the supposedly exhausted forward dropped 43 points and 25 rebounds on the state of Indiana's finest players, King's approach changed considerably.

"Hey, Larry," he said when the game ended. "We need to get you up to Terre Haute."

Hodges arranged for Bird and Beezer's brother, Kevin Carnes, to make a visit to Indiana State. Mark Bird also came along, and the three young men worked out for the coaches in jeans and tennis sneakers.

"This is how we play at home," said Bird when he refused the offer of gym shorts and basketball shoes.

Bird enrolled at ISU that fall and was required to sit out the season to be eligible under NCAA guidelines. He faithfully attended practice every day, tormenting the ISU players with his arsenal of basketball weapons.

The Sycamores were working on a defensive drill in which they would put three seconds on the clock and have their starters defend the last-second shot. Six times in a row, Bird beat the buzzer with an improbable bomb. The next day, when the starters were working on their full-court press, Bird took the ball to the middle and began shredding it.

"Bird!" King said. "Sit down!"

Larry was confused. Why was his coach so angry with him? He was putting on a show out there. No team in their right mind would press them with him handling the ball. It took him several minutes on the sidelines before it dawned on him why King was so irritated. Bird was making his team look bad.

He grabbed his sweats and marched out of the gym. Hodges, the assistant coach, followed after him and confirmed Bird's suspicions.

"Larry," Hodges said, "you're killing their confidence. We're losing them because of it."

"Well, I gotta go home and think about this," Bird replied. "I'm here to play ball. I *need* to play ball."

Hodges explained that his presence was demoralizing to the starters, who posted a 13–12 record that season. They were intimidated by him. Bird countered that practices were his games until he was eligible and his future teammates needed to toughen up.

"After that, I practiced all the time," he said.

Almost a year after watching, and waiting, Bird scored 31 points and grabbed 18 rebounds in his college debut against Chicago State. He was heartened to see nearly 5,000 people in the stands, especially since his teammates had forecasted a low turnout. Fan support in Terre Haute was often lackluster. It wasn't until after the game that Bird discovered why the crowd was so robust: free furniture was being given away at halftime.

The basketball climate in Terre Haute was about to change. Word of Bird's exceptional skills spread quickly. The team went 25–3 in 1976–77, his first season. I'm a Bird Watcher T-shirts sprang up all over campus. The tipping point was on November 28, 1977, when he appeared on the cover of *Sports Illustrated* surrounded by two cheerleaders whispering "Ssssh" so as not to reveal "College

Basketball's Secret Weapon." The cover transformed Bird into an overnight celebrity on the college basketball circuit. The avalanche of attention was an unwelcome development for a shy, understated country kid who preferred not to be noticed at all.

"That cover changed my life," Bird said. "People were all over me. There were some days I wished I had never been on it."

Magic Johnson, a freshman at Michigan State the day Bird became a cover boy, thumbed through the pages of *Sports Illustrated* in search of the story. He couldn't afford his own subscription, so every Thursday after practice at Michigan State he'd run into the coaches' lounge and pilfer their copy to see who was featured that week.

The day Bird graced the cover there was no accompanying feature. Larry had declined to be interviewed. Still, Magic found the brief blurb on the forward's hardscrabble life to be as eye-popping as his basketball numbers.

"Are you kidding me?" he said to Heathcote. "This guy is averaging 30 points a game, but before that he took a year off and told everybody, 'I'd be okay working the rest of my life.' Then he decides, 'Okay, well maybe I'll play after all.' Who does that?

"Unbelievable. I'm telling you, man, this guy is one interesting cat."

Magic identified with the pressure Bird felt to play basketball in his home state. Johnson had also narrowed his college choices to a larger, more prestigious university (Michigan) and the state school (Michigan State) preferred by his family. And like Bird, he had a multitude of other options: Maryland, Notre Dame, North Carolina State, and Indiana, to name a few. Each day dozens of schools inundated the Johnson family with letters, phone calls, and "coincidental" interactions. Finally, Earvin Johnson Sr. changed the phone number.

One cold winter morning, Detroit coach Dick Vitale showed up in Lansing just after 6 A.M. He knocked on the door of Magic's house and was told politely by Christine Johnson that her son had already left. He was up the street, shooting jump shots in the snow before school.

It was a common occurrence for recruiters to show up at odd hours of the day or night. NCAA regulations regarding contact with a student-athlete were far more lenient then, and Magic often waited at the bus stop for school in the morning with three or four suitors. When he went to lunch at Burger King, the assistant coach from Maryland loitered in the parking lot, hoping for a "chance" encounter with him.

Johnson was particularly flattered when he was contacted by UCLA coach Larry Farmer, and he bragged to his friends about "going Hollywood."

But Magic soon experienced the downside of big-time recruiting. Shortly after he cleared his schedule to fly out to Los Angeles, Farmer called back and told him to hold off. The Bruins were in hot pursuit of Albert King of Fort Hamilton High School in Brooklyn, New York, who had been rated the top prep player in the country, ahead of both Magic and another top senior, Gene Banks.

For the first time in his young life, Magic was relegated to second-class status. He moped around the house, cursing the Bruins, vowing to make them pay for snubbing him. When Farmer called back and tried to rekindle his relationship with Magic after King chose Maryland, the proud young point guard told him he was no longer interested in UCLA.

Another West Coast school, the University of Southern California, also invited Johnson out for a visit, but at the last minute Magic decided against making the trip. There was only one problem: he neglected to tell the USC coaches about his change of heart. When the plane arrived with no Magic on it, they frantically searched for their prize recruit in the Los Angeles airport before they reached his family and were informed that he was at home on Middle Street in Lansing, eating a sandwich.

Johnson visited Minnesota even though the school was on probation for recruiting violations, mostly because he was intrigued by their star, Mychal Thompson. The two connected immediately. They went to a party on campus, and by the end of the evening Johnson was surrounded by students, entertaining them with jokes and stories.

"It was like he was already enrolled there," Thompson said. "He made me feel great. It was almost like *he* was recruiting *me*.

"When he left, I told our coaches, 'We've got him. He's coming here. We're going undefeated next year!'"

Two weeks later, Thompson was stunned to learn that while Johnson rated Minnesota as his favorite recruiting trip, he couldn't possibly go anywhere in the Big Ten except Michigan or Michigan State.

Magic's mother and father favored him remaining in their hometown of Lansing, even though Michigan's campus in Ann Arbor was just 53 miles away. They weren't the only ones. Magic's teacher Greta Dart and her husband Jim, who were very close to the Johnson family and had no children of their own, were also MSU alums and pushing Spartan green.

The residents of East Lansing, desperate to keep their native son in the fold, signed a petition in the spring of his senior year of high school urging him to play for Michigan State. The petition had more than 5,000 signatures.

"I should have gone to Michigan," Johnson said. "It was the better basketball school and the better school academically. But it wasn't as simple as that. I had grown up around Michigan State. I had gone to all the games since I was a little boy."

Johnson was genuinely torn. He liked Michigan coach Johnny Orr and his assistant, Bill Frieder, who had been attentive and persuasive throughout the process. Unwilling to disappoint either school, Magic attended Saturday afternoon Michigan games wearing their trademark blue and yellow colors, then changed his sweatshirt to Spartan green before showing up at the MSU games on Saturday nights.

Just before Magic's senior year of high school, Michigan State fired head coach Gus Ganakas. His replacement was Heathcote, a gruff taskmaster who had no qualms about berating his players if they made a mistake on the floor. Just as he had been with Indiana's Coach Knight, Johnson was wary of playing for such a volatile personality.

Heathcote assured Magic that even though he was growing taller, he still envisioned him as a point guard who would run the offense. Johnson liked that idea. His decision was cemented once longtime MSU assistant Vernon Payne endorsed Heathcote even though Payne was moving on to Wayne State.

Magic's mother was relieved that her son chose State. Christine Johnson was a Seventh-Day Adventist, and her Sabbath ran from sundown Friday to sundown Saturday. Had her son gone to Michigan, she would have missed all of his Saturday afternoon home games. Earvin Johnson Sr. was happy because his son would be playing right up the street and the games wouldn't cut too much into his work hours. When Earvin Jr. announced his decision to attend Michigan State, he proclaimed at his press conference, "I was born to be a Spartan."

In his first season, the freshman helped turn a program that had gone 12–15 the previous season into a 25–5 powerhouse. Magic developed remarkable chemistry with Greg Kelser, an athletic forward who could run the floor and loved to slam home Johnson's carefully lobbed alley-oop passes. The Spartans advanced all the way to the Mideast Regional Final against Kentucky. The winner would go to the Final Four; the loser would go home.

The Spartans were up by 5 points at halftime and led by 7 with 19 minutes to go, but Kentucky, playing zone, swarmed Magic, forcing him away from the basket. He picked up his fourth foul with 9:19 left and began playing cautiously.

"Earvin changed his demeanor, and our team changed its demeanor along with him," Heathcote said.

Magic's shooting was off (2 for 10), his passes were ineffective (6 turnovers), and his team was in foul trouble. Michigan State ended up losing 52–49 in one of Johnson's worst games as a collegiate player. Kentucky's success stemmed in part from using Robey to set high post screens and lure MSU into foul trouble.

Johnson remained convinced that the Spartans lost because they stopped pushing the ball. As he and Kelser reviewed the film in the coach's office, they made a pact to play transition basketball on every possible possession the following season.

But first Magic planned to showcase his talents in the World Invitational Tournament, an opportunity, he felt, to show the country — and Joe B. Hall — that he belonged among the elite. When he looked down the roster, he was surprised and pleased to see Bird's name on the list. The *Sports Illustrated* cover had aroused his curiosity, and he figured he'd spend some time getting to know this Indiana State star.

Bird was aware of Magic's success but hadn't followed him closely, since Michigan State was neither in Indiana State's conference nor on their schedule. "I was more interested in what the Purdue guys were doing," he said.

The one name on the roster Bird was thankful to see was James Bailey, the Rutgers star whom he had toured with the previous summer in Sofia, Bulgaria. That U.S. team was coached by Crum, Bird's old H-O-R-S-E opponent, and they played four international opponents, including the Cuban national team. The U.S. team wound up in a bench-clearing melee against the Cubans, with fans spilling out of the stands and players punching and shoving each other.

Bailey was attempting to extricate himself from the mob when a security guard screamed to him, "Duck!"

He turned just in time to see his attacker heave a broken bottle at his head. Bailey punched the man in self-defense, but the bottle caught his elbow and ripped it open. He would require 54 stitches in all — 34 to repair the gash on his arm, and another 20 to sew up the wound on his right hand from the man's teeth.

The Bulgarian police, dressed in riot gear and toting rifles, finally separated the two teams. Bird, who had ducked for cover under the scorer's table, looked over at Bailey and asked, "What happened?"

Bailey, his face drained of color, was helped off the floor and taken to the hospital. Bird was so angry that he swore he'd never play in another international competition. It was a promise he did not keep.

International incidents have a way of bonding teammates, and Bailey and Bird developed a close alliance. They talked sports, compared upbringings, and found they had more in common than a white kid from the country and a black kid from the city would have ever imagined.

"I'd always heard Bird was kind of rough around the edges," Bailey said, "but I didn't find him that way at all. I was surprised how incredibly respectful he was of other people."

Bailey and Bird met again on the court in the spring of 1978 in the NIT tournament, just weeks before the World Invitational team was assembled. Rutgers nipped Indiana State in the final seconds on a Bailey basket, and as the two players walked off the floor together, the Rutgers fans burst through the ropes and stormed the floor to celebrate their win.

Amid the chaos that followed, an unruly fan charged Bird and jumped on his back. The forward shook him off with his elbow, knocked him to the ground, and kept walking.

"My coach wasn't very happy with me," said Bird. "But what was I supposed to do? The guy was hanging on my back."

If Hall was aware of Bird's little "incident" that spring, he never mentioned it. In fact, he didn't say much to Bird, Magic, or any of the other non-Kentucky players at all.

"I've never had a coach completely ignore me before," Magic said. "Joe B. Hall was the first."

Robey, one of the Kentucky chosen few, sensed the disconnect between his coach and the rest of the players. He befriended Bird and showed him the lodge where the Kentucky players stayed on campus during the school year. The accommodations were luxurious, complete with separate rooms and bathrooms for each player, a designated dining area with a cook, and a sitting area called the Wild Coyote Lounge, which had plush sofas, television sets, and pinball machines.

The lavish perks were later deemed an NCAA violation because they created an uneven playing field for recruiting, but it was clear to Bird that the Kentucky players were used to having the best.

Robey, who a year later became Bird's closest friend in the NBA, was funny, generous, and outgoing. He was difficult to dislike, but it was the situation that irked Bird, not the people involved. He objected to the way Hall doted on the Kentucky players and over-looked the others.

"We were kind of separate from the rest of the group," Robey ac-knowledged. "I'm sure there were better players than the Kentucky guys, but Joe already knew we could play together."

Because Magic was only 18, his body hadn't filled out yet. He was the youngest member of the World Invitational team, but he felt certain that once Hall spent some time with him he'd fall in love with his game and put him in the starting lineup where he belonged. The first two days of practice, Johnson dominated Macy, forcing turnovers, taking him to the basket, and running past him in the open floor. Yet, when the team played Cuba in its opening game on April 5 in the Omni, the starting lineup was Kentucky across the board.

"I'm thinking, 'Well, wait a minute,'" Magic said. "Sidney Mon-crief was sitting next to me on one side. James Bailey was sitting next to me on the other. Larry Bird was sitting next to James. Larry said, 'Forget about it. He's going with his own guys.'

"But when we scrimmaged at night, we were blowing 'his guys' off the floor. We embarrassed them. Macy and Robey and them couldn't keep up with us. And this was happening every time, not just once in a while."

The United States trounced the Cubans, who had only two play-ers who were 6-foot-6 or taller. Bird grabbed 7 rebounds in 14 min-utes of playing time, while Magic contributed 4 points and 3 assists in 13 minutes of a 109–64 win. News accounts of the game failed to mention either player. In fact, much of the ink was devoted to de-scribing the spectacular pregame warm-up dunks of James Bailey, Sidney Moncrief, and Louisville star Darrell Griffith, who was also on the team.

In the first few hours he practiced with Magic and Larry, Mon-crief recognized their exceptional court sense. Their pass-first, shoot-later approach was refreshing — and needed with a lineup of scorers who weren't used to sharing the ball.

"They were both so unselfish," said Moncrief. "It was a little un-usual."

After their first win, the team was walking up the staircase to exit the arena when they spotted Celtics general manager Red Auerbach descending on the other side.

"Hey, look, it's Red Auerbach," said O'Koren, nudging Bird.

"Who?" Bird asked.

After the opening game, Hall settled on a starting quintet of Givens, Macy, Robey, Moncrief, and Bailey. The Americans squeaked past Yugoslavia, the runner-up to the United States in the 1976 Olympic Games, 88–83. Although Kentuckians Macy and Lee were credited the following morning with helping the team pull away, it was the Indiana State forward who rattled in a 16-footer with five and a half minutes left to tie the game 72–72. Magic played 11 minutes in the game and tallied just one assist. He was pressing, trying too hard to impress in the short minutes he was given.

"You could see he was frustrated," Bird said. "I don't blame him. It was a joke. Kyle Macy over Magic? C'mon."

"It was crystal clear what was going on," Bailey said. "We just couldn't understand how Joe B. Hall could play those Kentucky guys when he had all this better talent in front of him — especially Magic and Larry.

"It was unfair. But if those two guys were disappointed, they never showed it."

During one practice when the starters were drilling on how to break the press, Bird and Magic instituted what Bird called the rat trap: forcing the ball handler to his opposite hand, then, as soon as he spun, bringing another player up and making the dribbler try to throw the ball over the top.

"Nobody told us to do it," Bird said. "We just did. We were stealing the ball and scoring on them like crazy. Then all of a sudden Hall just blew the whistle and stopped the drill. He was mad. Next thing you know, we're on to something else. He didn't seem very happy with us."

In their final game against the Soviets, which the Americans won handily, 102–87, Bird and Magic brought the fans out of their seats with their sizzling back-and-forth exchange. It was a snippet of brilliance, at least half of which Hall publicly acknowledged when the tournament was over. Pressed on how he chose his starting quintet of Macy, Robey, Givens, Moncrief, and Bailey over the talent he had on his roster, Hall said, "We felt that was our best unit. But today Magic came in with his road show and he blew them out of the press. He's a sensational player and real fine young man."

Moncrief and Givens were named to the All-Tournament team, while two Kentucky boys, Robey (20.0 minutes) and Macy (18.7 minutes) were among the team leaders in minutes played. Bird and Magic left content — they had made their mark in the privacy of the workout sessions.

"It's too bad we didn't play more," said Magic. "We were the crowd favorites. I'm not sure people had ever seen players like Larry and me."

Although they generated a large measure of respect for each other, the two players departed without having a single meaningful conversation. They arrived as strangers and left as mere acquaintances.

Eleven months later they met again, with the NCAA national championship — and their college legacy — on the line.

2

★ ★ ★

MARCH 25, 1979

Salt Lake City, Utah

THE DOOR TO THE gymnasium creaked open, unleashing a rush of disquieting noises. First it was a burst of boisterous laughter, then a thunderous commotion of bodies clomping toward the entrance.

Magic Johnson and his Michigan State teammates turned in unison to see who dared to interrupt Coach Jud Heathcote in midsentence, in mid-*strategy*, as he reviewed his team's defensive assignments for the final time in preparation for their NCAA basketball championship game.

The Spartans were down at the far end of the gym, huddled around their coach and a full-court heave away from the distractions that had punctuated their session, yet even from that distance the interlopers were unmistakable: the Indiana State basketball team, clad in jeans, boots, and ten-gallon cowboy hats.

The first person Magic looked for was their star, Larry Bird. He was amazed to see him standing there, his hat slightly askew.

Indiana State was scheduled to hold a shoot-around immediately following Michigan State's workout, but the allotted time for the

Spartans had not yet expired. The ISU players knew that, but guard Carl Nicks said, "Let's go in there and watch practice and flaunt our stuff. Let's let them know we're here.'"

There was an instant when the two basketball teams, one day away from playing in the most widely anticipated college title game ever, simply stood frozen in place and studied one another in silence.

Yet that moment was swiftly obliterated by the screeches of Heathcote once he checked his wristwatch and realized the Sycamores were encroaching on his precious practice time.

"We still have 20 minutes! You aren't supposed to be in here! Get out of my practice!" Heathcote howled.

As quickly as they materialized, Bird and his boys disappeared, slamming the door demonstratively behind them.

Magic was alternately stunned and amused by Indiana State's behavior, but Heathcote seethed for 10 minutes after the Sycamores left, teeth clenched and spittle flying.

"They don't respect you!" Heathcote roared. "They are trying to distract you! No one interrupts our practice! Do you see what they are trying to do?!"

Heathcote, who had been motivating college athletes for 15 years, recognized an opportunity when he saw one. He harped on Indiana State's antics until his players were sufficiently insulted and agitated.

The Spartans ran into the Sycamores one more time in the hallway as they departed. A handful of the ISU players chanted and sang the team's fight song as they passed.

"I'm not sure what they were trying to do," said Michigan State forward Greg Kelser, "but it was awful disrespectful."

As the Spartans filed onto the bus to return to the team hotel, the talk again turned to Indiana State's curious choice of attire.

"It just doesn't fit," Magic said to Kelser. "I didn't know they were cowboys. You just don't see that kind of thing in college.

"Just what are those country guys trying to pull?"

* * *

The 1979 NCAA championship game between Michigan State and Indiana State drew a 24.1 Nielsen rating, the highest in college basketball history, a noteworthy milestone that remained untouched three decades later.

It was the matchup every college basketball fan longed to see, not because the two schools had demonstrated a long history of success or a simmering, adversarial rivalry, but because of a more singular concept: Magic versus Bird, two prolific stars who led their teams with the perfect blend of superb passing, nerveless shooting, and, above all, a steely ability to withstand the mounting pressure that dogged each of them as their résumés swelled with success.

Their paths to the championship game in Salt Lake had not been nearly as smooth as their stellar records would indicate. Indiana State's unblemished 33–0 mark suggested a perfect season, yet it did not reflect the volatility that swirled around Bird, a demanding young player who would not tolerate anyone who failed to consistently submit the proper effort. It was of little consequence to Bird whether he was popular with his teammates. What he wanted — expected — from them was to match his intensity, and that was often a tall order.

"Larry would fight you," said Nicks. "He wouldn't back down. If he didn't like what you were doing, he was in your face, telling you."

Indiana State forward Leroy Staley learned that firsthand in preseason when he committed some sloppy turnovers and Bird began chiding him to pick up his game. Staley took out his frustration on seldom-used backup point guard Rod McNelly, cornering him as he brought the ball up the floor and kneeing him as he swiped at the ball.

As McNeely crumpled to the ground, Bird charged Staley, fists curled.

"Leroy was frustrated, I think," Nicks said. "He wasn't playing well, and he got too rough. But Larry wasn't going to let him get away with a cheap shot like that."

"I really don't know what happened," Staley said. "Larry was having a bad day. Next thing I know, he was swinging at me."

The two were eventually separated, but not before three Syca-mores hauled Bird away.

Nobody approached Bird after the altercation; they understood it was wise to let their volatile leader cool off on his own. Coach Bill Hodges called Bird and Staley in to clear the air, and both players agreed to move forward. When Larry returned, he was unapologetic and as steely-eyed as ever.

"We had a lot of skirmishes that year," Nicks said. "Every day in our practice was a dogfight."

Bird's mantra was simple: play the game the right way or stay away. In his mind, the previous season had been squandered by a lack of discipline, and he wasn't going to allow that to happen again.

"Leroy Staley is a great guy," Bird said. "He was also a good player and a good teammate who helped us a great deal. But you needed to stay on him, and he wasn't the only one.

"I didn't mind doing it. Those guys were intimidated by me. It was my job as the leader of the team to keep their intensity level up, even in practice. I knew that was the only way we could win a cham-pionship."

Bird was keenly aware of the inordinate publicity he received and stopped talking to the press in hopes that the media would promote other Sycamore players. Even so, he still had to contend with the perceived slights of his teammates, who grew tired of it all being about number 33.

"There was a lot of jealousy — still is to this day," Bird said.

Indiana State was projected to finish in the middle of the pack in 1978–79 when head coach Bob King suffered a heart attack and brain aneurysm and was replaced by assistant Bill Hodges. Up un-til that point, Staley, who had clashed with King, was planning to transfer to Florida State to play for coach Hugh Durham. Once Hodges received the promotion, Staley decided to stick around.

Transfers Nicks, Bobby Heaton, and Alex Gilbert brought new life and a fresh approach to the team and quickly became key com-ponents of the Sycamores' nucleus.

Nicks was a cocky guard from Chicago who went hard to the basket and wasn't afraid to take on anyone — defensively or offensively. Heaton, Indiana State's sixth man, was a savvy player with good court sense and a perimeter shot that would prove to be pivotal during ISU's remarkable run. Gilbert was a rebounder and shot blocker who possessed incredible leaping ability.

The other starters included defensive stopper Brad Miley and point guard Steve Reed, an inexperienced yet unselfish player who had great range but was a hesitant shooter.

The Sycamores' bench was short; the only other player besides Heaton who played significant minutes was Staley. The limited rotation earned the Sycamore regulars the nickname "the Magnificent Seven." And when a local car dealership featured them in one of their advertisements wearing blue cowboy hats, jeans, and boots, it became their signature look.

In the second game of the season, Bird led ISU to a 63–55 upset over Purdue, burning the Boilermakers for 22 points and 15 rebounds. Five days later, he dropped 40 points on Evansville, and then, on December 16, he punished Butler with 48 points, 19 rebounds, and 5 assists.

It was a remarkable string of basketball and Hodges, only 36 years old, drew great comfort from Bird's decision to play for ISU in his final season rather than bolt to the NBA. Hodges knew he was watching a once-in-a-lifetime player at work.

The previous spring Bird had become "junior eligible" for the NBA draft. Since Bird's career technically began in 1974 when he spent three and a half weeks at Indiana, he was considered a member of the class of 1978 in the eyes of professional basketball, even though he had never played a second for the Hoosiers and still had a year of eligibility left at Indiana State.

Under new guidelines of the NBA's collective bargaining agreement in 1976, a player could be drafted, return to college and play his final season, and then negotiate with the NBA team that had selected him. If an agreement was not reached by draft day, the team would forfeit its exclusive rights and the player would go back into the NBA draft pool.

Bird was unaware of the rules that had so direct an impact on him. In fact, he was blissfully ignorant of almost everything that had to do with the NBA.

"I just didn't care about the pros," Bird said.

The Indiana Pacers held the number-one pick in 1978, and their coach, Bob "Slick" Leonard, called Bird and invited him to Indianapolis for a visit to discuss his future.

Bird drove to meet Leonard with Ed Jukes, a local banker and trusted family friend. The meeting was held in downtown Indianapolis at the Hyatt Regency. As they walked into the hotel, Bird was struck by the long escalator that led to the second floor.

"It was the first time I had ever seen one," he said.

As they got situated in the hotel restaurant, Leonard asked Bird if he'd like a beer.

"Sure," Bird answered. "I'll have a Heineken."

Leonard gulped. He was a Terre Haute native and had grown up, as he liked to say, "walking the same dirt floors as Larry did." Yet even after becoming a professional player and NBA executive, Slick still drank Champagne Velvet beer, the locally brewed ale that was popular because it was inexpensive.

"On Friday nights it was Pabst Blue Ribbon, because we were probably going to drink a lot of 'em and that was the economical way to go," Leonard said.

"Only wealthy people drank Heineken. But I figured, 'Oh, what the hell.' I had one with him."

Leonard explained the dire situation of the Pacers franchise, which had recently merged with the NBA, along with the other teams in the American Basketball Association (ABA), and was on the verge of financial ruin. The team had offered its top free agent, Dan Roundfield, a $200,000 contract, "which was $200,000 we didn't have," Leonard said. But the Atlanta Hawks swooped in and offered Roundfield $450,000. Roundfield went for the bigger dollars and left the Pacers with a gaping hole in their lineup, as well as a difficult predicament to consider. Indiana wanted to draft Bird, but the franchise couldn't risk him going back to Indiana State for his senior season. They needed help immediately.

"Look, I can't wait a year," Slick told Bird. "Our franchise can't afford it. So if you are going back to school, you've got to tell me, because I'll trade the pick. But if you come out, I'll take you."

There was no hesitation in Bird's reply. He had promised his mother Georgia he would leave Indiana State with a degree. Although Georgia's financial situation was still tenuous, she remained steadfast in insisting that her son earn that diploma.

"My mom didn't care about the money," Bird explained. "She was hanging in there. It wasn't a life-or-death situation. If it was, maybe I would have made a different decision."

Leonard and Bird drained a couple more Heinekens before they amicably shook hands and parted ways. As he was leaving the Hyatt, Bird asked Jukes to hold on a moment. He hopped on the escalator, riding up, then down again, with childish delight.

Although he was disappointed that Bird would not be wearing a Pacers uniform, Slick was hardly devastated. At that time there were questions about Bird's body type, his quickness, and his temperament. No one was projecting him to be a first-ballot Hall of Famer.

"I liked Larry," Leonard said, "but, c'mon now. Nobody knew he was that good."

True to his word, Leonard dealt the number-one pick to the Portland Trailblazers in exchange for guard Johnny Davis, center Clement Johnson, and the number-three pick in the 1978 draft, which the Pacers used to select Kentucky big man Rick Robey.

Now it was the Trailblazers' turn to woo the reluctant ISU forward. Bird was barraged with phone calls at his French Lick home from Portland executive Stu Inman. After a while, Georgia Bird, able to distinguish Inman's voice, would politely but firmly hang up the phone.

Inman's sales pitch to Bird included the prospect of playing alongside a certain future Hall of Famer.

"Larry," Inman said, "you are missing out on an opportunity to play with Bill Walton. He is one of the greatest centers ever to play the game."

"He's hurt all the time," Bird bluntly replied.

(Although Bird, who would later play alongside Walton with the Celtics during their 1986 championship season, counts Walton among his closest friends, he was accurate in his assessment. In Walton's first two seasons in the league, he broke his nose, wrist, and leg. After leading Portland to an NBA championship in the 1977 season, Walton broke his foot in 1978, played in just 58 games, and demanded a trade during the off-season because of what he perceived to be unethical treatment from the team doctors. When the Blazers refused to deal him, the big redhead sat out the entire 1978–79 season in protest. The broken foot led to a myriad of problems that severely hampered his career and later required him to undergo fusion surgery on his ankle.)

Although Bird was as adamant with the Blazers about his intentions to return to Indiana State, Portland remained undeterred, emptying its Rolodex in attempts to reach out to numerous contacts to whisper in Larry's ear.

"I swear Portland had everyone working it," Bird said. "Total strangers would come up to me and say, 'I can't believe you're not going to the pros! You have a chance to take care of your family for life. Why do you need to go to school?'

"I kept telling them, 'No, I'm going back. I'm going back.' I wasn't changing my mind."

Inman made some inquiries about Bird and discovered he was fiercely loyal, uncommonly stubborn, and had a quick temper and a taste for beer. Inman had concerns about the forward's maturity and conditioning. On draft day, Portland selected Minnesota forward Mychal Thompson with the first overall pick. The Blazers' intent was to pluck Bird with their other first-round selection, the seventh pick, but Boston, selecting sixth, grabbed him before Portland had the chance.

Red Auerbach made the selection without ever speaking to Bird about his professional aspirations. The Celtics general manager already knew all about Indiana State's prized player. The day Larry's World Invitational Tournament teammates saw Red walking down the stairs, he was there to evaluate Bird. He had also been monitoring Bird through reports from scouts John Killilea and K. C. Jones. Killilea returned home from an extended road trip to the Midwest and gushed to Auerbach, "Red, I think I've just found the next Rick Barry. He can shoot from anywhere. And you won't believe what a great passer this kid is."

"I trusted Killilea," said Auerbach, "but I also thought he was exaggerating."

Auerbach placed a call to his friend Bob Knight, who assured him that Bird's missteps in Bloomington were nothing to be concerned about.

"In fact," Auerbach reported, "Bob told me he wished he had helped the kid along more. The way he put it was, 'The only thing Bird did wrong here was not check with me before he left campus.'"

On a balmy afternoon in June, Bird was playing golf in Santa Claus, Indiana, with his longtime friend Max Gibson when a stranger hollered to them, "Larry Bird! You just got drafted by the Boston Celtics!"

"What does that mean?" Bird asked.

"Hell, I don't know," he said.

Gibson and Bird plopped down their clubs and walked inside the lounge to have a sandwich. At around 4:00 P.M., they drove to the house where they were staying and turned on the television. Back then, without the benefit of 24-hour news scrawls, Internet access, and multiple ESPN channels, there was no other way to learn about the happenings of the day than to watch the six o'clock news. Bird and Gibson sat around talking about fishing, golf, and hunting until the NBA report finally aired. The forward listened, shrugged, then shut off the TV set. The magnitude of what Auerbach had done was lost on him.

"Max was a lot more excited about it than I was," Bird said.

Throughout Bird's senior season at Indiana State, members of the Celtics began appearing at the Hulman Center, often without warning. K. C. Jones, coach Tommy Heinsohn, Celtics star Dave Cowens, and even Auerbach himself intermittently appeared to check on their investment.

* * *

35

In the meantime, scouts from nearly every NBA team were also traversing the country with a Michigan State schedule in their pockets. They too had number 33 circled — Magic's college number with the Spartans. Johnson had already carefully mapped out his future basketball plans in his head. If all went well, he intended to turn pro after his sophomore season, and NBA executives knew it. In fact, Magic had nearly made the jump after his freshman year, even going so far as to meet with the Kansas City Kings, but the two parties couldn't agree on a suitable salary and Johnson went back to Michigan State, where he planned to cement his standing as a top draft pick.

In contrast to Bird, Johnson was a student of the pro game and had emulated his idols Wilt Chamberlain, Dave Bing, and Julius Erving on the playgrounds of Lansing.

Since he nearly always outlasted his friends, who grew tired of shooting or were called home to supper, Johnson often played 1-on-1 games with himself, counting his first crossover and jump shot as two points for Wilt and then his post move as two for Bill Russell.

"I wanted to play in the NBA in the worst way," Johnson said.

But first Magic wanted to win a college championship, and he was convinced that 1978–79 would be the year. Most of the nucleus of the MSU team that had advanced to the Regional Finals were back, including the reliable Terry Donnelly — whose timely shooting figured prominently in their postseason run — scorer Jay Vincent, and the rugged Ron "Bobo" Charles, who gladly handled the dirty work up front. Kelser was a senior, an explosive and gifted athlete who had meshed beautifully with Magic's game.

Heathcote was also excited about a highly touted freshman from Buchanan, Michigan, named Gerald Busby, who he felt could be a regular contributor before the year was out.

"Gerald had Jordan-like jumping ability," said Magic. "We had him marked down as a sure-fire NBA player."

Johnson was alone practicing perimeter jump shots in an empty Jenison Field House during the first week of September 1978 when

Heathcote waved him over to tell him *Sports Illustrated* had chosen him to appear on the cover of its college basketball preview issue. There would be no cheerleaders alongside him promoting college's best-kept secret: the word was already out on Magic.

For the cover photo of the November 27, 1978, issue, he donned a black tuxedo and top hat with a white vest and patent leather shoes. In the photograph, Magic is leaping through the air, laying the ball in wearing both the tuxedo and his trademark smile. The heading declares, "Super Sophs," and the tagline reads, "Michigan State's classy Earvin Johnson."

Magic was so anxious to see the cover that he didn't wait to swipe it from the coaches' lounge. He called his father, Earvin Johnson Sr., and told him to scoop up ten copies at the newsstand instead. When Earvin Sr. went downtown to buy the magazine, the racks were empty. The good people of Lansing had bought them all up. When Magic went home for his annual dentist's appointment, the receptionist lamented that someone had lifted their copy too.

"That was one special day in the Johnson home," said Magic's father. "For a young black man from Lansing, Michigan, to be on the cover of *Sports Illustrated*? I told my wife, 'Now I *have* seen everything.'"

Just as it had done for Bird, Johnson's cover shot raised his already considerable profile to new heights. Opposing fans from various Big Ten cities lined up, Sharpie pen and *Sports Illustrated* cover in hand, seeking his signature. Magic almost always obliged. Nine times out of ten, whether he was in Columbus, Ohio, or Minneapolis, he'd sign the magazine, receive a heartfelt "Thank you!" then absorb a raucous "Go Buckeyes!" or "Gophers rule!" as he turned to walk away.

Back in Terre Haute, someone showed Bird the glitzy cover with Magic decked out in formal attire.

"Good," was Bird's reaction. "Let someone else deal with all the attention."

Michigan State's first true measuring stick was a preseason exhibition game against the Russian national team, which was touring the United States and playing select colleges. The Soviets were a methodical team that simply could not keep pace with Johnson and Kelser. Michigan State ran them off the floor, 76–60, barraging them with repeated fast-break baskets.

The game, televised nationally on HBO, drew some interested observers: the Indiana State Sycamores, who gathered at Bird and Bob Heaton's off-campus house to watch the game. ISU was scheduled to play the Russians the following week, and while Bird tried to focus on the Soviets, he couldn't help but be dazzled by what Earvin "Magic" Johnson had done to them.

"At that point I knew very little about Magic," Bird said. "But I couldn't believe what I was seeing. Magic ran those guys like a pro team. Any miss and they'd be off, running the break. His angles on his passes were perfect. He looked kind of awkward bringing the ball up with that big body, but he was always one step ahead of everyone."

When Magic and Michigan State had completed their thrashing of the Russians, Bird turned to his teammates and said, "Boys, you are watching the best team in the country."

Bird began the evening sitting next to Nicks on a sagging couch and bragging about how he was going to dominate the Soviets. He pointed to one Russian forward and explained in explicit detail how he was going to embarrass him in the post. He pointed to another and promised to rain jump shots on his head. "There ain't nobody out there that can guard me," he boasted.

"That's what he started out saying," said Nicks. "But by the end he was saying, 'That Magic, he's incredible.'"

Bird backed up his bravado on November 20 as ISU stunned the Soviets 83–79 behind 22 points and 13 rebounds from their forward. Thus, Indiana State became one of just four colleges that beat the Russians.

Both Michigan State and Indiana State utilized their victories over the Soviets as a springboard to their regular season before departing for opposite corners of the country.

The Sycamores flew to Deland, Florida, where they easily dispatched East Carolina (102–79) and Cleveland State (102–71) to win the Hatter Classic.

At that juncture, Indiana State was 6–0, but Bird, the architect of the win streak who averaged over 31 points and 13.6 rebounds during that stretch, still wasn't impressed.

"We were winning, but we really hadn't played anybody yet," Bird explained.

For its Christmas tournament on December 18, Michigan State flew west to Portland, Oregon, where they were scheduled to play Washington State, Heathcote's alma mater. The Wazzus were ranked 10th in the country and led by Don Collins, who later played for the Washington Bullets in the NBA.

The normally effusive Heathcote was strangely closed-mouthed in the days leading up to the game against his beloved school, where he had also worked as an assistant coach for seven seasons.

"Like a bulldog, he was so tight," Magic said. "I could tell the game meant a lot to him. He had all of his old friends in the stands watching."

The day before the game, Magic called a players-only meeting and explained the significance of the matchup to Heathcote. "We can't let him down," Magic told them.

Michigan State trounced Washington State by 46 points. As they walked off the court, Magic nudged Heathcote with his elbow.

"Coach, that one was for you," he said.

The next day, just before Michigan State tipped off against Oregon State, Indiana coach Bob Knight, whose team had just beaten Oregon, shook Heathcote's hand and said, "C'mon now, Jud. Make it an all–Big Ten final."

Michigan State dispatched Oregon State by 8, then spanked Indiana 74–57 in the championship. Magic submitted 20 points and 7 assists against the Hoosiers.

The Spartan players were euphoric about their performance but also anxious to return home to ring in the New Year with friends and family. On December 30, they boarded a flight to Seattle that was supposed to connect them to a flight back home to Michigan, but a blinding snowstorm diverted them to Denver. There, with his team gathered around the baggage carousel, Heathcote received the official word: the new college rankings listed Michigan State as the number-one team in the country.

The newly minted team made it as far as Minneapolis the following day before inclement weather again left them stuck in a hotel, rinsing out socks and underwear on New Year's Eve.

By the time they finally landed in Detroit two days later, on January 2, the players were tired, cranky, and irritated. The wait for their bags was interminable. Ten, then twenty minutes passed. Heathcote approached an airline representative, demanding that their luggage be brought out to them. Another ten minutes passed.

"There was steam coming out of his ears," Magic said.

Finally, Heathcote could wait no longer. He climbed onto the conveyer belt and rode down the shoot after the luggage. Minutes later, he was escorted through a side door with a security guard on either arm, as his players convulsed with laughter.

"I get very impatient when I'm traveling," Heathcote said.

When the Spartans finally did return to Lansing, they had not practiced for a week. Although the team rallied to beat their next two opponents, they went on to drop four of the next six games, including a blowout loss to lowly Northwestern on February 3. That defeat dropped Michigan State to 4–4 in the Big Ten.

The number-one ranking was a distant memory, and so was the jubilation of their Far West Classic championship.

Heathcote called a team meeting and chastised his players for not submitting a solid defensive effort, not working hard enough on the glass, and failing to play with the proper concentration.

Then it was the players' turn to sound off. Kelser went first. "Our mistakes are exacerbated by your tirades," Kelser told Heathcote. "You need to back off. You are also relying on Earvin too much. It's made us too predictable."

One by one, the players weighed in. Vincent said he was playing tentatively because he was afraid if he made a mistake he'd get yanked off the court. Magic told Heathcote he felt stifled with the offense they were running.

"Coach," Magic implored Heathcote, "let me take the ball and go!"

The coaches and players had reached a stalemate. Heathcote and his staff wanted better fundamentals and a more consistent commitment. His players wanted more freedom and less harassment.

Reserve John Longaker, a Rhodes Scholar who rarely played key minutes but was respected by his teammates for his high basketball IQ, stood up and declared, "We're not playing Michigan State basketball. What happened to all that confidence we had earlier in the year? Earvin, what happened to all that cockiness you had that kept us going?"

"He was right," Magic admitted. "We weren't playing with the same swagger."

"I was glad John said something," Heathcote said, "because he was one of the only guys Earvin would listen to."

Longaker, who went on to become a physician at Stanford Medical School, spoke plainly to Johnson about his academic deficiencies and the need for him to apply the same self-discipline he exhibited in his workouts to his studies. He taught Johnson how to organize his assignments and budget his time.

Longaker was one of the few players who wasn't afraid to challenge Johnson. During that team meeting, he implored Johnson to stop pointing fingers and look at himself.

After each player aired his concerns, Heathcote pledged to provide his point guard with more leeway and agreed to make a concerted effort to scream a little less. The meeting adjourned without properly addressing one more unspoken issue.

Although the Spartans were a close team, there were occasions when Magic's gigantic personality became all-encompassing. That was occasionally bothersome to Kelser, who was the team's leading scorer and rebounder but who was clearly overshadowed by his dynamic teammate.

"The truth is, we had two superstars — Magic and Kelser — but

Magic was getting all the ink," Heathcote said. "Earvin understood it was a problem, but it was just his personality. He couldn't help that everyone loved him. He was such an easy guy to gravitate towards, and sometimes that was difficult for his teammates."

Kelser rarely vocalized his frustrations. He and Johnson were great friends and spent many nights dancing at the clubs in Lansing together. Yet Heathcote detected hints of Kelser's mindset in the locker room.

"Greg was always into his stats," Heathcote said. "We'd pass the sheet out after the game, and Earvin wouldn't even look at it. But Greg would devour that thing. He'd say, 'They've only got me down for six rebounds. I thought I had more, didn't you?'"

In 2006 Kelser published a book in which he detailed his memories of Michigan State's championship season. Included was a passage in which he discussed watching Magic score 20 points one night and becoming determined to score 25 himself the next time out so that Johnson wouldn't outshine him.

"There *was* jealousy," Magic said. "I didn't see it at the time, but I had stolen a lot of Greg's thunder. I didn't mean to. I didn't care about anything but winning.

"His comments in that book surprised me. He said I took away some of his glory. I was taken aback by that. It was kind of disappointing."

Kelser insists that he recognized Magic provided him with exposure he might not have ever received had he played without him and never meant to imply he wasn't grateful to his former teammate.

"I had no problem taking a back seat to Earvin," Kelser said. "But I did want to be recognized for what I accomplished. When our team was billed as 'Magic Johnson and the Michigan State Spartans,' I didn't appreciate that. But what was I going to do?"

The now famous Spartans team meeting is often cited as a catalyst to the team's turnaround, yet Heathcote believed that his decision to remove Ron Charles from the starting lineup and replace him with the smaller, quicker Mike Brkovich, who was a better shooter, had as much to do with the resurgence of his team as anything.

Teams had begun to recognize how damaging it was to allow Magic to grab the rebound off a miss and start the break himself. They adjusted by assigning a player to him with one specific goal in mind: block him out.

Brkovich provided another outlet pass and ball handler to facilitate the transition game. Heathcote also intended to make another change — to send Terry Donnelly to the bench and insert the freshman Busby into the starting lineup. But before Heathcote could promote him, Busby abruptly quit the team. He was homesick, bothered by his coach's gruff demeanor and his constant use of profanity. Busby decided a change of scenery was in order.

He transferred to Ferris State and performed well there, but Busby never came remotely close to winning a national championship — or making his projected jump to the pros.

"I'll always wonder what Gerald Busby was thinking," Magic admitted.

After the meeting and the lineup change, the Spartans ripped off wins in 10 of their final 11 games.

The lone loss down the stretch came when Wisconsin's Wes Matthews (who would later become Magic's NBA teammate for the 1987–88 championship in Los Angeles) connected on a wild last-second bank shot at the buzzer in the season finale, 82–80.

Initially, the last-second defeat stung the Spartans, who truly believed they were not going to lose another game. Kelser remembers that his teammates were uncommonly deflated before Magic started to work the room, pounding backs and whacking shoulders.

"It's okay, their season is over," Johnson told them. "We still have business to take care of."

Knocking off Indiana State was at the top of their list. Bird's team was the number-one overall seed in the field of 40, an astounding transformation for a school that had averaged less than 3,000 fans a game before he arrived.

Indiana State knew its fortunes had changed when the students who used to play on the courts after practice began showing up earlier and earlier. After a while, the number of people watching them work out had swelled to over 100 and Hodges was forced to close practice. That did not deter the "gym rats" from showing up anyway.

"I'd look through the windows on the gym doors, and you could see all these heads jostling to get a look," said Dr. Bob Behnke, the team trainer.

By the end of the season, fans were lining up outside the Hulman Center at 3:30 P.M. for a 7:30 game. Since the student section did not have assigned seats, when the doors opened at 6:00, there was a mad rush for the open spots. The fans were allowed into the gym in the middle level of a three-tier building. Bird and his teammates would stand in the tunnel on the first level and watch as their fellow students stampeded one another to get a better view of their beloved basketball team.

More often than not, the effort was worth it. Early in the season in a two-point game against Illinois State, Hodges called a time-out in the final seconds with the score tied and Indiana State in possession of the ball. Behnke remembered watching Hodges draw up an elaborate play on his chalkboard that involved double screens and back picks.

Nicks was assigned the task of inbounding the ball. As he and Bird walked out of the huddle and toward the court, Behnke heard Bird say to his friend, "Hey, Carl, just get it to me."

"So I did," Nicks said. "And you know what happened. Larry scored to win it."

The most titillating victory of the year, however, featured Bird in a supporting role. By February 1, 1979, Indiana State had won 18 in a row, but in a game with New Mexico State they were trailing by 2 points with 3 seconds to play. The Aggies' Greg Webb was at the line, while Bird and Nicks were stuck on the bench, having fouled out of the game.

Hodges called time-out, reminded his players to stay levelheaded, then went about divvying up responsibilities for the final seconds. Heaton, who was in the game, waited for his assignment, but in all the confusion Hodges had neglected to tell him where to go.

As each team broke from their huddle, the partisan New Mexico State crowd leaped to its feet bellowing, "18–1! 18–1!" Slab Jones, their star, sauntered past the Indiana State bench ribbing Bird and Nicks, "Too bad your streak is over."

Heaton, unsure of where to go, hustled underneath the team's basket, then realized he was too deep and would have no time to shoot even if he did get the ball. He migrated to half-court and waited.

Webb's free throw clanged short. ISU's Brad Miley controlled the rebound and quickly relayed it to Heaton. The player Bird affectionately called "Heater" didn't hesitate: he hoisted a 50-foot bomb just before the buzzer sounded.

"I thought it was going clear over the backboard," Heaton said.

Heaton groaned. The ball started its descent and, incredibly, banked in.

The shot pulled the plug on the New Mexico State celebration. Indiana State had improbably forced overtime, then went on to win in the extra frame.

"When New Mexico State scored their first basket of the overtime, no one even clapped," Heaton observed. "They were done."

Bird was elated for Heaton, a grinder with limited speed who compensated for it by making good decisions on the floor. It was also encouraging to see reserve Rich Nemcek make a couple of meaningful plays in a game of that magnitude.

"When Heater hit that shot, I thought, 'Maybe this year really is different,'" Bird admitted. "I saw something from our bench that night I hadn't seen all year. They played with confidence. They played like they were supposed to win."

Nine days after that thriller, Bird endured the only outing in his college career in which he scored in single digits. The opponent was Bradley, and Bird checked out with 4 points and 11 rebounds, but Indiana State rolled 91–72 behind 31 points from Nicks and 30 from Steve Reed. In defeat, Bradley coach Dick Versace declared afterward that his "bird cage" defense had been a success.

"He actually took credit for stopping me," Bird said. "That was funny to me.

"I didn't even *try* to score. I took two shots. They triple-teamed me the whole game by putting a guy in front of me, a guy behind me, and another one digging for the ball. We had players on the floor that weren't even being guarded."

It was a heady time for Indiana State. As the team's winning streak extended, so did the publicity surrounding their team. Bird was a campus celebrity, and not all of his teammates were comfortable with that.

"Guys were getting their due, but they thought they should have gotten more, I guess," Bird said. "I think some of them got so big in their mind, they thought they could probably do it without me."

"It was all about Larry," Nicks said. "I used to get disappointed a lot. Larry always tried to pull me in. I tried not to sulk, but there were times it was just so unfair. I was a valuable member of the team, but you wondered if anyone noticed."

The more attention Bird received, the more he shrank away from it. He began to case out side entrances, back doors, and less traveled routes whenever they arrived at a new arena. Media interviews were so unappealing to him that he often slipped out of the locker room before the reporters arrived. His behavior was initially puzzling to Nicks.

"I'm thinking, 'Wow, this is unique,'" Nicks said. "You've got to remember, I'm this stud from Chicago who is used to telling everyone what I've got. But Larry taught me not to get caught up in the limelight. I found myself trying to emulate him."

Not everyone took the same approach. One day the team was discussing on the bus where to stop to eat and one of the reserves, his voice dripping with sarcasm, sneered, "Whatever Larry wants." If such comments were hurtful to Bird, he never expressed that. Instead, he simply pushed his teammates harder.

"Some of those kids just didn't understand that Larry had elevated them to a height they never in their lives would have reached without him," Behnke said. "They were on a trip of a lifetime, but a couple of them were too jealous to enjoy it."

"Somebody asked me once how I felt about all that," Bird said. "I told them, 'Hell, I'm jealous of them too. I'm jealous because I never got to play with a Larry Bird.'"

Bird was an imposing figure, even to his friends. When it came to basketball matters, they warily conformed to what their star demanded. It was clear who the leader of the team was, "and if one of them got out of line, they'd be stopped," Larry said.

During one practice early in the season, a couple of ISU players were horsing around instead of conducting the drills outlined by Hodges. Before the coach had to admonish them, his star player took care of it.

"If you don't want to be here, then get the hell out," Bird shouted.

When he wasn't playing, Bird was content to be just another guy on campus. He was at his happiest when they went down to the local college hangout, the BallyHo, and threw back a couple of drafts. When ISU played St. Louis, Hodges arranged for the team to take a side trip to the city zoo, where the players walked around wearing their cowboy hats and licking ice cream cones and making faces at the gorillas. "Like a bunch of little middle school kids," Nicks said.

The team loved their trips to Tulsa, Oklahoma, where they frequented an all-you-can-eat spaghetti factory that offered several varieties of pasta and excellent saucy meatballs. The other highlight was being taken out to dinner after a big win by Bird's friend Max Gibson when he came to town. On those nights the players knew they were going to enjoy the biggest and best meal of the year.

Indiana State's final regular season game was against Wichita State, the only time all year the Sycamores were on national television. A major snowstorm enveloped Terre Haute, and when the team went to the arena to conduct their shoot-around on game day, the roof was leaking.

"It was snowing like crazy," Bird said. "I felt sure they'd cancel the game."

Georgia Bird weathered the near-whiteout conditions to arrive at the Hulman Center and report that the roads were slippery, barely plowed, and most definitely unsafe.

The teams played anyhow. Bird scored 49 points and grabbed 19 rebounds in front of a full house with Al McGuire offering breathless commentary courtside.

By the time the conference tournaments wrapped up, both Indiana State and Michigan State were awarded first-round byes in the NCAA tournament. The only way their paths would cross was if both teams advanced to the Final.

But first the Spartans needed to eliminate a Lamar team, coached by the colorful Billy Tubbs. Michigan State destroyed them, 95–64, behind Magic's triple-double — 13 points, 10 assists, and 17 rebounds.

In his postgame press conference, Coach Tubbs strode up to the podium and tore up a fistful of papers. It was the scouting report he had purchased from Bill Bertka's respected scouting service, Bertka's Views. Bertka, a veteran coach and scout who has been involved in the Lakers organization for more than 30 years, had identified the Spartans as a half-court team that walked the ball up the floor.

"Obviously Bertka couldn't see all the games himself, so he hired high school coaches to scout teams for him," Heathcote said. "Well, the high school coach that scouted us came to our game at Indiana. Bob Knight knew we wanted to run, so every time the ball went up he sent four guys running back to midcourt. We never could get our fast break going, so I told Earvin, 'Scrap it. Just walk it up.'"

From there, the Spartans rolled 87–71 over Louisiana State, then punched their ticket to the Final Four by upending Notre Dame, which was loaded with seven future NBA draft picks: Bill Laimbeer, Orlando Woolridge, Kelly Tripucka, Bill Hanzlik, Bruce Flowers, Tracy Jackson, and Rich Branning.

Heathcote told his team the night before the game on March 17, St. Patrick's Day, "Men, this game is for the national championship. This is the best team you will play this season. Even better than Indiana State."

Heathcote fine-tuned his matchup zone, which was quickly becoming one of the most heralded defenses in college basketball, to fit the Fighting Irish personnel. Then he lathered his team into an emotional frenzy by reminding them that Notre Dame had refused to come to Jenison Field House during the regular season to play them. He also brought up the fact that Notre Dame was on television every Sunday.

"We were on once — a national game against Kansas," Heathcote said. "I asked my guys, 'Hey, aren't you tired of watching these Notre Dame players?'"

Michigan State beat Notre Dame with 34 points and 13 rebounds from Kelser and 19 points and 13 assists from Magic. The Spartans shot 63 percent in the second half.

Indiana State cruised through its first two tournament games with an 89–69 win over Virginia Tech and a 93–72 win over Oklahoma. Bird averaged 25.5 points and 14 rebounds in the two games, which were impressive numbers considering he had fractured his left thumb in the Missouri Valley Conference Final against New Mexico State. Behnke fashioned a makeshift splint to stabilize the thumb, but he could do little to limit the considerable pain Bird would be experiencing every time the ball made contact with the area.

"I can't say the injury impaired him, but it had to hurt," Behnke said. "But there was never a discussion of him sitting. He was playing, no matter what. That was his mentality."

Indiana State's final obstacle in its quest for a Final Four berth was Arkansas, led by Sidney Moncrief, Bird's former teammate in the World Invitational Tournament. The afternoon before the Arkansas game, Bird fielded a call from Auerbach, who was in town to watch the tournament and wanted Bird to come up to his hotel room for a few minutes.

"Look, Larry," Red said, "when your team gets beat in the tournament, we'd love for you to come to Boston and finish the season with us."

"You mean after the tournament?" Bird asked.

"After you get beat here," Auerbach answered.

"Well, Red, I don't think we're going to get beat," Bird answered. "I think we can take Arkansas."

"We'll see, kid," retorted Auerbach.

Bird scored 31 points and grabbed 10 rebounds against the Razorbacks, but it was his roommate, Heaton, who'd earned the moniker "Miracle Man" for his last-second heroics, who again launched the winning shot.

With the score tied 71–71 in the final seconds of the game, Heaton looked to get Bird the ball, but Bird was double-teamed. Heaton drove the lane with his natural right hand, and as Arkansas forward Scott Hastings slid over to help, Heaton switched the ball into his left hand and rolled in a shot as the buzzer sounded. Indiana State was going to the Final Four, and Auerbach was going home without his prized draft pick.

The Terre Haute campus was a cauldron of excitement, with Sycamore mania bubbling over to the classrooms, the restaurants, even the city library.

The semifinal matchups in Salt Lake City, the site of the Final Four, pitted Michigan State against Penn, the plucky Ivy League team that had shocked North Carolina earlier in the tournament, and DePaul against Indiana State.

Michigan State's surprise opponent was a heavy underdog against the Spartans, but Penn's brash star Tony Price declared beforehand, "I don't fear Michigan State. They're just a bunch of dudes who play ball."

The "dudes" demolished the Quakers 101–67. It was 50–17 at halftime, and Johnson added yet another triple-double to his résumé: 29 points, 10 rebounds, 10 assists.

Midway through the second half, Michigan State couldn't help but break an old cardinal rule in sports: they started to look ahead.

"Now stay focused, let's take care of this game first," Heathcote instructed his players.

Magic looked directly at Heathcote.

"C'mon, Coach, they're the Ivies! We're not going to lose to them!" he said.

By the midway point of the second half, Heathcote admitted, all of the Spartans were thinking about one thing: "How are we going to stop Bird?"

In the final moments of their thrashing of Penn, the Michigan State fans began chanting, "We want Bird! We want Bird!" The Sycamore fans responded in unison, "You'll get Bird! You'll get Bird!"

Larry's Indiana State boys did not breeze into the championship like Magic's club. DePaul stars Mark Aguirre and Clyde Bradshaw made it clear they planned on playing a physical game and promised there would be no easy baskets for Bird.

"They were talking all this trash about how they were going to manhandle us," Nicks said. "I think it really pissed Larry off. And that's never a good idea."

Michigan State's players sat in the stands and watched in disbelief as DePaul came out and guarded Bird in single coverage. Magic turned to Kelser and declared: "Big mistake."

"Larry was hitting shots from all over the floor," Magic said. "I wasn't keeping stats or anything, but at one point I said, 'Hey, has that guy missed at all?'"

Bird finished the game with 35 points on 16-of-19 shooting. His curious stat line also included 11 turnovers, a gaudy number that normally would have spelled doom for Indiana State. Nicks attributed the miscues to two factors: a hyperactive Bird and nervous teammates who had trouble hanging on to his creative (and often unexpected) passes.

"Those turnovers were my fault," Bird said. "Back then, I had a habit of passing off while I was jumping in the air. Too many times my teammates were already turning around to get in position for the rebound."

Heathcote didn't notice Bird's turnovers. He was too mesmerized by Bird's unwavering confidence in his own shot and his ability to choose the perfect pass for the open man.

"I don't mind telling you Bird scared me," Heathcote said. "He was the kind of guy whose passing skills were so sharp, he could cut your defense to ribbons."

With the desired dream matchup of Bird versus Magic set for the NCAA Final, the two teams arrived the day before the championship game for their respective press conferences. The national media anticipated that Larry would be a no-show, but he surprised them by taking his designated seat at the podium.

The normally taciturn forward was both revealing and entertaining, even if some of his answers were not particularly loquacious. When asked, for instance, how his thumb felt, the self-described "Hick from French Lick" answered, "Broke."

On the subject of what he'd do with the hundreds of thousands of dollars that awaited him in the NBA, Bird cracked, "I might buy everyone on the team a new car — and Brad Miley a jump shot."

As Kelser and Johnson bounded into the press room with smiles and belly laughs and handshakes and high-fives for some of the local reporters, Bird retreated to the side with Bill Hodges and did not make eye contact with either of his opponents. Magic took one step toward his former World Invitational teammate, but backed off when Bird made no motion to meet him halfway.

"All I was doing was trying to say hi to the guy," Magic said. "Normally at those things you shake hands, make some small talk, but Larry wasn't having any of that."

Johnson turned to Kelser and whispered, "Okay, then. I guess this isn't going to be a friendly one. You know what? Larry Bird, he's kind of a jerk."

Once Magic was seated, he congenially answered the same questions over and over with a new twist for each reporter. As he watched Johnson court the press, Bird understood who the media darling would be when the session was over. He found "the Magic touch" to be grating.

"I just couldn't be like that," he said. "I didn't want to be like that. All that hand-slapping stuff, it seemed phony to me."

Bird had his reasons for snubbing the Michigan State players. He was angry to see both Kelser and Johnson representing the Spartans. His sidekick, Carl Nicks, was back in the locker room instead of sitting with him, a slight he knew bothered his teammate deeply.

"They had two guys up there," Bird said. "Why couldn't we?"

When Kelser and Magic arrived back at their hotel, Kelser gathered the team together and told them to start locking into their game assignments.

"This Bird guy is really serious," Kelser reported. "He's already got his game face on."

Heathcote spent his entire practice before the championship game devising ways to slow Bird. His frustration grew as one after another of his subs impersonated number 33, yet failed to duplicate the kind of offensive firepower Heathcote knew was coming.

"This isn't working," Heathcote said. "You guys don't play anything like Bird. Earvin, you be Larry — you play just like him, only he has a jump shot."

Magic bristled, grabbed the ball, and said, "You want the real Larry Bird? Just watch me."

Johnson began launching 15- and 20-foot shots, which were well beyond his normal range. He hit fallaways in the post, long baseline jumpers, and turnarounds in the key.

"I was loving it," Magic said. "I think I hit about 15 in a row."

Now Heathcote was agitated with his defense. "Play him like he's Larry Bird!" he admonished them. "Are you going to give Larry Bird all those shots?"

After Magic buried his 10th in a row, Heathcote, his face crimson, blew the whistle and waved it off.

"I was so far out, my foot was out of bounds," said Magic.

The evening before the championship game, Johnson organized a team trip to the movies. When the Spartans arrived at the theater, they spread out in different rows to watch the film. As the lights came up, they were chagrined to discover that some of them had been sitting near players from the Indiana State team.

"We heard a lot of comments," Nicks reported. "Things like, 'It's on, man. You're going down.'"

Nicks reported these developments to Bird, who had not accompanied the Sycamores to the theater.

"Who cares what they say?" Bird asked Nicks.

"Larry didn't care, but some of our other guys were intimidated," Nicks said. "It seemed to me we had some guys who weren't feeling good about our chances."

In the hours preceding the championship game, two college stars bunked down in the same city but in separate hotels, wrestling with their bed sheets and obsessing over the other one's talent.

Bird could not eliminate the image of Johnson prancing up the court and setting up Kelser for one of his thunderous acrobatic alley-oop slams. He tried to visualize how his team could prevent the Spartans from running them off the floor. The problem, he quickly determined, was that Magic was too big for Nicks to guard and too quick for Miley to guard. And if the Sycamores resorted to a double team, either Kelser or Vincent was apt to exploit it.

Magic kept replaying Bird's offensive arsenal against DePaul in his mind and worrying about the versatile ways in which he was able to hurt them. Most of the other top college players they faced had one particular signature move.

"The problem with Larry was he could score from anywhere," Magic said. "It was the first time in my life I was scared of another player."

While Bird experienced his share of trepidation over Magic, he was equally concerned about the shortcomings of his own team. Two of their starters, Brad Miley (50 percent) and Alex Gilbert (28 percent) were horrendous foul shooters, and Bird knew that sooner or later it was going to catch up with them.

His concern about free throws proved to be prophetic. ISU would hit only 10 of 22 from the line in the championship game, while Bird, who went on to be a career 88.5 percent free throw shooter in the NBA, would hit only 5 of his 8 free throws.

On game day, Bird and Heaton sat side by side on adjacent training tables, minutes before the tip-off. As Behnke taped Bird's thumb, Heaton asked, "Larry, how you feeling?"

"I feel sick, like I always do before every game," Bird answered. "I just want to get out there. The waiting is killing me."

Hodges chose the 6-foot-8 Miley to guard Magic instead of Nicks, who had been making noise all week about wanting a piece of the Michigan State star.

Just 15 seconds into the game, Magic upfaked once and easily drove left past Miley. Magic tripped over Miley's feet, stumbled awkwardly, and was called for a travel, but he knew he was on to something.

"I'm thinking, 'Okay, I'm going to have my way with this guy,'" Magic said.

Johnson was shocked that Nicks didn't draw the assignment. After watching several hours of film on Nicks pressuring guards, he had braced himself for an assault of full-court pressure. With Miley guarding him, he knew that was no longer a worry.

Steve Reed drew first blood for Indiana State with a jumper from the top of the foul circle, thereby negating the "early knockout" punch Magic and Heathcote were seeking.

"But I didn't care about that basket," Johnson said. "It wasn't Larry that took it."

Bird swished a long corner jumper to give Indiana State an 8–7 edge. Although he couldn't have known it at the time, it was the last lead Bird's team would have in the game.

Heathcote angrily called for a time-out even though the game was still in its infancy. "We played the whole season to get here, and we went over the game plan again and again, and you guys are blowing it," Heathcote bellowed. "Now do what I told you! Get in Bird's face!"

Michigan State responded with a 9–1 spurt, and when Heathcote went to a bigger lineup of Kelser, Magic, Brkovich, Vincent, and Charles, the Spartans threatened to blow the game open.

"I knew when they started getting 4-on-1 fast breaks, we had problems," Heaton confessed. "No one had done that to us before."

Michigan State led 30–19 when Magic picked up his third foul angling for an offensive rebound. Johnson sat the final three and a half minutes of the half, but Michigan State still jogged off with a 37–28 advantage at the intermission.

Bird was somber as his team limped to their locker room. Michigan State was doing a masterful job of not only limiting his shots but also sealing off his passing lanes. And every time he tried to put the ball on the floor, two defenders choked off the lane.

"I knew we were in trouble right away," Bird conceded. "Things weren't going right. Their quickness, their defense . . . and our guys were tensed up more than any other time we played."

Michigan State's strategy was to work as fervently to prevent Bird from passing as they did to limit his shooting. That left Nicks as ISU's best hope at generating some offense. With Bird struggling, Nicks admitted, he found himself forcing the issue.

"I rushed too many shots," Nicks said. "What scared me to death was Larry couldn't hardly get anything off. He couldn't find a way, and I had never seen that before. I was thinking, 'This is bad.'"

On the other end of the court, Bird also struggled to contain the quicker, more athletic Kelser, who drove on him repeatedly in hopes of exploiting him defensively.

Michigan State was ahead 44–28 and on the verge of breaking the game open when Kelser received the ball on the right side of the key and tried to take Bird to the middle off the dribble. Bird jumped in the passing lane and drew contact. It was a clever maneuver by a player who was at a disadvantage athletically but one step ahead of the play mentally.

Kelser was whistled for his offensive foul, his fourth, which sent him to the bench and provided the Sycamores with one final flicker of hope.

"I'm thinking, 'Oh no, Greg,'" Magic said. "The only chance they had was if one of the two of us were out and we couldn't spread the floor and beat them with our speed."

In the ISU huddle, as Hodges called on his club to pick up the Spartans in a full-court press, Bird implored his teammates, "C'mon, one more run at 'em."

Nicks, Heaton, and Staley each came up with big baskets, but Michigan State's steady Terry Donnelly matched each of them with clutch perimeter jumpers. He would finish the game a perfect 5-of-5 from the floor.

Just as Bird feared, errant free throws hurt Indiana State down the stretch. Bird missed a key free throw after forcing Brkovich into a turnover, and after a Bird fallaway cut the deficit to nine points, Nicks went to the line with a chance to shave it to seven. Instead, he missed both.

The Sycamores would never get closer than six points. With less than five minutes to play, Magic orchestrated a textbook backdoor cut, received the ball from Kelser, and jammed it over the outstretched arms of Heaton. Not only was Johnson credited with the basket, but he was also awarded two free throws for a flagrant foul, a dubious call that even Heathcote concedes could have gone either way.

The image of Magic soaring over Heaton appeared on the cover of *Sports Illustrated* a few days later, declaring Michigan State the national champions.

In the final four minutes, without a 24-second clock to limit their time of possession, MSU went to a spread offense and ticked off as much time as they could by passing the ball around the perimeter. Bird, frustrated by their stall tactics, swatted the ball out of Magic's hands as he was inbounding it, then laid it in for two. The basket was waved off, and Bird was called for a technical. He did not react to the call; he merely turned and ran back down the floor, his blond head bowed.

Once the buzzer sounded and Michigan State's 75–64 victory was officially in the books, Bird quickly located Johnson, shook his hand, and congratulated him for having the better team.

Bird checked out with mortal numbers: 19 points on 7 of 21 shooting attempts with 13 rebounds and 2 assists. Yet what haunts him to this day are the missed free throws.

"It's the one thing I'll never get over," Bird said.

Magic was too busy celebrating with his teammates to notice the anguish of his opponent. It wasn't until later, with his arm draped around a young announcer named Bryant Gumbel, that Magic noticed Bird sitting on his bench, his face buried in a towel. Johnson had just been named the game's Most Outstanding Player on the strength of his 24 points, 7 rebounds, and 5 assists, but suddenly he felt a pang of sympathy for his rival.

"I spent all week wanting to beat Bird in the worst way, but when it happened, I found myself feeling kind of bad," Magic said. "I knew how much it meant to Larry. I cried the year before when we lost to Kentucky."

Bird declined to attend the postgame press conference. He remained, head down, choking back tears in that towel for several minutes after the game ended.

"What hit me most was it was all over," Bird said. "I didn't know where I was going. I hadn't signed with the Celtics yet, and I had no clue what was next. And it was just killing me we were out there playing so hard and no matter what we did, it wasn't going to happen."

In subsequent years, as the stature of Bird and Magic increased, the championship game was rehashed and rescrutinized hundreds of times. Bird conceded that, if the two teams played again, Michigan State would beat Indiana State nine times out of ten.

"Maybe even ten out of ten," he admitted.

Their epic game sparked an interest in college basketball that exploded in subsequent years. Three decades later, the NCAA basketball tournament was one of the most hyped and eagerly anticipated events in sports, its roots firmly planted in the drama of Magic and Larry.

After their showdown, both players went home to a hero's welcome. The Spartans were treated to a ticker-tape parade featuring Magic lounging in a convertible, waving to his adoring public.

The Sycamores were greeted by more than 10,000 smitten fans upon their return to Terre Haute, and Bird was later presented with a key to the city.

Heathcote spent 16 more seasons at Michigan State, earning legendary status for guiding the team to the first title in school history.

Hodges was dismissed from Indiana State three seasons later and never given another opportunity to coach a major college program.

Bird and Magic moved on to professional basketball — together, of course.

Whenever Hodges ran into Heathcote, he'd whack his rival on the back and say, "Remember, Jud, you're the one who ruined my life."

Bird vowed to make sure he would never have to say the same to Magic Johnson.

3

★ ★ ★

MAY 16, 1980

Philadelphia, Pennsylvania

THE ROOKIE WAS SITTING in the captain's seat.

Usually only veterans claimed dibs on the roomier bulkhead rows on the commercial airlines, which were not designed to comfortably transport athletes with an average height of 6-foot-6 across the country.

Had Lakers captain and perennial All-Star Kareem Abdul-Jabbar been on board, he would have assumed his customary spot on the bulkhead aisle. But Abdul-Jabbar was back in Los Angeles nursing a badly sprained ankle, and the timing of the injury couldn't have been worse. The Lakers were playing the Philadelphia 76ers in the 1980 NBA Finals, and as they headed east for Game 6, they were forced to depart without Kareem, the epicenter of the Lakers offense, a towering combination of skill and finesse with a trademark skyhook that was one of the most effective weapons in the league.

The notion of playing without Abdul-Jabbar at the most critical point of the season, with LA ahead 3–2 in games and on the cusp of winning it all, was momentarily paralyzing.

Lakers coach Paul Westhead announced in practice he would plug Kareem's hole with Earvin "Magic" Johnson, the precocious rookie who had skipped into training camp as the number-one pick in the 1979 draft. Westhead's strategy puzzled some of his veterans. Magic was a point guard accustomed to running the show. Now, it appeared, he *would* be the show.

"I wasn't sure what Westhead's intent was," confessed veteran Jamaal Wilkes. "I guess he was saying, 'We just lost our best player, but we have this young, charismatic phenom who is going to make it all right.'"

If there was any question whether that young phenom was up to the task, Magic eliminated all doubt when he boldly walked past his more seasoned teammates and settled in Kareem's premium seat for the flight to Philadelphia. As the 20-year-old turned around, he flashed his pearly whites and declared, "Never fear. E.J. is here!"

Magic could see the players' spirits were flagging, but felt with the smaller, quicker lineup the Lakers could strike with their transition game. It was a huge mistake, he believed, to write off Game 6 and pin their hopes all on Game 7, when Abdul-Jabbar might or might not be back.

"Okay, fellas, you know what?" Magic said. "We're looking at a wide-open game here. This might be all right. Let's put our track shoes on and run these guys out of the building."

Johnson pulled big man Jim Chones aside and asked him how he should defend Caldwell Jones, who, at 6 feet, 11 inches, would enjoy a height advantage. Chones reminded Magic that Jones was not a threat from the perimeter but an exceptional rebounder who needed to be boxed out completely.

"One more thing," Chones cautioned. "Caldwell likes to come over from the weak side to block shots. Be aware of it, or he'll make you look bad."

On game day in Philadelphia, the rookie breezed through the locker room selling LA's potentially catastrophic hole in their lineup without Kareem as an opportunity, an adventure.

"Hey, Norm," he said to veteran guard Norm Nixon. "We're so

worried about how we're going to stop them. Well, who is going to guard us?"

Michael Cooper watched Magic working the room like a night-club singer in a cocktail lounge. Professional athletes generally become jaded as the years pass, scoffing at the rallying cries of youngsters who have just exited the college ranks and still believe in pompoms and fight songs. As Johnson stopped at each locker preaching his gospel of optimism, Cooper mused, "He's giving his own pep rally."

The rally was successful because Magic's energy was contagious. Wilkes, often a facilitator for Kareem, started envisioning himself slashing to the hole. Nixon perked up at the idea of more shots. Chones volunteered to hound the massive Darryl Dawkins, a force in the middle whose self-proclaimed nickname, Chocolate Thunder, indicated the power with which he played the game.

"We went from thinking we couldn't win to talking like we would win," Cooper said.

On the night of Game 6 of the 1980 NBA Finals, Celtics forward Larry Bird sat with a small group of friends in a Boston club awaiting the Lakers-Sixers showdown. The elimination of his Celtics team by Philadelphia in the Eastern Conference Finals had deprived him of the opportunity to face Earvin "Magic" Johnson and even the score of their increasingly personal rivalry.

Unlike most of America, which was forced to watch the game on tape delay because no major network was willing to run the NBA Finals in prime time during its sweeps period, Bird watched the game in real time. He had a friend in the television business who arranged for a live feed to be pumped into the restaurant.

As he lamented his own rookie season, which he felt ended prematurely at the hands of Julius Erving and the Sixers, Bird admitted to his buddies he was curious how Magic would fare. He knew by charting Magic's productive box scores that he had become LA's everyman, yet even so, when Bird saw his rival step into the circle for the opening tap, he guffawed.

"You gotta be kidding me," Bird said. "Magic can't jump!"

Johnson didn't win the tip, but that was the only moment when his game fell short that evening. He was a catalyst offensively, driving the lane and knocking down fallaways. He was an agitator defensively, using his strong body to knock Philly off the ball. He was, as always, the most expressive player on the floor. He led Los Angeles on a 7–0 run to start the game and never looked back.

"I found myself rooting for him even though I didn't like him," Bird said.

Although the game was tied 60–60 at halftime, Johnson was buoyant. Chones, as promised, was thwarting Dawkins. The Sixers, as Magic predicted, were flummoxed by the Lakers' new lineup. When Johnson started hitting shots over Caldwell Jones, they switched Erving onto him. Then they tried Bobby Jones. It didn't matter. None of them could derail Earvin Johnson's momentum.

"I knew exactly how Magic was feeling," Bird said. "There are times when you get it going and you are in this incredible place, this zone, where you are controlling the game. You feel no matter what you try, it's going to work. It's the greatest feeling in the world, because no one can stop you.

"And nobody was going to stop Magic that night."

The Lakers won the title with a 123–107 victory. Magic was an NBA champion on his first try, without his captain, a future Hall of Famer, in the lineup. He logged 47 out of a possible 48 minutes, was a perfect 14 of 14 from the free throw line, and finished with 42 points, 15 rebounds, and 7 assists.

It was an unprecedented performance. Johnson was the youngest Finals MVP in history and the first rookie ever to win the award.

Bird witnessed Magic's brilliance with conflicting emotions. He marveled at his ability and his poise under pressure, but was also overcome with envy. He left the bar feeling unsettled.

"I was jealous and ticked off, but at the same time I was in total awe of what he had done," Bird said.

By the time he arrived home, Bird had calmed down — until he watched Johnson's highlights on the news and became agitated all over again.

"Damn," Bird said. "I've got to win one of these things [championships]. This guy's got two in a row. He's making me look bad."

Earvin "Magic" Johnson had a knack for making things look easy, yet his decision to turn professional and subsequent indoctrination with the vaunted Lakers was stressful, emotional, and, in the beginning, painfully lonely.

Magic was a pleaser, and in the spring of 1979, while he was still plucking confetti from Michigan State's championship victory parade out of his afro, his Spartan teammates were already pleading with him, "C'mon, man. Stay with us. Let's go for two championships."

For a moment, he was legitimately tempted. Johnson had two seasons of eligibility left, loved being "the Magic Man" on campus, and felt the Spartans could repeat as champions if he stayed in school. Yet the lure of the NBA was irresistible.

Greg Kelser was graduating and had already hired an agent who promoted himself, in part, by saying he had done some work for NBA star Julius Erving.

Erving was one of Magic's idols. Dr. J signed with the Virginia Squires of the ABA after leaving the University of Massachusetts early and had thrived as a professional. Forbidden by NCAA regulations to dunk in college, Erving became the master of high-flying slams, and when the ABA merged with the NBA, Dr. J became one of the league's first bona-fide superstars.

"Do you think your agent could hook me up on the phone with Dr. J?" Magic asked Kelser. "I'd like to ask him his advice."

Erving knew all about Johnson and his gifted passing skills. He not only agreed to talk with him, he invited Magic and Kelser to stay at his suburban Philadelphia home during the 1979 NBA playoffs. They bunked in the guest room, fussed over by Erving's wife Turquoise, and were given passes into the Sixers locker room. Both players were amazed at how big the pro players were, far more imposing than they appeared on 24-inch black-and-white television sets.

Dr. J sat down with Johnson and briefed him on the challenge in front of him. Erving had left school as a college junior and by doing so missed an opportunity to be an Olympian. Magic would also be giving up that dream if he went pro, he said. Dr. J explained that, whatever decision he made, someone would be disappointed.

"If you go pro, some of your college teammates will resent you," he said. "If you stay in school, your family might be upset you won't be in a position to assist them financially."

Erving also outlined the difference between a college basketball season and the long, often grueling lifestyle of a professional basketball player.

"Are you ready to be in a man's world?" Erving asked. "This is 82 games now, not 30. Can you handle the demands on your body? Can you handle the drudgery? It's going to be totally different. You think you know, but trust me, you don't. Be ready for the ups and downs, because they're coming."

Magic was ready. He'd been waiting for this moment since he was 12 years old. He declared himself eligible for the NBA draft and braced himself for the inevitable commotion it would cause.

His decision was indeed a newsmaker, but not in the manner he expected. An article by Joe Falls of the *Detroit Free Press* detailed why Johnson would not make a good pro. Falls questioned (correctly at that time) whether Magic had the range or the accuracy to be a legitimate outside shooter. He maintained that Magic's no-look passes wouldn't be successful in the NBA and called into question Johnson's defensive capabilities. Falls was also skeptical that a player of Johnson's size could succeed as a point guard in a league that put a premium on quickness and athleticism.

Magic had known Falls since high school. He was an influential columnist, and his words were stunning. They also ticked Johnson off.

"Did you hear about this?" he asked Kelser, whom he roused out of bed with an early morning telephone call.

"Did you read Joe Falls this morning?" said Magic to Heathcote when he arrived at the Spartans gym.

"Ah, don't worry, that's just Joe," Heathcote said.

Johnson was already motivated to make his mark in the NBA, but Falls's prose became the impetus he needed to stay an extra hour, shoot an extra hundred jump shots, and run through an extra set of defensive slides.

"Joe Falls did me a favor," Magic said. "He helped me get ready for the NBA as much as anybody."

Johnson's new NBA home would be determined by a coin flip between the Chicago Bulls and the Los Angeles Lakers to see who selected first in the 1979 draft.

After meeting with Johnson, Bulls general manager Rod Thorn and coach Jerry Sloan, an old-school coach who abhorred glitz and flair, were giddy at the prospect of building around him.

"Magic was just so disarming because of his charisma," Thorn said. "We were asking him questions, but the next thing you know, he was interviewing us. Even Jerry was getting excited."

Magic's visit with the Lakers also went well. He walked out convinced they would take him if they selected first—until he read an *LA Times* article on the plane ride home discussing general manager Jerry West's fascination with Arkansas star Sidney Moncrief, the team's plans to bring in UCLA forward David Greenwood for an interview, and speculation that the Lakers could use the draft selection to trade for a power forward.

"Maybe they don't like me as much as I think," he confided to his father.

What Magic didn't know was that Dr. Jerry Buss, the future owner of the Lakers who was about to buy the team from Jack Kent Cooke, told the Lakers front office that he expected the team to draft Magic.

"They resisted because Jerry West really liked Moncrief too," Buss said. "But I told them, 'It's Magic, or find yourself another buyer.'"

The coin flip was determined over a squawk box in an empty conference room. Thorn was in Chicago, Lakers executive Bill Sharman was in Los Angeles, and the NBA's legal counsel, David Stern, was in New York presiding over the toss.

The Bulls capitalized on the event as a promotional opportunity to let the fans vote on whether the call should be heads or tails. The Chicago fans voted heads.

"It came up tails," Thorn said. "They got a Hall of Famer in Magic Johnson, and we got David Greenwood."

Greenwood played six years for the Bulls and enjoyed an unremarkable career that spanned twelve seasons and four teams.

Larry Bird's NBA destination was already secure in the spring of 1979, but the timing of his arrival in Boston remained in doubt. When Indiana State's season finally ended in heartbreak in Salt Lake City at the hands of Michigan State, the Celtics made a pitch to sign Bird for the final eight games of their season. He declined in order to complete his student teaching obligations so he could finally earn his diploma.

That meant reporting to West Vigo High School in Terre Haute as a physical education and health teacher and assistant baseball coach. Bird was scheduled to begin in March, but each time Indiana State advanced in the tournament, he called West Vigo's baseball coach, Dave Ballenger, to apologize and postpone his arrival. After the third call, Ballenger finally told Bird, "What are you apologizing for? I'm going to the game!"

Although Auerbach was persuasive in his argument to lure Bird to Boston, informing Bird that he would be the first player in history to compete in both an NCAA game and NBA game in the same month, the young forward opted instead to teach flag football, badminton, and dodge ball. His duties also included teaching a CPR course and driver's education.

While the Celtics dropped seven of those final eight regular games, Bird tooled around with high school students in a specially equipped vehicle that had a brake on the passenger side in case the young drivers panicked. "We had some close calls," Bird said, "but I always had my left hand ready in case I needed to grab the wheel."

Bird's most difficult — and rewarding — assignment at West Vigo was the three or four times he taught a classroom of mentally disabled children. He spent the majority of the class chasing his students down the hall and ushering them back to their seats after they bolted upright and scampered out of the room without warning.

"It was an unbelievable experience," Bird said. "And at times very overwhelming. I can't tell you how much respect I have for people who have made it their life's work to help those kids."

In the evening, Bird played basketball at the Boys and Girls Club in Terre Haute and occasionally filled in for Bob Heaton's softball team. One night in early April, he arrived at the diamond to discover that his brother Mike was on the opposite team.

Bird was manning left field when Mike lofted a line drive toward him. The fly ball started out straight, then sank dramatically at the last moment, like a Tim Wakefield knuckleball. Larry bent down on one knee to make a basket catch, but the ball smashed his finger and bent it backward. He felt an odd tingling sensation, and when he picked up the ball and tried to throw it, his finger curved around at an unnatural angle, as though he was a Saturday morning cartoon character with exaggerated, elastic limbs.

"I looked down," Bird said, "and my finger was all the way over to the other side of my hand."

Bird's mangled finger was so grotesque that his brother Mike nearly vomited when he examined it. Bird's girlfriend, Dinah Mattingly, rushed him to a nearby hospital where emergency room personnel took x-rays and immobilized his finger in a splint.

He slept fitfully that night, with his throbbing finger robbing him of any prolonged sleep. Bird's alarm was set for an early morning wake-up call to go mushroom hunting, and he was hell-bent on sticking to his plans. There is a six-week period each year when rare morel mushrooms grow in Indiana. They range in size and color, depending on the month, and they are extremely difficult to find. Bird had been hunting mushrooms for years and was annoyed that his aching finger threatened to ruin his day. It never once occurred to him that it also might ruin the upcoming season of the Boston Celtics.

He popped a couple of aspirin and went hunting anyhow. After emerging from the woods just before dark, his brother informed him, "There's a doctor looking for you. He checked your x-rays, and you need to get to Indianapolis right away."

The news was alarming: Bird's knuckle was shattered, and he needed surgery to remove bone chips and insert several pins to stabilize the finger.

"How long is it going to take before it's healed?" Bird asked the surgeon.

"Healed?" the surgeon replied. "Son, I'm not sure it will."

After the procedure, the doctor attempted to immobilize the finger by putting a clip behind Bird's fingernail. Then he attached a mechanism running the length of his wrist to hold the finger in place. One evening, while Bird was watching television, the clip gave way and the fingernail ripped off, leaving Bird yelping in pain and splattered with his own blood.

He had not yet signed a contract with the Celtics, nor had he informed them of his injury. When Auerbach learned of his draft pick's surgery, he summoned Bird to Boston. By then, the forward was working out again, yet he still visited the godfather of Celtics basketball with some uneasiness.

"I just didn't have the same feel for the ball as I did before," Bird said. "I was sure Red would notice."

Team physician Dr. Thomas Silva didn't like what he saw. He told Auerbach that the knuckle would never repair completely and Bird would not have the same range of motion. In his estimation, the young forward was damaged goods. The Celtics boss listened, then directed Bird out to the court. He threw him the ball and told him, "Shoot it."

Bird buried one jumper. Then another. Then another. Although his feel wasn't the same, his range was intact. So Auerbach threw him a bounce pass, then a chest pass, then an overhead pass. Bird nimbly caught them all.

"If he was in pain," Auerbach said, "he did a pretty good job of disguising it. He was one tough kid."

The general manager put his arm around his young forward. "I'm not worried about this," Red said.

For the first time since he arrived in Boston, Bird exhaled.

As time went on, Bird's finger built up calcium deposits and became grossly disfigured. Once, while Bird was posing for a cover shot for *Sports Illustrated*, the photographer told Bird to hold up his finger to signify that he — and the Celtics — were number one. But when Bird held up his ghastly digit, it looked more like "We're number ten." The photographer shot him using his opposite hand instead.

Although he still went on to bury some of the biggest shots in NBA history, Bird concedes nearly 30 years after the fact that Dr. Silva's diagnosis was correct. "I never could shoot as well again," he said.

Magic Johnson spent the better part of August 1979 working solely on his own perimeter game. Dr. Charles Tucker, a school counselor from Lansing and a former ballplayer who became Magic's agent, warned him that teams would sag off him and double-team Kareem until the kid proved he could stroke the jumper.

"No one is going to sag off me without paying for it," Magic grunted in between sessions.

He signed a five-year, $2.3 million contract with a $175,000 signing bonus, and he couldn't imagine what he'd do with all that money. Buss asked him to move to Los Angeles to get acclimated to his new home, and Johnson happily obliged.

Magic was 19 years old. He didn't know anyone and was overwhelmed by the sprawling, glittery city and its daunting freeways. His new teammates were much older, and many of them were married with families. His first month in his new city he was completely alone.

Buss owned an apartment complex in Culver City and suggested the rookie move in there since it was near the practice facility, the airport, and the Forum. Johnson bought himself a new color television and spent his days watching *Perry Mason* and dialing home.

He missed the chaos of his house in Lansing, which always seemed too small, too loud, and too cluttered but now seemed so inviting. On Sunday nights, he'd call and ask his sister Pearl to describe what his mother Christine was cooking. Then he'd hang up and order takeout — again.

One morning, Buss called to check on him.

"Do you like football?" the owner asked.

Three hours later, Magic was on the field at the USC game standing next to the coaches and the players. The Lakers' season hadn't started, and Magic had yet to play for LA, yet he was serenaded by the college football crowd with doting cheers of "Mag-ic, Mag-ic!"

"Dr. Buss!" Magic exclaimed. "They know who I am!"

Buss and Johnson, the two new guys on the Lakers' block, became constant companions. They both loved chocolate doughnuts, which they shared on Saturday mornings. They enjoyed shooting pool and competed in epic Ping-Pong battles. The owner liked to frequent exclusive nightclubs, and while Johnson was not a drinker, he went along anyhow, socializing with some of the wealthiest people in Los Angeles.

Buss took Magic to fellow real estate mogul Donald Sterling's famous annual Malibu party. Sterling, who would later purchase the Los Angeles Clippers, owned a stunning waterfront home and served aqua-colored martinis and cocktails with miniature umbrellas floating on top. Magic was awed by the music, the food, and the women, but mostly he was mesmerized by the rolling surf.

"I was from Michigan," he explained. "I had never seen the ocean before."

When he got home from the party, he called Greg Kelser, his childhood friend Dale Beard, his girlfriend Cookie, and his mother. "You won't believe where I was tonight," he told each of them. "I was at the beach. Right on the water. With all the movers and the shakers!"

A week later, Buss took Magic to Friday night at the Playboy mansion. It was movie night, only Magic couldn't concentrate on the film because there were too many beautiful women to distract him. That prompted another series of phone calls back home to say, "Guess where I was?" — except this time he left his mom and Cookie off the call list.

Buss took his point guard to the exclusive Pip's in Beverly Hills to dance alongside the biggest Hollywood names. "There's Prince, there's Sylvester Stallone, there's Michael Douglas," Johnson would say, rattling off the parade of stars.

"It blew me away," Magic admitted. "And what blew me away even more was, they knew me."

Night after night, he and Buss toured the town. Buss brought lots of women with him on their excursions, and he'd dance disco, the waltz, and the tango with them for hours. When he got tired, he'd turn to Johnson and say, "Earvin, dance with these ladies."

Sometimes Buss and Magic would go to Vegas, where Buss would win (or lose) thousands of dollars in a half-hour. Whenever the Lakers' owner decided he had reached his limit, they'd go dancing again.

Although they spent countless hours together, they rarely talked about basketball. Buss wanted his prize investment to think beyond that.

"Earvin, take care of your money," Buss told him. "What do you want to do after basketball?"

The goal of the Lakers' flamboyant owner was to create a basketball team with Hollywood flair. Doris Day and Frank Sinatra were already regulars at the Forum, but Buss knew he'd made it when Sean Connery called him one evening and asked if there was room for agent 007 in his box.

"Once people saw Magic play," said Buss, "everyone wanted in."

Before Johnson's arrival, the Lakers' summer league games typically drew around 3,500 people. For Magic's first outing, more than 10,000 fans showed up.

There was a similar buzz in Boston, where Bird was already being billed as the savior who would turn around a franchise that had won only 29 games the previous season. Bird was wary of the city, especially after looking out the window of his downtown hotel room at the Parker House and watching a flock of Hare Krishnas dressed in robes chanting on the Common.

His owner, Harry Mangurian, was not interested in nightlife, casinos, or scantily clad women. He was a racehorse enthusiast who shook Bird's hand once and left it at that.

"He didn't seem all that interested in basketball," Bird said. "It was his wife who was the big fan."

While Boston certainly had its share of exclusive restaurants and trendy nightclubs, Bird did not frequent any of them. He was content to drink a six-pack of beer in the kitchen of his modest Brookline home. The team went to a steak house one night before the season to have dinner, but the rookie did not attend. He was busy mowing his yard.

He was thankful that Dinah was moving to Boston with him. Bird could be impetuous and hotheaded, but Dinah was his valued alter ego. Just as he was about to make a rash decision, she would pointedly tell him, "I'd think about that if I were you."

"She talked me out of doing a lot of dumb things," Bird said.

They met at Indiana State during one of the more chaotic times of his life. His father had committed suicide a year earlier, and his family was struggling financially. Bird married a childhood friend, Janet Condra, right after he enrolled at Indiana State, but the couple divorced in 1976. During a brief (and failed) reconciliation, Condra became pregnant and had a daughter, Corrie. Bird's attorneys asked for a paternity test, and by the time it was proven that Corrie was Larry's child, she was already a toddler who had seen very little of her father. Larry was dating Dinah by then and refused to be a part of his daughter's life, a decision that haunts him to this day.

It was Dinah who urged him through the years to make contact with Corrie and attempt to forge a relationship with her. Dinah, who later became his wife, also helped him navigate a private life that became very public as his stature grew.

"She has always been the mature one," Bird said. "I was a difficult guy to live with sometimes, especially when I was playing. She probably loved it when I came back from shoot-around and took a nap so I was out of her hair.

"I was lucky. Dinah was always independent, but she always supported me too. And there were times when I really needed it."

In the beginning, Bird didn't venture out in Boston much. Like Magic, he knew no one in his new city, and he couldn't have picked his coach, Bill Fitch, out of a lineup. When Bird attended his introductory press conference in Boston, he was anxiously waiting for the proceedings to begin when a portly gentleman came up to him and began discussing the Celtics personnel. Bird politely answered his questions, but was nervous and distracted and wanted the man to leave him alone.

Finally, when it came time for the press conference to start, Bird excused himself and took his place on the dais. To his surprise, the man joined him.

"Larry," he said, "I'm your coach, Bill Fitch."

Fitch would soon become unforgettable. He was a disciplined tactician who held his players accountable for every detail. He was organized and unyielding, and his basketball knowledge left an indelible impression on Bird. Fitch became the standard by which Bird would later model his own coaching career.

The other major influence in his early years was Red Auerbach, the legendary Boston sports hero who built the Celtics dynasty, first as a coach and then in the front office. Red's signature move was to light up a cigar when his team had a game clinched. Often he did this on the bench, during the game, in a building that was clearly marked NO SMOKING.

Auerbach didn't believe in mincing words, and that suited Bird just fine. The 62-year-old patriarch was fiercely competitive and fiercely loyal. Bird liked him immediately. In fact, the two men were alike in many ways. Both had the uncommon ability to size up people in a matter of minutes, and each could be horribly stubborn.

When Bird reported to rookie camp, Auerbach coaxed him into playing tennis in between sessions. Then, when the regular season started, Larry became Auerbach's regular racquetball partner.

"Red was an angles guy," Bird said. "I hate to admit this, but he did cheat on the score. He really hated losing."

Occasionally Auerbach would take Bird to eat at his favorite Chinese restaurant in Marshfield, Massachusetts, where the team's rookie camp was held. It was there that Auerbach would recite the proud history of the franchise Bird was joining.

"It's an honor to be a Celtic," Auerbach told him. "You should never forget that."

The Celtics' summer league digs were no-frills accommodations that included courts with rims of varying heights. Auerbach ran a summer camp for kids there, and his pro players were expected to eat with the campers in the mess hall and lecture the kids in between workouts. Normally veterans didn't bother to attend, but once word got out that Bird was in town, M. L. Carr and Dave Cowens just happened to drop in.

Cowens was a Celtics favorite, an undersized center who played All-Star basketball with uncommon passion and energy. He was the best front-court player on the team when Bird arrived. Carr was a wily veteran who had come over from Detroit, where he led the league in steals. Auerbach warned Bird ahead of time that Carr would jump his passing lanes and try to distract him with his non-stop banter.

"I got this one," said Carr, pointing to Bird the first time they scrimmaged.

Carr poked him, banged him, muscled him. "C'mon, rook," he said, in a voice low enough for Bird and no one else to hear, "is that all you've got?"

Because Auerbach had tipped him off, Bird was careful to step forward to meet the ball, thereby cutting down on Carr's opportunities to pick off the pass. He also refused to be rattled by Carr's chatter. Bird was content to feed his new teammates with scoring opportunities while eschewing most of his own.

"I've never seen anyone who could beat you with the pass the way Larry did," Carr said. "He'd bait you and bait you like he was going to shoot, and sucker the defense in, then deliver the pass to someone else on the money."

By the time training camp started, Bird's initiation was almost complete. There was one veteran left who wanted a piece of him, and that was Cedric Maxwell, a slender forward who was as proud of his trash-talking as he was of his low-post moves. He played 2-on-2 after practice with Bird, Carr, and Rick Robey and led Bird onto the block, where he spanked him with a series of upfakes and step-backs.

"He didn't really know how to play defense yet," Maxwell said.

When it was Bird's turn on offense, Maxwell stood with his hands at his side, daring the rookie to beat him. Bird started drilling shots. He hit them from 15 feet, then moved back to 20 feet, and then, finally, to 25 feet. By then, Maxwell was frantically trying to halt the comeuppance by blanketing him with his spindly arms. It was too late. Larry Bird was torching him.

"Damn," Maxwell said to Carr. "That white boy can shoot."

Once the Celtics veterans were done challenging Bird, they went about the business of protecting him. There was resentment among some black players who couldn't understand why there was so much hype surrounding a white rookie who, as far as they could tell, couldn't run or jump. Carr recalled forward Maurice Lucas telling him before a game in Bird's first season, "I'm going to take down the great Larry Bird."

"Oh, yeah?" Carr said. "Well, you're going to have to go through me first."

Magic underwent a similar rite of passage in Lakers training camp. Coach Jack McKinney put him on the second team and left him there for days. He stressed to Johnson that his decision-making would be the most important component of his job description. McKinney advised the rookie to remain respectful and to know his place.

Johnson willingly fetched Kareem's paper, bought him hot dogs in the airport, and nicknamed him "Cap" so there was never any doubt who ranked atop the Lakers' hierarchy. And yet, Magic was a born leader on the court and couldn't suppress those tendencies.

"It was potentially a big problem," Buss said. "The way Earvin played the game, he just had to be in charge. At the same time, you had this Hall of Fame player who had already won before."

Johnson endeared himself to his teammates with his hustle and his unselfishness. Norm Nixon nicknamed him "Buck" because he was always galloping around like a young deer. Although the veterans knew Magic spent time with Buss, nobody was aware of how close the owner and the rookie had become, and therefore no one objected.

"The extra hand-holding made sense because he was so young," Wilkes said. "I don't think Earvin had any intentions of crossing the line. I'm not sure he even understood he was crossing the line."

Johnson may have been a teenager, but he played with the swagger of a veteran. In his first practice with the Lakers, he turned it over twice because Wilkes, a three-time All-Star, wasn't ready for the pass.

"Magic!" McKinney reprimanded him. "You can't make those passes. This isn't college."

Johnson fumed. He was embarrassed to be singled out and furious that Wilkes didn't make the play.

The next time down the floor, Magic waited until Wilkes cut through the key, then the moment Wilkes turned, fired the ball at him. "Jamaal," he said evenly, "I'm going to keep hitting you in the head until you look."

Wilkes became the ideal complement to Magic's exceptional court vision. He moved gracefully with or without the ball (hence his nickname "Silk") and had great hands. He also knew how to use a pick better than anyone Johnson had ever played with before. He didn't object to the rookie's admonishment because, Wilkes said, "he was right. After that, I always looked."

Not everyone responded as positively to the confident rookie. Johnson was outplaying teammate Ron Boone in practice, and when the two went up for a rebound, Boone purposely whacked Magic in the back of the head. As they ran down the floor, Magic said, "You better know I'm going to get you back."

"Keep moving, rookie, you're not going to do anything," Boone replied.

Magic delivered his payback in the form of a fist to Boone's neck. Boone crashed to the floor and came up swinging.

"Don't you ever do that shit to me again!" Johnson shouted.

"Magic, get off the floor!" McKinney barked.

"Bullshit!" Magic retorted. "He hit me first, and when I retaliate, you're going to throw me off the court?"

"Get off the floor," McKinney repeated.

"I might be a rookie, but none of you are going to punk me," Magic said. "You're dealing with the wrong guy if you do."

Johnson sat on the sideline for the remainder of the practice, then left without speaking. For the next six days, he dominated practice, knocking down shots and firing pinpoint passes, each delivered with his teeth gritted. Jerry West tried to calm him, but Magic was unmoved.

"Jerry," he said, "I can smile nice, but I can fight mean too if I have to."

On October 12, 1979, Magic Johnson and Larry Bird made their pro debuts on opposite ends of the country.

Bird, operating on East Coast time, was in the starting lineup against the Houston Rockets in Boston Garden. His performance was unremarkable from a statistical standpoint because he was in foul trouble for most of the night and watched the Celtics pull away for a 114–105 win from the bench. His coming-out party proved to be the next night in Cleveland, where he poured in 28 points.

Because California was three hours behind Boston, Bird was showered, dressed, and settled in his family room to watch Magic's first professional regular season game in San Diego. When Johnson fed Kareem for a skyhook at the buzzer to win it, Johnson was so ecstatic that he jumped into the big fella's arms.

"What the hell is he doing?" Bird said to Dinah.

Kareem wondered the same thing. When they got back to their locker room, he reminded Magic that they still had 81 more games to go.

"He'll burn out in a week if he keeps going at this pace," Norm Nixon observed.

Nixon was wrong. The young buck played at one speed every day: full speed. He never wanted a day off, never ran easy, never let up. His energy level was a constant.

"He charged ahead at everything," Wilkes said. "And what it did was put tremendous pressure on the rest of us to match that kind of commitment."

One month into his professional career, after lighting up the Denver Nuggets for 31 points, 8 assists, and 6 rebounds, Magic confessed, "There are some nights I feel like I can do anything out there."

Four weeks later, Bird pinned a triple-double (23 points, 19 rebounds, and 10 assists) on the Phoenix Suns and wryly noted, "Some nights the game just seems really easy."

The NBA couldn't believe its good fortune. It had been saddled with drug scandals, image problems, and dwindling revenues, but this budding rivalry between two remarkable rookies had revitalized two of its kingpin cities. Boston's vice president Jan Volk sensed something special was going on when the team played a Wednesday night game against Utah against the televised World Series — and sold out anyway.

"None of our fans could name a player from Utah," Volk said. "They were coming to see Larry."

They only played each other twice during the regular season. Just as he had done during the NCAA Final, Bird refused to engage in any banter with Johnson. During their December tilt, the only time the two exchanged words was when Bird leveled Magic as he drove to the basket. The two rookies stared each other down before teammates stepped in.

"I thought Larry and I had some kind of connection after the NCAA championship," said Magic. "I guess he was making it clear he didn't feel the same way. So I made up my mind, 'I'm done trying to be nice to this guy. I'm just going to beat him instead.'"

The Lakers went on to take both regular season games that season, irritating Bird even further.

Bird circled his first trip to Los Angeles for a number of reasons. It was a chance to play Magic again, but also to be on the same court as Abdul-Jabbar, who represented one of his first introductions to pro basketball. Bird grew up a block and a half from a poolroom called Reeder's. The owner was a midget who loved sports and took Bird's brothers to a Chicago Cubs game each summer. Bird was too young to go, but one night, when Abdul-Jabbar was scheduled to play against Elvin Hayes in the old Houston Astrodome, Bird convinced his parents to let him go down to the pool hall and watch the game.

"I thought Kareem was the greatest," Bird said. "Every time I came across him in the pros, I flashed back to sitting in that pool hall, staying up until eleven o'clock to watch him play. I was asleep by eleven-thirty, but I remembered every move he made."

Practicing alongside Abdul-Jabbar and his Lakers teammates only further convinced Magic that he had a lot to learn. Cooper and Nixon showed him how to break down film and decipher the tendencies of opposing guards, like Gus Williams's preference to dribble twice before he pulled up at the free throw line or "Downtown" Freddie Brown's habit of gravitating to the corner.

Nixon ran the projector and pointed out that when the San Antonio Spurs ran "4," that meant George Gervin was curling off a screen, while "2" meant he was coming off a single double screen.

Nixon was helpful in other matters as well. One morning when the Lakers were on the road, Magic was having breakfast with a woman. As he hugged and kissed her goodbye before he got on the team bus, Nixon called him over.

"Don't ever do that again," Nixon said.

"Why? She's just a friend. We're having breakfast together," Magic protested.

"I don't care who she is," Nixon said. "When you walk out to the bus with a girl like that, Coach is going to think you spent the night with her. And God help you if you play bad."

"Okay," the rookie said. "I got it."

* * *

By the time the Celtics started their regular season, Bird was spending most of his time with Robey and Cowens, drinking suds and watching sports. In the late seventies and early eighties, the home NBA team was required to provide the road team with a case of cold beer in the locker room after each game. Players drank as much as they wanted, then left the rest behind. The Celtics rarely had any surplus on the road because Bird and Robey grabbed pillowcases from the hotel and stuffed them full of cans of beer.

When the 1979–80 regular season ended, the Celtics had won 61 games and the Lakers had won 60. LA weathered an unexpected coaching change when McKinney fell off his bicycle on his way to play tennis with assistant coach Paul Westhead and suffered severe, life-threatening injuries. After Westhead took his place and named radio announcer (and former Lakers player) Pat Riley as his assistant, the team sailed on.

Both rookies filled the stat sheets from wire to wire. Larry's and Magic's skills, contrasting personalities, and dueling franchises couldn't have been better scripted on Madison Avenue.

"For once," said longtime NBA executive Donnie Walsh, "the hype was real."

The Lakers easily advanced past Phoenix and Seattle in the postseason, and Boston swept Houston in the first round, but the more experienced Philadelphia 76ers, led by Dr. J and Darryl Dawkins, put an abrupt end to Bird's first season and killed any hopes of a Lakers-Celtics Final.

Bird finished third in the league MVP voting and was a first-team All-NBA selection, yet none of that was of any consequence to him. His only focus was winning a championship, preferably over Magic. "And then all of a sudden, it was over, just like that," Bird said. "It was a shock, really."

Magic prepared for the Finals with mixed emotions. He was thrilled to be on the league's biggest stage, but wished he would be competing against someone other than Erving. The generous man who eleven months earlier had opened his home to a young college sophomore with a life-altering decision to ponder would now be trying to wrestle a championship away from him. When Dr. J and Johnson met on the floor before the game, Erving embraced his protégé and said quietly, "Forget everything I told you."

The Finals were a blur to the rookie. The intensity and the pressure and the attention was initially overwhelming. Magic marveled at Kareem, who approached each game with the same blank expression and the same measure of calm. The captain burned the Sixers for 33, 38, and 33 points in the first three games. He had already scored 26 points in the third quarter of Game 5 when he crashed to the court grabbing his ankle. Abdul-Jabbar was taken to the locker room, but returned late in the fourth quarter to score 14 points down the stretch and give the Lakers a 3–2 series lead.

When Abdul-Jabbar left the locker room on crutches, the Lakers recognized that they'd be going to Philadelphia without him — and, if they believed the rest of the NBA, without a chance.

The day before Game 6, Bruce Jolesch, the Lakers' public relations director, grabbed Magic after the team's workout.

"I've got some disappointing news," he said. "Larry Bird won Rookie of the Year."

"How close was it?" Magic asked.

"Not close," Jolesch answered.

Bird won the award by a 63–3 margin. The lopsided vote was demoralizing. Magic called to commiserate with Earvin Johnson Sr., who bitterly told him, "This is a complete injustice."

Magic expressed mild disappointment publicly, nothing more. But privately he seethed over the lack of respect he was given. The fact that Larry Bird dominated the vote only made it worse.

"I was jealous, and I was mad," Magic said. "I thought I had a great year. When I heard I only got three votes, I took it out on the Sixers. I wanted people to recognize my play the way they had recognized Larry's.

"It wasn't anything personal against Larry . . . well, actually, it was."

By the time he dominated Game 6 as Kareem's fill-in, no one was talking about the Rookie of the Year any longer. They were trumpeting the incredible Magic, who brought championship glory back to Los Angeles.

"I think we can win a few of these," said Magic, cradling the championship trophy in the afterglow of his superb showing.

The Celtics had other ideas. With the number-one pick in the 1980 draft, courtesy of a previous trade with Detroit, they went shopping for a front-court player to help contain Kareem. After briefly pursuing Virginia center Ralph Sampson, who maintained he would not come out of college, Auerbach turned his attention to the graduating senior prospects, among them Purdue center Joe Barry Carroll and Minnesota forward Kevin McHale.

Auerbach didn't like Carroll's game but deftly convinced everyone in the league that he was about to select him. Golden State, which also needed help in the middle, wanted Carroll badly. Auerbach ended up trading the number-one and number-thirteen picks to the Warriors for the number-three pick (which Auerbach used to take McHale, the player he wanted all along) and an underachieving center by the name of Robert Parish, who, Auerbach surmised, would be an able backup to Cowens.

The Big Three was born, although it would be five more seasons before McHale became a starter. Parish was not projected to be a starter either, but on October 1, 1980, while the team was in Terre Haute, Indiana, waiting to take the bus to Evansville for an exhibition game, Cowens walked up the top step and announced he was retiring.

"I'm sorry, guys," Cowens said. "My heart just isn't in it anymore."

Bird was stunned. Not only did he look up to Cowens, but the big redhead had become one of his closest friends on the team. Cowens had given Bird no indication he was feeling this way.

"I was a little mad," Bird said. "I thought we had a great team with Dave. But without him? Robert wasn't ready. And Kevin? Who knew, really?"

Bird turned to Parish, who was sitting three seats behind him on the bus, and said, "You better get into shape."

Although Parish was one of the favorite targets of the hard-driving Fitch, the coach whipped him into condition, and Parish's game flourished accordingly. The seven-footer ran the floor like a long-legged gazelle, dutifully filling the lanes in transition even though most of the time he never saw the ball. Bird became so appreciative of the center's commitment that he made sure he held the ball back a couple of times so Parish could come down as the trailer and be rewarded with two points.

The transition from Cowens to Parish, whose weapon of choice was a high-arching rainbow jumper, was more seamless than anyone could have hoped. Yet Bird couldn't shake the lingering feeling that Cowens had let them down.

"I just couldn't understand why he couldn't wait and leave at the end of the season," Bird said.

Boston averaged 109.9 points in 1980–81, a byproduct of a deep front line and a resourceful little point guard named Nate "Tiny" Archibald. True to his moniker, the former New York City hotshot stood about 5-foot-8 (although he was listed officially as 6-foot-1), but compensated for his lack of size with considerable guile and quickness. Tiny went around big men and small men, under screens and over screens. He could drive, shoot, and distribute the ball.

"He literally made us go," Bird said.

McHale, the new rookie, was 6-foot-10 with shoulders so broad it looked as though he'd forgotten to remove the coat hanger from his shirt. He was long and agile and every bit as easygoing as Bird was single-minded. It made for a fascinating relationship between two successful forwards who approached their craft in vastly different manners.

"Larry was relentless," M. L. Carr said. "He was there when we came in to practice, and there when we left. One day I said to Kevin, 'Why don't you be like Larry?' He said, 'Hey, man, I've got a life.'"

Throughout the early portion of the 1980–81 season, Magic was grounded by torn cartilage in his knee that left him in street clothes for 45 games. Magic had never been seriously injured before and was impatient to return. As the Celtics pounded opponent after opponent, Magic became concerned that he wouldn't recover in time for the postseason.

He returned on February 27, and Buss printed up buttons that declared THE MAGIC IS BACK! to celebrate the occasion.

Norm Nixon rolled his eyes. He was tired of Magic stealing all the press and dominating the ball. He had taken over the point position during Magic's injury, and the team had played well. Once a mentor to Johnson, Nixon was increasingly becoming his foil.

Westhead, in his first full season as Lakers coach, scrapped McKinney's flowing motion offense and implemented a system that was predicated on pounding the ball inside to Kareem. Showtime had been reduced to Slowtime, and Magic was frustrated, especially since he often found himself playing in the front court.

"Paul ran this system where I was supposed to only run down the floor on my designated side, the left side," Magic said. "I'm saying, 'Are you kidding me? I can only use the left side of the floor?'"

"Coach," he said to Westhead after practice, "we need to get back to running."

"Magic," Westhead answered, "stick to the game plan."

The fractured Lakers were stunned by the Houston Rockets in the opening round of the best-of-three series. Magic shot 2 of 13 from the floor in the final game and threw up an air ball on the final play as he drove to the basket. His squabble with Nixon went public, and "the whole thing," Johnson said, "went up in smoke."

Boston had survived a grueling Eastern Conference Finals with the Sixers by overcoming a 3–1 deficit. Bird was immense in the deciding Game 7, picking off numerous Sixers passes and banking home the game-winning shot.

Just as Magic had done the previous year against the 76ers, Bird willed his team to victory.

"I never heard the term 'point forward' until I met Larry," said Tiny Archibald. "He was a professor. He dissected the game, and he dissected the players. He knew when to shoot and when to score better than anyone I've ever seen.

"He wouldn't let us lose to the Sixers. He simply would not allow it."

LA's stunning postseason fall left Bird feeling like a prizefighter who had just been told his heavyweight opponent was TKO'ed before he got to throw a punch. He wanted Magic and the Lakers in the Finals, but instead he got Moses Malone and the Houston Rockets.

Malone willingly played the role of Boston's villain, declaring the Celtics were "really not that good." Even after the Green took a 3–2 series lead, Malone dismissed them as "chumps," not champs.

Bird was effective as a rebounder and a passer against the Rockets, but until the deciding Game 6, he was shooting only 38 percent from the floor. Houston forward Robert Reid was credited with being a Bird stopper, which only served to irritate the Boston forward further.

"Try stopping this," he said to Reid, when he connected on a 15-footer in the third quarter.

"Stop that," he said again, after he drilled his only three-pointer of the series late in the fourth quarter.

The Celtics won Game 6 behind Bird's 26 points on 11-of-20 shooting. He celebrated his first championship by puffing on one of Auerbach's trademark stogies. Then he partied with his teammates through the night in the team hotel. The Celtics were young and healthy and their future was limitless.

As Magic sat at home in Lansing with his father watching Boston's victory celebration, he fidgeted uncomfortably in his chair.

"That's it," said Magic, who got up and called Tucker, who lived in Lansing and owned his own basketball court. Twenty minutes later, Johnson was dressed in his practice gear, going through a full workout at his agent's house in the middle of the night.

"I was so pissed watching Larry smoke that cigar," he said, "I couldn't stand it anymore."

That summer, Buss offered Magic a 25-year, $25 million contract. It was an outlandish deal, both in dollar value and years. No one expected Johnson to play another two and a half decades, so the inference was clear: Buss had plans for him beyond his basketball days. Suddenly, Magic's teammates were revisiting his cozy relationship with Buss.

Abdul-Jabbar, who had carried the Lakers for six seasons, was particularly insulted by Magic's windfall. The morning after the contract was announced, Kareem wondered aloud in the papers, "What is he, player or management? We don't know."

Johnson's new deal was a problem — a big problem. An irate Nixon met him in the hallway and said, "Buck, what's going on? The guys are talking. They say you are hanging all the time with Buss. That's a no-no in this business."

"I didn't know that," Magic said. "Dr. Buss is my friend."

"Players and management don't hang out together," Nixon said.

"Hey, I'm hanging with Dr. Buss. That boat has already sailed," Magic replied.

"Well, I'm just telling you, we don't know how to take you," Nixon continued. "If something is said in the locker room, we don't know if you are going to take it back."

"What are you talking about, Norm?" Magic said incredulously. "I've already been in your locker room for two years. Has anything we've said gotten back to Dr. Buss?"

Nixon shrugged. For the next couple of weeks, Magic was on an island. The only player he trusted was Cooper, who was busy fighting for a niche on the team. Magic wasn't the only player who chafed at Westhead's style. Neither Wilkes nor Nixon liked it either, but only the young buck spoke his mind.

Magic's frustration spilled over on November 18, 1981, in Salt Lake City. The Lakers were in the middle of a tight game with the Utah Jazz when Westhead called time-out. As the team gathered in the huddle, Magic began talking about the miscues of the previous two plays and how the Lakers could correct their mistakes.

"Magic," Westhead said, "be quiet and pay attention."

"We're just going over what we need to do," Magic said.

"I don't want to hear anything out of your mouth," Westhead retorted. "That's your problem. You talk too much."

Johnson flinched. He turned away from the huddle and moved toward the water cooler.

"Get back here!" Westhead hissed. "You're busting the system. You're not doing your job."

Cooper ushered his friend back into the huddle. "Forget about it, Buck," Cooper said. "Just play."

Los Angeles hung on to win 113–110. As Magic walked off the court, his coach was waiting for him in the hallway. Westhead pulled him into the coach's room and warned him, "You better get with it, or we're going to have problems."

"You've stopped us from running, and you're blaming me," Magic said. "The other guys don't want to tell you, but they don't like playing this way either."

The argument escalated. Reporters lingered in the hallway, capturing the scene. Johnson emerged from the office and angrily kicked the water cooler in the hallway. Then he went back to his locker and announced he wanted to be traded.

Pat Riley witnessed all of it. He knew tensions were building between Westhead and Johnson. He could sense Magic's frustration with playing a slower pace, and he knew Westhead's patience had been running thin with the outspoken guard.

"I should have gotten involved," Riley said. "Maybe I could have stopped it. It was an awkward situation. I loved Earvin, but I was working for Paul."

When the team returned to Los Angeles the next morning, both West and Buss were waiting for Magic. They told him that his decision to go public with his complaints was inappropriate and immature. Then they told him they had fired Westhead, something West had been planning to do anyway.

Magic was relieved. The team played San Antonio at home the next night, and he wanted to get back to Showtime. In a curious arrangement, Riley, whom he liked and trusted, was named the head coach — but West would be moving down to the bench to help him as a "consultant."

On the night of November 20, Johnson arrived earlier than normal to the Forum in case Riley wanted to review any game details. He was anxious for a new start and couldn't wait for the game to begin.

"I was thinking everything was back to normal," Magic said.

The boos started the moment he joined the lay-up line. Magic glanced around to see who they were directed toward. It took him a moment to realize the Forum fans were targeting him. They booed him during introductions, and they booed him the first time he touched the ball. Magic looked at Cooper, holding back tears. "They're blaming me for this?" he asked.

Johnson played through all of it, recording a triple-double (20 points, 16 assists, and 10 rebounds) and leading the Lakers in a 136–116 blowout win. By the end of the game, the boos had subsided, but it would be a long time before Johnson forgot them — or the lack of support he received from his own bench.

"The worst part about it was my teammates," Magic said. "They hung me out to dry. None of them backed me up. Coop was the only guy. He wasn't in a position to do it publicly, but he did it privately. The rest of them couldn't be bothered, and I took it personally.

"It made me realize who I was dealing with. I thought, 'Okay, I guess this is what they mean when they say it is a business.'"

For the next month, Magic's life on the road was miserable. He was the resident NBA bad guy, the spoiled, petulant coach killer, and nothing he could do or say would alter that image. At first, the adversarial reception was upsetting, but after a while it was merely another source of motivation.

Bird was puzzled by the national furor. Magic was averaging double figures in assists. How could anyone call him selfish or spoiled? "I felt kinda bad for him," Bird said.

After Riley took over, the Lakers won 17 of their next 20 games. He rejuvenated the Lakers' transition game and spread the wealth among his major offensive weapons. Six players averaged double figures in 1981–82, including Magic. Riley took a conciliatory tack, asking his players for input and admitting freely he was learning on the job. Johnson became his confidant, and his friend.

Eventually Magic's world was realigned. He was back in the fans' good graces, the team was playing up-tempo again, and his new coach was about to embark on a meteoric career path. The team breezed to the Finals and awaited an Eastern opponent.

"I was hoping for the Celtics," Magic said.

The 1982 Sixers avenged the previous year's playoff loss to the Celtics by clinching the Eastern Conference Championship on the hallowed Boston Garden parquet. As Philadelphia closed out the win, Boston's fans urged Dr. J and his club, "Beat LA! Beat LA!"

Magic, watching on television from Los Angeles, merely smiled. So did Riley, his new coach.

"I just felt, after all we'd been through that season, our guys were ready for anything," Riley said.

The Lakers beat the Sixers to win the 1982 NBA Championship, and Johnson was named the Finals MVP with 13 points, 13 rebounds, and 13 assists in the clincher. Asked which of his two NBA titles was sweeter, Magic slung his arm around Cooper and said, "Any championship is special."

Long after the crowd thinned, Magic recapped the tumultuous events of the 1981–82 season with his father. It had been a grueling year, one that made him realize that winning was fleeting and team chemistry was fragile. He believed the Lakers had the talent to be good for the long haul, but he worried that egos and contracts would get in the way.

There was also the matter of Larry Bird and the Boston Celtics.

"One of these times," Magic said to his father, "you just know we're going to see them."

4

★ ★ ★

JANUARY 31, 1982

East Rutherford, New Jersey

THE 1982 NBA ALL-STAR GAME seemed to have all the trappings of an entertainment bonanza. The East squad featured three members of the 1981 World Champion Boston Celtics, with forward Larry Bird as the headliner, and the West squad boasted three members of the Los Angeles Lakers, including Magic Johnson, who had spurred his team on to the title in 1980 and would win another for them later that spring.

It should have been an easy sell: Celtics and Lakers! Magic and Larry! East versus West! Come watch the battle of the stars!

Except that, in 1982, nobody was buying it. Although the Lakers-Celtics rivalry had begun percolating again, the two teams had not yet met head-to-head in the Finals, and while Magic and Larry had already become obsessively entrenched in each other's psyche, the public's awareness of their heated rivalry was still evolving.

Then there was the All-Star Game itself, a stand-alone, no-frills event that lacked sponsors, imagination, and national appeal. Three days before the event was held at the Brendan Byrne Arena in East

Rutherford, New Jersey (capacity 20,049), league officials, facing the potential public relations disaster of a cavernous arena with empty seats, called an emergency meeting to strategize on how they could boost anemic ticket sales.

David Stern, who was the league's executive vice president at the time, took a proactive approach. He called all of his family ("including some uncles I wasn't sure I had"), then all of his friends, then every acquaintance he could locate in his Rolodex. His solicitations were anything but subtle.

"Would you like some tickets to our All-Star Game?" Stern would ask.

"Sure," they'd answer. "How about six?"

"How about sixty?" he'd reply.

The event was listed as a sellout but should have more appropriately been labeled a handout.

The players provided a spirited competition fueled by the West's objection to the general consensus that the East was the superior conference.

Magic submitted 16 points and 7 assists in a 120–118 West loss. Bird was named MVP of the game with 19 points, 12 rebounds, and 5 assists, but he left with the lingering feeling that Parish, who contributed 21 points and 7 rebounds and held Abdul-Jabbar to 2 points on 1-of-10 shooting, should have been given the trophy. There was one clear reason why Parish didn't: his teammate Bird scored 12 of the final 15 points to win it.

Throughout the weekend, Bird barely acknowledged Magic. His focus was on dismantling the Lakers, not fraternizing with them, even in an All-Star setting. He pointedly ignored his gregarious nemesis, who was omnipresent throughout the proceedings.

Johnson greeted most of his Eastern All-Star opponents by grabbing them, hugging them warmly, then asking, "So how's the season going?" But when he bumped into Bird in the corridor, he nodded silently, then moved on.

"At that point," Magic acknowledged, "there was a real dislike on both sides."

Magic was irritated by the inordinate amount of media attention directed Bird's way. Johnson wasn't allotted the same offensive free-dom (or shots) with the Lakers that Bird enjoyed with the Celtics. Magic's primary role was to facilitate others, specifically Kareem. Because Bird scored more and had bigger numbers, he generated more headlines.

"Did I resent the attention he got for that? Of course," Johnson said. "Shoot. I had some game too. But people don't count assists the way they do points. There was nothing I could do about it."

Bird spent All-Star weekend hanging with Boston teammates Parish and Tiny Archibald and lamenting the lost opportunity for some time off. The Celtics traditionally embarked on a West Coast road trip following the All-Star break, and Bird would have pre-ferred to stay home rather than participate in what he felt was a second-rate event.

"To be honest with you, before Stern became commissioner, I thought the All-Star Game was a whole bunch of bull," said Bird.

Each year the All-Stars were feted in an oversized ballroom where they ate dry chicken on a raised dais and were entertained by a series of miscast comedians. In 1983 in Los Angeles, Jonathan Winters left NBA staffers convulsing with laughter in the green room while he was awaiting his introduction, but when Winters hopped up on stage and quickly took stock of the mostly African American athletes staring him down, it occurred to him that he had nothing in common with his audience.

"He kind of froze," Stern recalled. "He got up there and started doing a routine about killing Japs. I wanted to disappear."

Subsequent years proved to be equally uncomfortable. Comedian David Steinberg's monologue about artificial insemination and de-positing its contents into a bottle left Stern, who happened to be seated next to Dallas owner (and born-again Christian) Donald Carter, sinking further and further in his seat.

Magic Johnson also slid down low in his chair, but it was bore-dom, not embarrassment, that altered his posture. He dreaded the entertainment portion of the program and planned once the lights went down to slip discreetly out of the ballroom. His cohorts in-cluded Isiah Thomas, George Gervin, Norm Nixon, and Dennis

Johnson, and their exodus was done two by two, under the cover of darkness and crude punch lines. By the time the lights came back up, the room was more than half-empty.

In 1984 Bird sat adjacent to Kareem Abdul-Jabbar in yet another All-Star ballroom, this time in Denver, perspiring from the white-hot lights bearing down on him.

"This sucks," Bird said.

"These damn lights are giving me a migraine headache," muttered Abdul-Jabbar, who stood up and walked out.

Although the players were unaware of it, their fortunes were about to change. On February 1, 1984, one day after the All-Star Game, David Stern replaced the retiring Larry O'Brien and was sworn in as the new NBA commissioner. Although he was not widely known outside the league, from within Stern was heralded as a bright, innovative attorney who had been tirelessly advocating for change. No matter was too insignificant to escape Stern's notice: whether researching a stipulation of the collective bargaining agreement or choosing the color of the cloth napkins for a staff luncheon, he immersed himself in every detail. He was a marketing master with a portfolio full of new ideas for his struggling league.

He was also an accessible executive who solicited his players' opinions. When Bird said that he abhorred the pregame All-Star banquet format, Stern replaced it with a private room and buffet meal where players could come and go with their families. When Magic complained that the entertainment didn't reflect the interests of the athletes, Stern hired singer Jeffrey Osbourne, who was so dynamic that he had the crowd on their feet pumping their fists and hollering "Woo! Woo!" instead of trying to slink out the back door.

"Overnight the whole feel of the league was different with David Stern," Magic said. "He understood what we needed. He also understood what he had. Larry and I were right there, waiting to take the NBA to the next level."

Although he had watched the 1979 NCAA championship game between Michigan State and Indiana State, David Stern wasn't salivating over Magic and Bird's potential to infuse new life into the

NBA. He was more focused on the fact that the announcers were forbidden to mention the NBA during their telecast. The NCAA had no interest in promoting the next landing spot for its stars. The colleges were wrangling with pro basketball for publicity, airtime, and consumer dollars, and they were winning.

The marketability of Larry and Magic simply was not pressing enough to sit atop the to-do list of either Commissioner O'Brien or his chief lieutenant Stern in 1979.

"We were too busy trying to get through the day," Stern said.

O'Brien, a political strategist by trade, had run the senatorial campaign for a young upstart Democrat from Massachusetts named John F. Kennedy in 1959, then eventually followed him to the White House. He stayed on as part of Lyndon B. Johnson's team, was named postmaster general, and in the early seventies became chairman of the Democratic National Committee, which led to his office being targeted in the famous Watergate scandal that destroyed the presidency of Richard Nixon. O'Brien's résumé was captivating, but his background in politics did not impress his basketball brethren, who often found the commissioner to be aloof, unapproachable, and indifferent regarding matters of the game.

Financial concerns had left the NBA weighing the possible contraction of its Denver and Utah franchises. League attendance was spotty, the television package was modest, and NBA marketing strategies were rudimentary. The majority of the athletes playing professional basketball were African American, and corporations were openly skeptical that a league of mostly black players would be appealing to their customers, who were overwhelmingly white. The forecast for the NBA in the early eighties was gloomy, with prominent media outlets regularly predicting its demise.

"The only time we ever made *60 Minutes* was when Rudy Tomjanovich got punched by Kermit Washington, or when they showed a bunch of empty seats and Rick Barry sitting on the bench as the only white player," Stern said. "It was always something negative."

In an attempt to capitalize on the anticipated arrival of Magic and Bird in the NBA, the public relations department took the highly unusual step of putting the rookies on the cover of the *NBA*

Register and Guide. The cover was mildly unsettling to Stern, who oversaw the league's marketing department and felt it would be a slight to proven stars such as Abdul-Jabbar, George Gervin, and Julius Erving. He consulted his marketing team, which consisted of one person — himself — and ultimately gave in to the recommendations of the PR staff.

Prior to the arrival of Bird and Magic, securing sponsorships for the league was a daunting challenge. In May 1982, Stern hired Rick Welts to create new marketing partnerships for the NBA. Welts, an avid basketball fan and former ball boy for the Seattle SuperSonics, had been working for Bob Walsh & Associates, one of the first sports marketing firms in the country. Once in the employ of the NBA, he put on his best suit and called on McDonald's, Coca-Cola, and General Motors. He never got past the lobby. He suffered similar indignities when he tried to tap smaller, less prestigious companies.

"Most of them wouldn't even see me," Welts said. "And those who did just laughed at me. The NBA had such a bad reputation in the business community."

As one gifted player after another fell prey to substance abuse in the late seventies and early eighties, the NBA tried to debunk the damaging perception that their league was flush with drug users.

David Thompson, a three-time college All-American with a 44-inch vertical leap, should have been an NBA superstar. Instead, the former North Carolina State star developed drug and alcohol problems and was out of the league by the time he was 30 years old. John Lucas, a superb athlete who played in the U.S. (Tennis) Open when he was 13 years old and was the number-one pick in the 1976 NBA draft, developed cocaine and alcohol problems and entered drug rehabilitation. He later opened his own drug treatment facility in Houston designed specifically to assist troubled athletes like himself. Sly Williams, a promising young talent with the New York Knicks, became notorious for binges of abuse and once called in to say he was going to miss a game because "there was a slight death in the family."

Four participants in the 1980 All-Star Game — Phoenix star Walter Davis, New York guard Micheal Ray Richardson, Atlanta guard

John Drew, and Atlanta swingman Eddie "Fast Eddie" Johnson — ended up battling addiction.

Fast Eddie managed to amass more than 10,000 career points in spite of his cocaine habit. His teammate Drew scored more than 15,000 points, even as he started freebasing. Drew entered drug rehab in 1983, returned as the league's Comeback Player of the Year in 1984, then relapsed again two years later and became one of the first players to be banned for life by the NBA.

Coaches and general managers tried to navigate the landscape of the drug culture with few resources and no set guidelines. Former Atlanta Hawks coach Hubie Brown recognized that drug use was rampant, both in professional sports and in the entertainment industry, but the NBA bore the brunt of the criticism because of the high profiles of the players who got caught. Brown tried to educate himself on how to assist his troubled players, including consulting a psychologist, but conceded, "What did I know about cocaine or freebasing?"

The league's security office reached out to law enforcement officials in each NBA city so they could identify who sold the drugs, then tried to limit the flow of activity between their players and the dealers. Stern invited federal drug enforcement officials to the league meetings so they could brief coaches, general managers, and owners on how to detect a player who was battling a drug or alcohol problem. Counseling was made available to the athletes, yet there were few takers.

"It was all about race, drugs, and overpayment," Stern said. "The perception of our players was, 'They are black, they make too much money, and therefore because they are black and have too much money, they spend it on drugs.'"

Terry Furlow, an African American who led the Big Ten in scoring for Michigan State the season before Magic Johnson became a Spartan, tragically fit the profile. He befriended Magic after watching him dominate one of his high school games.

"Hey, kid," he told Johnson. "Meet me after school, and we'll play some ball."

Magic showed up, and Furlow trounced him 15–0 in the game

of 1-on-1. The next day the score was the same. For weeks Furlow toyed with Magic on the court before finally Johnson slammed the ball down in disgust.

"I quit," Magic said. "I'm tired of you beating me all the time."

"Now, you listen," Furlow said. "If you quit now, you'll never be nothing. You stay right here and take this whooping until you learn how to score."

Magic stayed. Furlow forced him to his left and made him shoot with either hand. He used his body to seal Johnson off and showed him how to execute a proper drop step. The games became closer. Magic lost 15–5, then 15–7. A year later, he grew three inches, and suddenly Furlow had all he could handle.

"See you in the NBA, kid," Furlow told Magic the day the Philadelphia 76ers made him the 12th pick in the 1976 draft.

Four years later, Furlow was dead — killed after ramming into a pole with his car on a highway in Ohio. Police reported there were traces of cocaine and valium in his system. Furlow was 25 years old and employed by the Utah Jazz at the time.

Magic knew drugs were part of the sports culture, but until Furlow's death, it hadn't touched anyone he knew. That soon changed. Although Johnson witnessed no evidence of cocaine use on the Lakers, he knew some of his championship teammates were smoking marijuana on a regular basis.

"I never said anything," Magic said, "but there was always a part of me that wanted to ask them, 'Hey, aren't we trying to win this thing?' Because you weren't at your best when you were doing that stuff — I don't care what anyone says."

Bird was stunned when former player Paul Westphal was quoted in the eighties as saying more than half of the NBA players used cocaine.

"I didn't see it," Larry said. "I didn't know what guys did when they left the gym, but I couldn't imagine how they could play at such a high level if they were doing that stuff."

When he was in college, Bird and his friend went to a fraternity party on the Indiana State campus. One of the girls was acting strangely, and when Larry inquired about her, his friend told him, "Oh, she's been snorting."

"Get me the hell out of here," Bird said.

"Hey, Larry, what's wrong, it's no big deal," his friend protested.

"I'm gone," said Bird.

Larry adopted the same theory in the NBA: he avoided large parties and confined his fun to more intimate, manageable settings. The Celtics were decimated by two high-profile tragedies in the eighties and nineties — the death of draft pick Len Bias from cocaine intoxication, and the shocking passing of teammate Reggie Lewis from heart trouble, which his physician, Dr. Gilbert Mudge, later alleged may have been linked to cocaine use. In both cases, Bird never saw it coming.

"I missed a lot," Bird conceded. "I missed a lot because I didn't want to know."

By 1981, Magic's and Larry's second season in the league, cash-strapped owners, trying to keep their franchises viable, decided to open their books to their athletes to reveal their tenuous future. At the time, 60 percent of the gross revenue, which was hovering at $118 million, was being paid out to the players. The formula had to change or the league was going to be out of business.

In March 1983, the NBA and Players Association president Bob Lanier hammered out an unprecedented agreement that implemented the first revenue-sharing plan in league history. Although O'Brien was still the commissioner, Stern acted behind the scenes as the architect of the deal. The pact included a salary cap that would pay the players 53 percent of the league's defined gross revenue (television and radio revenues and gate receipts) and a guaranteed $500,000 a year in licensing. The revenue-sharing concept proved to be a model for major sports franchises.

Six months after the new collective bargaining agreement was implemented, the league announced a landmark substance abuse policy that specifically targeted cocaine and heroin use: repeat offenders caught using or selling drugs were dismissed for a minimum of two years from the league.

The agreement also provided treatment and rehabilitation for players who willingly came forward to disclose their problem. Lanier and the union identified family stresses, boredom on the road, a lack of knowledge on how to manage money, and the adjustments of former college stars struggling to accept a lesser role in the pros as some of the factors that led to substance abuse.

Lanier, who is African American, was offended by the suggestion that all black NBA players were drug users. He was heartened that Magic Johnson proved to be such a dynamic African American role model who not only eschewed drugs but also didn't smoke cigarettes or drink alcohol.

"He came at the perfect time," Lanier said. "Magic had this great face that just radiated. Same with Larry Bird. He was such a competitor, anyone could appreciate what he was doing. We needed guys like that."

In 1984 Welts infused new life into All-Star weekend by starting both the slam-dunk competition and the Old-Timers' Game (which was later scrapped because of too many injuries). The NBA was able to attract Schick, American Airlines, and a tiny company based in Indiana called Gatorade as sponsors, in part because of the compelling personal stories surrounding the participants. That, Welts determined, was what his fan base wanted.

Larry and Magic fit the bill. They were East Coast versus West Coast, the Lunch Bucket Brigade versus Showtime, the gritty leader versus the flashy star.

"It was as if they came out of central casting," Welts said. "We couldn't have asked for a better fit.

"It provided us with the foundation to build on the idea of the player as the hero."

Although their exceptional court vision was a shared talent, Johnson and Bird were a study in contrast. Magic was effusive, emotional, and engaging. Bird was stoic, reserved, and enigmatic. There was also one undeniable difference between the two: the color of their skin. Neither ever gave that component of their rivalry much consideration, but whether they liked it or not, it quickly became a factor.

"There was clearly a racial element to their relationship," said former Celtics coach K. C. Jones, who is African American. "Larry was a dominating, highly intelligent individual, and he was white. Magic was a dominating, highly intelligent individual, and he was black.

"None of that mattered to the coaches or the players, but it did matter to the public. Larry created an admiration and following among whites, and Magic created an admiration and following among blacks. And with that came some animosity between the two groups when the Celtics and Lakers were playing. Larry never liked it. He didn't want to be the Great White Hope. But he didn't have a choice."

Magic noted the racial divide when the topic of Larry Bird was raised. His black friends from Michigan State constantly degraded Bird's game, while his white friends from the same college tended to overstate Bird's talents.

"The country was split over Larry and me," Magic said. "After a number of years, it was okay for people to admire both of us, but in the beginning the black guys backed Magic and the Lakers, and the white folks rooted for Larry and the Celtics."

His first week in training camp, Bird was serenaded with catcalls of "the Great White Hope" from Cedric Maxwell. He didn't pay him much mind. Bird had grown up playing against African Americans who worked at the Valley Springs Hotel in French Lick, and their heritage was irrelevant to him.

"All I cared about was finding the best game," Bird said.

The rest of America was not quite so enlightened at the time. According to Magic, white players were routinely dismissed as "overrated" by black fans who felt the white stars were built up by the biased, predominantly white media. White fans often sniffed at black players as undisciplined and lacking fundamentals. They didn't want to pay to watch the "street ball" of African Americans. The arrival of Bird and Magic helped dispel false assumptions on both ends of the racial spectrum.

Magic frequented the Morningside Barber Shop on Crenshaw Boulevard in Los Angeles and was astonished to hear the "elders" discussing Bird one afternoon. Magic had never heard them mention a white ballplayer before, not even the legendary "Pistol Pete" Maravich.

"I got to give it to you, that white boy can play," his barber said.

"I told you that the last time I was in here," Magic said.

"You did," the barber replied. "But I wasn't buying none of that until he put on that show in the Finals against the Rockets. That boy made Moses [Malone] look silly!"

Bird, the forward who allegedly possessed no agility or athleticism, won over the barber shop patrons when he pulled up for a jumper from the foul line against the Rockets, but sensed immediately it was off target and streaked down the right side of the floor in pursuit of the rebound. He grabbed the ball as it came off the rim and then, in midflight, switched it from his right to his left hand and coaxed it back in. That acrobatic move became the signature clip of Boston's 1981 championship title over Houston.

Soon after that, minority kids began showing up at the playground wearing Bird's number 33 jersey. Magic was surprised the first time he saw it, particularly because it was on a blacktop in Los Angeles. When Lanier frequented his barber shop in Milwaukee, he too noted the old-timers extolling the virtues of Bird's moxie.

"Most of the brothers came up on the playground," Lanier explained. "They talked a lot of smack. So Bird comes into the league, and he's talking all the time. But if you talk smack and you back it up, then you are considered one bad mother. And Larry always backed it up."

Bird's habit of baiting his opponents was quickly becoming part of NBA lore. During Indiana Pacers forward Chuck Person's rookie season, his team traveled to Boston Garden a week before Christmas, and Bird was waiting with a holiday greeting.

"I've got a present for you," Bird told Person as he walked past him before the game.

Late in the second half, Bird ambled up the court and drilled a three-pointer right in front of the Pacers' bench, where Person happened to be sitting.

"Merry f——ing Christmas," said Bird.

Although Bird and Magic helped to shatter some of the old stereotypes that had become cemented in American sports culture, it was a gradual process. Magic was one of the most cerebral players to ever play the game, yet rarely was he lauded for a "high basketball IQ," a moniker that black athletes claimed was reserved exclusively for white players. Conversely, in spite of Bird's highlight reel of amazing basketball feats, there are some who still refuse to recognize his natural ability.

"Larry was a debate," Michael Jordan said. "He still is. People ask me all the time who my all-time five top players are, and when I start saying Larry, they interrupt me. They say, 'You've got to be kidding me. He can't play with LeBron James!' I tell them, 'You guys don't get it. Larry is far better than any small forward who played the game, and to be honest, I'm still not sure if he is a small forward or a power forward.'

"To appreciate Bird fully, you need to know the game. You have to be a basketball person to be able to give him his due. He's not jumping out of the gym. He doesn't dunk on anyone. He doesn't show any quickness. That's why some people can't see the value of his game. Now, is that racial? I suppose you could see it that way, since he doesn't possess the athleticism of some of the black guys in the league, but I never bought that.

"If you walked into Madison Square Garden, a mecca of basketball, and said, 'What do you think of Larry Bird's game?' the answer is going to be, 'He's a great player because he can do so much.' And that has nothing to do with the color of his skin."

For black athletes in the city of Boston, it was often difficult — sometimes impossible — to be colorblind. Former Celtic M. L. Carr said the residual effects of Judge W. Arthur Garrity's decision in June 1974 to integrate the Boston public schools by implementing forced busing were still palpable when he arrived in the city in 1979 as a free agent.

Garrity's decree polarized the city's communities and ignited spasms of violence. During the height of the tension, police arrived at Boston public schools each morning to help load and unload students, snipers were dispersed on rooftops poised to strike down potential threats, and metal detectors were installed in school hallways.

The lasting image of the racial unrest was captured by *Boston Herald* photographer Stanley Forman on April 5, 1976. Black attorney Theodore Landsmark was on his way to City Hall when he came across anti-busing protesters. A Charlestown youth speared Landsmark with the point of an American flag, and the photo, which appeared across the nation, became a shameful symbol of Boston's turbulent racial history.

Carr remembers the picture well. He signed with the Spirits of St. Louis, an ABA franchise, a few months after the incident, and the racial attack was a recurring topic of discussion in the dressing room. "The guys all said the same thing," he said. "There's no way we'd ever play in Boston."

Carr was more open-minded. He was impressed by general manager Red Auerbach's recruiting pitch and comforted by Auerbach's own résumé, which included assembling the first all-black starting five in NBA history and appointing the league's first African American coach.

When he signed with the Celtics in 1979, Carr settled into the tony suburb of Weston in a beautiful home with a spacious fireplace. Teammate Dave Cowens ordered him a cord of wood and had it delivered to Carr's house. The following day, he had a visit from the local authorities.

"Mr. Carr," the policeman said, "we've got a problem."

"What is that?" Carr asked.

"See that wood you have out there? Some of your neighbors say it looks an awful lot like the wood they had delivered to their house."

"Oh, really," Carr said. "Which neighbors would those be?"

The policeman declined to identify the accusers.

"Are you sure that's your wood?" the officer asked.

"Are you sure you want to ask me that again?" Carr replied.

Robert Parish, born and raised in Louisiana, was strolling

through the North End of Boston one night and was stopped and searched by police without provocation. The next time he frequented the popular Italian section of the city, it happened again. After that, he found another part of town to have his supper.

It was far more challenging to find a highway where Parish would not be pulled over in his luxury vehicle. On half a dozen occasions, he was stopped by police for no apparent reason.

"I wasn't speeding, I wasn't swerving, I was just driving," Parish said. "And when I asked them why they pulled me over, I got the same answer every time: there were reports of 'suspicious activity' in the area. I guess that's code for: 'There's a black guy driving a nice car down the highway.'"

K. C. Jones, an avid golfer, tried to join a local country club but was told the wait was several months. Two weeks later, he bumped into a mutual friend who had applied and been accepted in a matter of days.

"The only difference between the two of us was he was white and I wasn't," said Jones.

Jones lived in the wealthy town of Wellesley in a quiet, tree-lined neighborhood. Many of the neighbors were cordial but distant. He didn't discover until he had lived there a few months that his realtor had been warned not to sell the house to a black family.

Most of the time, Jones said, the slights were subtle. Other times, the racial bias was appalling. In the late sixties, he walked into a suburban Boston restaurant for lunch with a white friend. Before they were seated, the owner nervously motioned to his friend.

"You can't stay here," he said. "All of my patrons are white."

After a couple of racial incidents involving his family, the affable Carr carried a registered gun with him at all times, including game days to and from Boston Garden, a practice he continued when he became coach.

"I never had to fire it," said Carr, "but that doesn't mean I didn't have to use it."

City officials worked tirelessly to ease racial tensions, but in some cases Boston's reputation had already been cemented among professional athletes. A handful of Major League Baseball players had clauses written into their contracts that allowed them to veto a trade to Boston.

Maxwell went home to his native North Carolina to visit family and was chagrined to learn that none of them were rooting for his basketball team.

"Plain and simple, black people didn't like the Celtics," Maxwell said. "They were too white — or at least that's how they were presented. You had John Havlicek, who was white, so you never heard about Jo Jo White, who was black. You had Dave Cowens, so you never heard about Paul Silas. And then later you had Larry Bird, who was the Great White Hope in a white town that was perceived by most black people as the most racist city in the country at that time."

According to Maxwell, the first time the Celtics played the Lakers in the Larry and Magic era, the majority of black America monitored the 1984 Finals very carefully. Even though the barber shop elders admired Bird's game, they still passionately booed him and his Boston team.

"They were rooting for Magic and the Lakers, and when Larry Bird and the Celtics won instead, it was one of the worst black eyes you could have given black America," Maxwell said. "Now, I was a black man playing for the Celtics at the time. We had a bunch of black guys that year, but it didn't matter. We were still perceived as a white team, and Larry was front and center.

"You couldn't find any black people rooting for us, even in our own town."

When Magic Johnson landed at Boston's Logan Airport for his first playoff game against the Celtics, an older African American man chased after him and extended his hand.

"You gotta beat those Celtics," he said.

"Where are you from?" Magic asked.

"I'm from Boston," the man answered.

"I thought everyone from Boston loved the Celtics," Magic said.

"Son, I am a black man," he said. "Why would I root for those white boys?"

106

Bird was oblivious to the racial undertones. He didn't care what color you were as long as you cut to the right spot, boxed your man out, and dove for a loose ball if it came free. He was an equal opportunity motivator: whether you were black or white, he was going to be in your grill if you messed up. The first time he barked at Maxwell, his teammate quietly burned.

"We grew up in a time of segregation," Maxwell said. "I'm looking at Larry, and he's from the French Lick area, a center of Klan activity. If you were a black man in Indiana, once you got past Indianapolis, you didn't stop for nothing.

"So for me, in the beginning, it was crazy to be playing alongside a guy from there. But it stopped being an issue pretty quickly. Race was never ever an issue with Larry Bird. He was no racist.

"He was just a guy who wanted to kick some ass and win."

Stern demonstrated a keen sensitivity to the racial climate of his league and set about transforming the NBA into one of the most diverse entities in sports. He championed African American players, coaches, and general managers and pushed tirelessly for minority ownership. As the popularity of Bird and Magic increased, the NBA marketed them in a way that transcended racial stereotypes. They became the optimal story line for corporate America, and companies began lining up to capitalize on their success.

Stern had already developed a cordial relationship with both Johnson and Bird, although his initial instinct was to keep a respectful distance. Bird, who insisted on calling the commissioner Mr. Stern, liked him immediately. Stern found Bird to be a man of few wants and even fewer words, but he said, "I was good at reading grunts, so I was pretty sure I knew what he meant."

Magic was more vocal and proactive. He regularly presented Stern with a flurry of ideas on how he could better exploit the growing rivalry between the Celtics and the Lakers, as well as the tantalizing subplot of Larry versus Magic.

Stern genuinely loved the game of basketball and made it a priority to attend every NBA Finals game. Through 2009, he had missed only one in his tenure — to attend the 80th birthday celebration of his wife Diane's Uncle Martin.

In the earlier playoff rounds, Stern traversed the country in an attempt to drop in on every postseason team. When a team fell behind 2–0 in a best-of-five series, Stern would fly in on the chance a franchise was about to be eliminated, earning him the moniker "Grim Reaper."

His first Finals as commissioner was the 1984 series between Los Angeles and Boston. The Celtics were up 3–2 in games when Stern, riding in an elevator before Game 6, struck up a conversation with a group of men wearing number 33 Celtics jerseys.

"So where are you from?" Stern asked.

"We're from Indiana — we're friends of Larry," one of them answered.

"Jeez, tell Larry to take it easy on us," Stern cracked. "We need this series to go seven games."

It was an offhand joke, but when the Celtics lost Game 6, Bird publicly berated the new NBA boss.

"He's the commissioner. He shouldn't be saying anything like that," Bird declared. "The NBA wanted a seventh game because they wanted to make more money, and they got their wish. There's no reason to lie. He said it. He's a man and he'll live up to it.

"He may have said it in jest. But I'm out here trying to make a living and win a championship."

Bird's attack on Stern instantly became headline news. The comment threatened to derail the commissioner's tenure in its infancy, and he was mortified. For the first time in his life, he shut off his phone and locked himself in his hotel room. "What have I done?" he asked himself as the messages piled up.

With a pivotal Game 7 looming, Stern correctly assumed his misstep would quickly fade into the background. It did. Bird and the Celtics prevailed, and Stern's first minor controversy receded from view.

Nearly 25 years after he called out Stern, Bird recalled the incident with regret.

"I was wrong," Bird said. "I never should have said it, but that's how I felt at the time. Stern shouldn't have been joking about something so important either, but two wrongs don't make a right.

"If you have never been in that situation, if you've never laced them up, then you don't know what the players are thinking. It's so intense, so *big*, and it was my first time to play Magic [in the Finals] since college, so it was stress city."

Buoyed by the star power of Bird, Magic, and later Jordan, Stern realized he needed to shore up his marketing coffers. He reached out to NFL commissioner Pete Rozelle and baseball commissioner Bowie Kuhn and sat in on their meetings, asked questions, took notes, and formulated a strategy for his own league based on the success of two of America's favorite sports.

Stern canvassed his own NBA franchises and identified who was having the most success generating income for their teams. Billy Marshall, a retail buyer for the department store Jordan Marsh, had been selling Bird jerseys in his shop and had accounted for almost 10 percent of NBA merchandising sales at the time. Stern offered Marshall a job, and within two years he had placed merchandise in 18 of the league's 23 cities.

In 1984 the NBA's retail merchandise generated $44 million. By 2007 that number had jumped to a staggering $3 billion under Stern's watchful eye. In the mid-eighties, the two most popular team jerseys were easily identifiable: Magic's number 32 Lakers jersey and Bird's number 33 Celtics jersey.

The arrival of Bird and Magic also fortuitously occurred at the same time cable television overtook the sports market. For years most viewers had three networks and one local station to choose from. With the advent of networks like Fox, which tied its success to televising NFL football, the landscape changed dramatically. In the meantime, a fledgling network based in Bristol, Connecticut, called ESPN, believed it could make a business out of a 24-hour sports channel. Stern was initially skeptical, but the NBA's relationship with ESPN blossomed as the network grew.

When Stern began looking to upgrade the NBA's entertainment division, he hired Ed Desser, the executive producer of *California Sports*, and queried him on how to package a highlight show, what constituted a compelling pregame lead-in, and which camera angles were most viewer-friendly.

In 1982 the NBA couldn't afford to buy a 30-second spot to promote its Saturday games on CBS and was dependent on the network for a "charity promo" on Thursday nights. As Johnson and Bird rejuvenated the fortunes of NBA franchises, the network was happy to use them as their advertising hook. It was "Come see Magic and the Lakers and Larry and the Celtics," a marketing strategy that did not sit well with the new commissioner.

"I was happy for the publicity," Stern said, "but I didn't think it was so fair to Kareem and McHale and Parish and Worthy."

The rest of the league understood why it worked. Doug Collins, an NBA player, coach, and broadcaster, said Bird and Magic added a new wrinkle to competition. It was no longer who could score the most points, but who could make the better pass, or whose team could win more championships.

"Having two team-oriented superstars like them really helped save our game," said Collins.

Hubie Brown's Atlanta Hawks went to the playoffs three straight seasons, but their only sellouts were against Philadelphia, Boston, and Los Angeles. It was no coincidence that those teams featured Dr. J, Larry Bird, and Magic Johnson.

"In the mid-eighties, Larry and Magic were the two 'must-see' guys on your schedule," Brown said. "And we were in no position to say anything but, 'Great. We'll take it.'"

The explosion of the television market, combined with the drama of Magic and Bird, attracted a new generation of viewers. In 1979 the league's four-year deal with CBS was worth $74 million. By 2002 the league had inked a six-year deal with ABC, ESPN, and TNT valued at $4.6 billion.

There were other factors that fueled the growth of the league, among them Stern's push for top-notch arenas with luxury suites, which proved to be a valuable source of revenue, and his globalization of the game.

Stern, whose unquenchable thirst for new frontiers has come to define him, plunged into the international market. He attended sporting goods conferences in Munich and Milan. He developed relationships with European professional basketball teams and asked them about the structure of their league, their television contracts, the talent level of their players, and their facilities.

He visited Israel, Africa, Mexico, and China. Stern scheduled exhibition games overseas and worked closely with the Olympic committee to lay the groundwork for NBA players to be eligible to participate in the Games. He developed a strong relationship with FIBA (the French acronym for Fédération Internationale de Basketball Amateur), the international governing body, paving the way for foreign players to play in the NBA. That led to untapped marketing dollars worldwide.

"But all that was possible because of Magic and Larry," Collins said. "It started with them. They captured the imagination of the entire basketball world. People ask me all the time which one was better. My answer is, 'Flip a coin.' If you win and I pick second, I wouldn't have lost. You couldn't possibly lose with those two."

In the spring of 1984, ten-year-old Derek Fisher plunked himself in front of his television set in Little Rock, Arkansas, and watched the most exciting basketball series he'd ever seen. When the NBA Finals between the Lakers and Celtics were over, Fisher grabbed his ball, ran out back, and practiced his "Magic" moves. Halfway across the country, nine-year-old Ray Allen, mesmerized by the sweet shooting motion of the Bird man, tried to replicate the forward's high-arching delivery in his own driveway.

A new era was dawning, and the future stars of the NBA were tuned in.

5

★ ★ ★

JUNE 12, 1984

Boston, Massachusetts

HE COULD HAVE SHUTTERED the curtains and cranked up the volume of the television. Instead, Magic Johnson acted on his perverse need to witness the celebration that was unfolding around him, staring blankly out the window of his Boston hotel, fixated on the sea of green below.

Thousands of fans clogged the streets, many wearing shamrock-colored T-shirts, creating a gleeful gridlock of traffic in the already historically congested city. Car horns honked, fireworks crackled, and grown men danced Irish jigs in celebration of the Celtics' Game 7 victory over the Lakers to win the 1984 NBA Championship.

"It was bedlam," Magic said. "I made myself watch it. It made me feel worse, but I deserved to be miserable."

His two close friends, NBA stars Mark Aguirre and Isiah Thomas, remained sequestered in the room with him, attempting to console him. Back then, there were no team charters to whisk professional athletes home immediately after the game. The Lakers flew commercial and were forced to wait until morning before they could escape Boston and their glaring errors, which were highlighted hourly on the local news channels.

Aguirre turned off the television, and Thomas ordered room service: a feast of chicken, ribs, mounds of fruit, and baskets of rolls and pastries. Most of it went untouched. Johnson had no appetite for anything except self-loathing.

His friends broached various topics with the aim of distracting him — music, cars, women — but as the hours droned on, Magic kept doubling back to missed free throws, errant passes, and dribbling out the clock.

"We should have won that series," Johnson said quietly. "I've always prided myself on getting it done in crunch time. What happened?"

He already knew the answer. Larry Bird happened. His rival dominated the series, copping the Finals MVP trophy with timely shooting, relentless rebounding, and uncanny court vision, a trait he and Johnson shared from the moment they lined up opposite one another.

By morning, Magic had been saddled with a new nickname for himself (Tragic) and his team (the Fakers). That was humiliating enough, but something gnawed at LA's normally ebullient star beyond that, something he wouldn't even share with his trusted confidants.

"It was losing to Larry," Magic admitted. "That was the most crushing part. It was my first time in an LA-Boston series, and he got the best of me."

Three miles from Magic's hotel, in a team van driven by the Celtics' assistant equipment manager Joe "Corky" Qatato, Larry Bird and teammate Quinn Buckner were mired in the celebratory traffic. Their plan was to ride in the van to Hellenic College in Brookline, where their cars were parked, then drive back downtown to join the team celebration at Chelsea's, a local watering hole in a tourist section of the city called Faneuil Hall.

But the traffic wasn't moving, and Bird was impatient. He reached across the driver's seat and thrust the van into park.

"C'mon, Quinn," Bird said. "We'll get our cars later."

The MVP of the '84 Finals leaped out the van, crossed over by foot to the other side of Storrow Drive, a major Boston thoroughfare, and began hoofing it back downtown.

A bemused Buckner followed behind, chuckling at the absurdity of their actions.

It was only a matter of seconds before they were recognized. A car with three fans driving inbound stopped in amazement when they spotted their franchise forward striding along the curb.

"Larry Bird?!!!" the driver asked.

"Sssh," Bird answered. "Listen, you got any room in there for Quinn and me?"

The young man opened the door and motioned for his companions, resplendent in their Bird team jerseys, to move over for two of the city's newly crowned champions. As Buckner and Bird crammed their oversized basketball frames into the back of the economy car, the passengers howled with delight and astonishment.

"Larry Bird is in our car!" shrieked the driver, pounding the steering wheel for emphasis.

"Oh, my God, are you kidding me?! This is unbelievable!! I'm wearing your shirt!!!" howled the passenger in the rear seat.

"All right now, calm down," Bird said. "If you want us to stay, you gotta keep quiet."

They tried. But as they weaved through traffic with the object of every Celtics fan's desire lounging in the back seat, it was impossible not to holler out "MVP!" or "Lakers suck!" They were traversing the heart of downtown Boston with the most famous and popular athlete in the city.

"So, Larry," said the driver, as they approached Chelsea's, "can we come with you?"

"Sorry, champions only," declared Bird, punching Buckner in the shoulder.

When Bird and Buckner reached Faneuil Hall, they thanked their blue-collar chauffeurs and skipped through the roped security entrance to Chelsea's.

Inside, the two players clinked beer bottles and toasted to their title. Bird, normally reserved in victory, disarmed Buckner with occasional gleeful outbursts of "We did it!" Hours later, amid the singing and the drinking and the reveling, Bird grabbed Buckner and slung his arm around him.

"I finally got him," Bird said. "I finally got Magic."

The Lakers and Celtics began the 1983–84 season with unfinished business to address. Los Angeles had cruised to the Finals the previous June but was unceremoniously dumped by Julius Erving, Moses Malone, and the Philadelphia 76ers in four straight games. The Celtics had suffered a shocking sweep of their own, falling to the Milwaukee Bucks in the Eastern Conference Semi-Finals.

Bird bitterly referred to the 1982–83 campaign as a lost opportunity to capitalize on a nucleus of talent that should have, in his opinion, yielded a championship. It further irked him that Los Angeles would have been the opponent in the Finals had the Celtics advanced. It was (and had been since his arrival in the NBA) his fervent wish to battle Magic and LA head-to-head for the title, yet four seasons into their professional careers, that matchup had not materialized. Bird was acutely aware of what his nemesis was accomplishing on the Other Coast, even though he rarely acknowledged it.

"Did you see Magic had 21 assists the other night?" Larry's teammate Chris Ford asked.

Bird didn't respond, but he already knew about Magic's numbers. He had checked them first thing in the morning.

"I was keeping my eye on him," Bird admitted. "It got to a point where I really didn't care about anyone else. The focus had to be Lakers, Lakers, Lakers."

Two thousand eight hundred miles away, Magic Johnson woke up each morning, poured himself a glass of orange juice, spread out the newspaper, and checked the paper to see how Larry Bird and the Celtics had fared the night before. He painstakingly charted not only his rival's points but also his assist count.

"When those assists started going up," Magic said, "I knew he was doing what I was doing: making everyone better."

In 1984 it became increasingly apparent that Los Angeles and Boston were on course to meet in the Finals. Bird was submitting MVP numbers, and Magic was orchestrating a transition game that ran rampant over alleged Western Conference rivals. The Celtics and the Lakers crushed opponents in their respective conferences with one eye on the other.

"You knew pretty early on it was going to be one of the greatest rivalries in sports," said former Lakers guard Byron Scott. "There was an edge to the games. You had two teams that genuinely disliked one another, and then you had Magic and Bird, who wanted to beat each other's brains out."

The Lakers objected to Bird's cold stare, his trash-talking on the floor, and his stubborn unwillingness to acknowledge LA's accomplishments. The Celtics dismissed Magic's toothy smile, his flashy fast-break baskets, and what they perceived to be his false cheerfulness.

"We hated Magic Johnson," confirmed Celtics forward Cedric Maxwell. "All that Showtime, the Hollywood glitz, the phony smile. He was all style, and we were all substance."

That summation of the Lakers was precisely what had rankled coach Pat Riley to the point of fury. Riley had worn Lakers purple and gold for nearly six NBA seasons, establishing himself as a hard-nosed, intelligent player. When he became head coach of the Lakers, he established a demanding, unrelenting practice regimen that required both physical and mental stamina.

"For anyone to suggest we were soft, that we were 'Showtime,' I'd like to see them get through one of our practices," Riley sniffed.

Yet even he understood that until the Lakers reversed their fortunes against Boston, the perception, however erroneous, would stand. Riley, Magic, and Kareem were all trying to buck a historical trend that had come to define both franchises.

From 1956 to 1969, the Celtics won eleven championships in thirteen seasons. They met the LA Lakers in the Finals six times

A stoic Larry (second row, third from left) celebrates a big win with his Springs Valley High School team. *M. Gibson/Courtesy of Larry Bird*

Magic and his high school coach, George Fox, team up to win Everett High School a state title.
Courtesy of Magic Johnson

Larry and his mother, Georgia, in 1979 in Salt Lake City, where Indiana State played Michigan State for the NCAA title. *Courtesy of Larry Bird*

Magic and Larry keep their eyes on the ball in the 1979 NCAA championship game. *James Drake/Sports Illustrated/Getty Images*

LEFT TO RIGHT: Celtics owner Harry Mangurian, general manager Red Auerbach, Larry, and attorney Bob Woolf at a press conference to announce Bird's signing with the Celtics.

Steve Lipofsky/Basketballphoto.com

Earvin Johnson Sr. and Earvin Johnson Jr. are all smiles after Magic signs with the Lakers.

Marty Lederhandler/AP

Magic shares a championship moment with his friend and team owner Jerry Buss after the Lakers win the title in 1980.

Gene Pushkar/AP

Magic becomes the first rookie in NBA history to be named Finals MVP in 1980. *AP*

Larry rises above the crowd in the 1981 Finals.
Steve Lipofsky/Basketballphoto.com

Larry, seated next to his pal Rick Robey and coach Bill Fitch, watches the final seconds of a loss to Philadelphia in the 1982 Eastern Conference Finals. *Peter Morgan/AP*

Magic and his confidant Isiah Thomas share a belly laugh at the 1983 All-Star Game.
Andrew D. Bernstein/NBAE/Getty Images

Larry enjoys being a fan. *Dick Raphael/NBAE/Getty Images*

Magic and Larry go head-to-head in the 1984 Finals.
Dick Raphael/NBAE/ Getty Images

Kevin McHale's takedown of Kurt Rambis in Game 4 of the 1984 Finals changed the tenor of the series.
Peter Read Miller/Sports Illustrated/Getty Images

Larry and Magic put on their best face in a promotional campaign for the league.

Andrew D. Bernstein/NBAE/Getty Images

Larry, going casual, accepts his 1984 league MVP trophy.

Steve Lipofsky/Basketballphoto.com

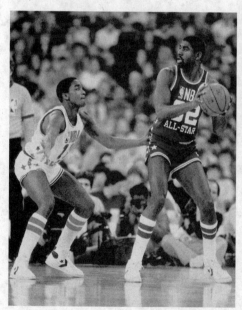

Isiah Thomas guards Magic at the 1985 All-Star Game in the Hoosier Dome.

Andrew D. Bernstein/NBAE/Getty Images

Michael Jordan stands alone at the 1985 All-Star Game, where he believed Magic and Isiah Thomas conspired to freeze him out of the game action.

Andrew D. Bernstein/NBAE/Getty Images

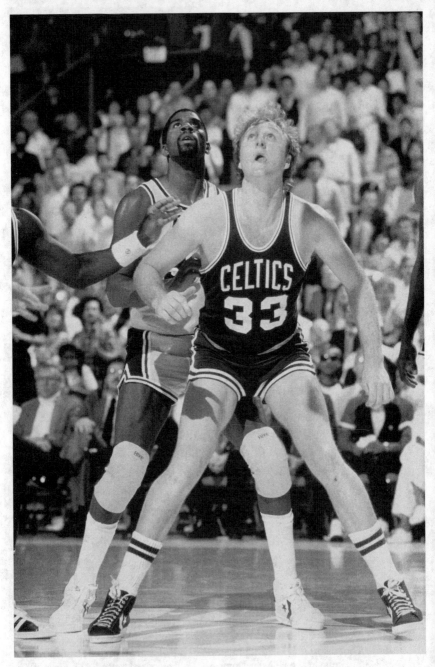

Magic and Larry vie for a rebound. *Andrew D. Bernstein/NBAE/Getty Images*

and won all six. The misery was etched into the faces of Lakers general manager Jerry West and Riley, both of whom were a part of the franchise's futile attempt to exorcise the demons of Celtics patriarch Red Auerbach's arrogant victory cigar.

For fourteen seasons, West excelled with such precision that the NBA logo was modeled after his likeness. He scored 25,192 career points, dished out 6,238 assists, and was nicknamed "Mr. Clutch," but he won only one championship — in 1972 — at the tail end of his distinguished career. He retired having never beaten the Celtics in the NBA Finals.

There were many occasions when he came excruciatingly close. West and Elgin Baylor, the skilled forward who averaged 38.3 points and nearly 19 rebounds a game, anchored a 1961–62 Lakers team that had it all: shooting, defense, and versatility. But midway through the season Baylor was called into the army reserves in Fort Lewis, Washington, and was relegated to playing only on weekends or with an occasional day pass. In preparation for the Finals against Boston, the Lakers set up shop in a local gym adjacent to Baylor's army base so he would be able to practice with the team.

The series came down to a winner-take-all Game 7 at Boston Garden, and a tie score with the clock down to 0:05 — five seconds. Franklin Delano Selvy, named after President Roosevelt, was charged with getting the ball inbounds to his Lakers teammates. Celtics guard Bob Cousy's assignment was to distract him as much as possible.

"Arnold [Red Auerbach] told me to jump up, scratch, wave my hands, shout, whatever I had to do," Cousy said.

Cousy leaped into the air, flailing his arms. Selvy waited until Cousy reached the top of his jump, then dumped the ball in to "Hot Rod" Hundley and quickly sprinted to the left corner, his favorite spot on the floor. By the time Cousy landed, then raced after Selvy, he realized he was a step behind.

"Oh, God, I blew it," Cousy thought to himself. "I'm going to be the guy that cost us the championship."

Hundley was supposed to deliver the ball to either West or Baylor, but both were smothered by Celtics defenders. He was startled to see Selvy alone on the baseline. West, struggling to free himself from a double team, was also encouraged to see one of his team's best shooters with the ball in his hands and a chance to win it.

"It was about as good a look as you could hope for," West said.

Selvy, a two-time All-Star, launched his 12-foot shot just before Cousy arrived to challenge it. (Selvy later claimed Boston's guard pushed him, but there was no call from the referee.) The jumper bounced high off the back rim — then out. West held his breath as the shot hit iron — then exhaled in disappointment as Celtics center Bill Russell gathered in the rebound. The buzzer sounded, the game went into overtime, and Boston prevailed.

As the Celtics players jubilantly hoisted Auerbach onto their shoulders, the Boston fans streamed out of the stands and swarmed the court. West tried to skirt away from the oncoming crowd, which barreled past Baylor and Selvy and him as if they were invisible. Once safely ensconced in the cramped visitors' locker room, West remained in full uniform, replaying the final possession in his mind. "If it goes in," West said ruefully, "then history is altered."

For years afterward, Hundley intermittently picked up the telephone and called his old Lakers pal.

"Hello?" Selvy would say.

"Hi, Frank. Nice shot," Hundley would answer. Then he'd hang up the phone.

And so it went. Each year the Lakers believed it would be different. Each year it wasn't. In 1968–69, with Cousy retired and Russell in his final season as player-coach for Boston, the Lakers acquired Russell's chief rival, the irrepressible Wilt Chamberlain. Chamberlain, who once scored 100 points in a game, enabled Los Angeles to win 55 games and capture home-court advantage throughout the Finals against — who else? — Boston. Predictably, the Lakers-Celtics showdown went seven games, but this time the new champion was to be decided on the Lakers' home court, the Forum.

Lakers owner Jack Kent Cooke felt so confident about his team's chances that he ordered thousands of purple and gold balloons and perched them high above courtside in the rafters, nestled in netting, waiting for the perfect moment to release them and ignite the Lakers' celebration.

As West ran out for pregame warm-ups, he noticed the balloons above and shook his head. He was embarrassed by his owner's arrogant gesture.

"The Celtics deserved better," West said.

With a minute to play and Boston clinging to a one-point lead (103–102), West poked the ball free. In the frenzied scramble that followed, Celtics sixth man Don Nelson picked up the loose ball and lofted a shot from just beyond the free throw line. It clanged off the back rim and shot straight up into the air — but, unlike Selvy's jumper, the Boston player's shot dropped through the strings.

The Celtics won. The Lakers didn't.

Again.

West dropped to his knees as the buzzer sounded. He looked up one more time at the balloons before he shuffled to the dressing room. He had played the final three games of the series with a strained hamstring, and his leg was throbbing. As he stood in the shower with cascades of water streaming down his body, West briefly contemplated quitting.

"It was the most devastating moment of my career," he said. "If I had something else I liked to do in terms of competition, I probably would have done it. It would have been best for me to get away from basketball at that point."

The balloons were donated to a children's hospital. West, who had submitted 42 points, 13 rebounds, and 12 assists, became the first MVP of the Finals to play for the losing side. The series epitomized his professional legacy: brilliance in defeat against Boston.

"Jerry never talked much about it," said Magic, "but he didn't have to. It showed on his face. The man had been tortured by the Boston Celtics."

By 1984 there were new players and new story lines to explore in the Celtics-Lakers rivalry, but the presence of West and Riley and Auerbach and K. C. Jones, who had starred with the Celtics on the court and was now their coach, only added to the intrigue.

"It was impossible to ignore the history," said Lakers forward

Kurt Rambis. "Even if we wanted to, we couldn't. There were news articles, stories, conversations, remembrances.

"It wasn't just about us. We were playing for Wilt Chamberlain and Jerry West and Elgin Baylor."

Bird won his first of three consecutive league MVP trophies that season, averaging 24.2 points, 10.1 rebounds, and 6.6 assists a game.

Magic's numbers were also gaudy—17.6 points, 7.3 rebounds, and 13.1 assists—but he had not yet reached the elite status of his rival. The individual tension developing between the two wasn't restricted to Larry and Magic. Each Celtic and Laker was instructed not to cross the line into enemy territory.

"I used to love two of the old Celtics—Jo Jo White and Hank Finkel," said LA forward James Worthy. "When I got to LA and was told I had to hate Boston, I thought to myself, 'What do I have to do with this history?' But then I realized I was part of it as long as it said Lakers across my chest."

Bird was aware in general terms of the Lakers-Celtics wars of the past, but he wasn't particularly interested in learning the nuts and bolts of the rivalry. While he had great respect for the players before him, he wasn't inclined to study their accomplishments. His developing rivalry with Magic was already being compared to the epic battles of Russell and Chamberlain, yet those debates were of little consequence to Bird.

"Obviously I had heard of Bill Russell and the championships he won," Bird said. "But if anyone had pressed me on which years, I wouldn't have known. When I was 23 years old, I thought Bill Russell was 100 years old. That's the way it is when you are 23.

"You don't care what happened before. You want to make your own history."

Since both Magic and Larry had already won an NBA championship, dethroning one another became the salacious subplot. Magic was tired of hearing about the "gritty" Bird, and Larry was sick of the "dynamic" Johnson. By playoff time, both stars were aggravated by comparisons and questions regarding the other. The competition between them had ratcheted up yet another notch.

"It was annoying," Magic said. "We were both trying to carve out our own niche, on an individual and a team level, and everyone kept linking us together. I didn't like it. I kept telling people, 'I'm nothing like him.' We didn't even play the same position."

That did not prevent basketball pundits from engaging in a reoccurring debate: who is better, Larry or Magic? Both Johnson and Bird feigned indifference, yet each knew their first head-to-head clash in the pros would give whoever won the edge.

"Magic didn't sit around and talk about Larry," said Rambis. "But clearly he was on Earvin's mind. He was on *all* of our minds."

He should have been. An ornery Bird spent the better part of 1983–84 ruminating over the collapse of his team the previous spring. After losing to Milwaukee in the 1983 playoffs, Bird punished himself with rigorous off-season conditioning drills in the searing southern Indiana sun. During his long, arduous runs through the hills of Orange County, Bird cursed his team's inability to focus and their preoccupation with upstaging their coach, Bill Fitch.

The nucleus of the freewheeling group that won an NBA championship with such flourish two years earlier in 1981 had disintegrated into a collection of dispirited, divided, and, in some cases, openly defiant players. Although Bird resolutely stood by Fitch publicly and privately, even he could see the coach had lost the team.

"It was the petty stuff that turned us on him," explained Carr, one of Fitch's chief antagonists.

During a road trip to New York in 1979, his first season with Boston, Carr made plans to meet some family after the game at Charley O's, a restaurant directly across the street from Madison Square Garden. As he was about to leave, Boston trainer Ray Melchiorre informed him that Fitch's rule was that every member of the team was required to go back to the hotel on the team bus.

The hotel was nearly 15 blocks uptown. Carr stared at Melchiorre in disbelief.

"You mean to tell me you are going to make me drive on this bus 20 minutes, then take a cab back to the exact spot where the bus is parked?" he said.

"That's right," Melchiorre said.

Carr threw down his towel in disgust, grabbed his bag, and stomped off. As he made his way to the back of the bus, he complained, "I signed a five-year deal to be treated like this?"

Despite their dissatisfaction with their coach, the Celtics initially appeared to be poised for another title run in 1982–83. They broke out of the gates winning 16 of their first 20 games. Bird was averaging 22.9 points a night and tended to describe to some hapless defensive opponent in painstaking detail how he was going to score on him before carrying out the deed in exactly the fashion he outlined.

He developed a friendly but competitive running dialogue with Knicks trainer Mike Saunders, and whenever Boston played New York, he'd call his baskets as he ran past the Knicks bench.

"Bank shot," Bird would inform Saunders, then fly down the floor and kiss the ball in off the glass.

"Twenty-footer, left side," Bird would announce, before he stuck a long jumper in Knicks defender Trent Tucker's face.

"I always considered myself a pretty confident person," said former Celtics player Danny Ainge, "but I've never seen anyone who believed in himself like Larry did."

Even so, team chemistry was an issue. Mindful of the blossoming talents of Magic, Auerbach acquired rugged defensive specialist Quinn Buckner from Milwaukee with hopes he could help neutralize Johnson.

"I was sure we'd be seeing the Lakers in the Finals that spring [of 1983]," said Auerbach. "I don't mind telling you that Magic worried the hell out of me. He was so big and so strong. We needed someone who could be physical with him."

The addition of Buckner left Tiny Archibald, an All-Star the previous season, on the bench. Archibald struggled to accept his reduced role (the team would waive him shortly after the season ended), while Parish, McHale, Maxwell, and Carr chafed at Fitch's persistent prodding.

Maxwell was sitting in the locker room with his headphones on after the team had lost a close game when Fitch strode toward him and tapped him on the shoulder.

"If you ever have those headphones on again, I'll break them in half," Fitch said, and demonstrated the motion of snapping them in two. For the rest of the season, Celtics players walked up to Maxwell and mimicked the same snapping motion, reducing Maxwell to gales of laughter and further antagonizing the coach.

Boston won 56 games that season but finished 9 games behind Philadelphia in the standings. By the time the postseason rolled around, the players were at their breaking point. Fitch installed a curfew, and one night in Houston sat in the lobby waiting to make sure each of them adhered to it. McHale and Carr waited until seconds before the curfew before sauntering inside to their rooms.

"It was a bad season," Ainge said. "Max and Chief weren't listening. They had totally tuned Fitch out. And Kevin wasn't happy either."

"It was a professional mutiny," said Buckner. "They just wouldn't play for Bill Fitch. They spent half a season trying to embarrass him. That's not an environment I was familiar with. Bill deserved better."

In Game 1 of their best-of-seven series with the Bucks in the 1983 Eastern Conference Semi-Finals, the Celtics were thumped 116–95 on their own floor. Fitch, infuriated by the insubordination of his players, humiliated his starters by making them check back into the game in the fourth quarter of a blowout. The home crowd booed lustily.

Boston's performance deteriorated from there. In Game 4, with the Celtics already trailing 3–0 in the series, Buckner recalled Fitch imploring the players to push the ball up the floor.

"Instead, it looked like three guys were literally taking the ball up at a pace three times slower than it should have been — on purpose," Buckner said.

"I admit it," Carr said. "Our goal in 1983 wasn't to win a championship. It was to get rid of Fitch."

After the Bucks' sweep, McHale caused a stir when he declared he could "hold his head high" following the playoff debacle. A somber Bird contradicted McHale's assessment by saying all Celtics should be embarrassed, and he promised things would be different next season — or else.

"I was ticked off," Bird said. "After the game I told Red, 'Hey, look. We've got no leadership here. If you want me to lead this team, I will. But we've got to get back to winning championships and forget all this other crap, because it's killing us.' And I meant it."

Bird didn't limit his exasperation to a conversation with Auerbach. Once the locker room door was closed, he leveled a brutally honest assessment of their shortcomings at his teammates, including their poisonous attitude toward Fitch. Though Bird didn't single out any player by name, he did not hesitate to talk specifically about issues he had with players' commitment, conditioning, and attitude.

"Most of what he said was unprintable," Buckner said. "And he was very pointed in his comments. Most of the guys were looking around the room as if to say, 'He's not talking about me.' But they must have gotten the message, because everyone came back in better shape the next season."

Fitch was fired that summer and K. C. Jones was elevated from assistant to head coach. Bird was not pleased that Fitch was designated to take the fall for a team that quit on him. "As much as I loved playing with some of those guys, they were the ones who should have been shipped out," Bird said. "I told them, 'Someday you'll look back and realize Bill Fitch was the best coach for this team.'"

Bird retreated to his newly constructed home in West Baden, Indiana, complete with its full-length outdoor court. He added a stepback jumper to his arsenal, refining it by shooting 800 of them a day. Buckner came to visit Bird that summer and agreed to participate in his morning workout. They awoke at 7 A.M., put on their track shoes, and ran five miles — uphill. Buckner was amazed by the steep incline of Bird's regular route and was walking by the halfway mark. Bird was not a fast runner, but he had long strides and the determined look of an athlete scorned. He and Buckner did not discuss the Bucks' sweep, but Bird's dissatisfaction was implied in the intensity of his workouts.

After his uphill run, Bird hopped on his bicycle and pedaled 20 miles around the county. Then, with the burning sun at its peak, he spent an additional hour and a half shooting 500 jumpers and 500 free throws.

"I was getting ready for a whole lot of years of us and the Lakers," Bird said. "We were young and they were young. They had Kareem. They had Magic. They were making moves. I wanted to make sure we kept up."

Auerbach felt the same way. Still in search of a physical player to offset the brilliance of Magic, he acquired Dennis Johnson on June 27, 1983, from the Phoenix Suns. The price was Robey, Bird's sidekick and drinking companion. Bird's teammates insisted in subsequent years it was no accident that number 33 won his first MVP trophy after his buddy Robey had moved on.

At the time, the move to bring in D.J. was viewed as somewhat of a gamble. Although his talent was unquestionable, he had developed a reputation as a difficult player. Seattle coach Lenny Wilkens had branded him a "cancer," and the image lingered. Yet D.J. had proven to be a legitimate hindrance to Magic in the Western Conference, able to offset his strength with physical play of his own.

Johnson and Johnson were hardly strangers. They played against one another in Los Angeles during the summer months and occasionally dined together with their wives. That tradition came to a screeching halt once the trade was made and D.J. became a Celtic. The summer after the deal, he ran into Magic just as he was completing his workout.

"In the past it would have been, 'Hey, man, how you been? Where you going to be later? Let's hook up,'" D.J. said. "Not this time. It was, 'Hey, how are you doing? See you later.'"

"Once he started wearing Celtics green, we were done socializing," Magic confirmed.

While the Celtics reinvented their backcourt by acquiring Dennis Johnson, the Lakers had done some maneuvering of their own in preparation for the 1983–84 season. Norm Nixon, a mainstay in the Lakers' rotation for the previous six seasons, was swapped along with Eddie Jordan to San Diego for seven-footer Swen Nater and the rights to rookie Byron Scott.

West wisely recognized that the Lakers needed a lethal perimeter threat to exploit the double teams that Abdul-Jabbar and Magic were drawing. Yet the trade was not well received in the LA locker room. Nixon was popular with his teammates and the players were wary of the rookie Scott, who had starred at Arizona State and grew up rooting for the Lakers, but quickly realized he was going to have to bide his time before he would be accepted as a member of the Lakers' inner circle.

Scott made some early overtures to Magic, who at 24 was the closest to him in age, but the reception was tepid at best. In the ensuing years, Scott would become one of Johnson's most valued friends, but in 1983–84 he was just another rookie who was going to have to prove to Magic that he belonged.

The Lakers' nucleus of Magic, Kareem, Worthy, Bob McAdoo, Cooper, and Wilkes (who was stricken with an intestinal infection that restricted him to limited duty in the postseason) represented the optimal personnel for playing an up-tempo style. The Lakers averaged 115.6 points a night and shot 53.2 percent from the floor. Magic, who led the league in assists that season with 13.1 a game, distributed the ball with alarming ease.

"Sometimes," Wilkes said, "I think he knew where I was cutting before I did."

Boston relied on a half-court game that pounded the ball inside to Maxwell, Bird, Parish, and McHale. The Celtics steeled themselves for a long, grueling season in the rugged Eastern Conference, hoping they could slug their way past physical teams like New York, Milwaukee, and Philadelphia.

"I always said the problem with our rivalry was the Lakers could be out there playing at 80 percent and still get to the Finals, but we had to bang and scratch and beat our way to get there," Bird said. "It was just a fact the East was stronger and more physical. We were taking a huge beating on our way to the Finals, and the Lakers were just sitting back, waiting for us to arrive."

Although each roster was loaded with future Hall of Famers, both coaches found themselves obsessing over the two young stars. Magic's size and his exceptional passing skills were only half the reason he was so dangerous, according to K. C. Jones.

"Magic pulled everybody in," said the Celtics coach. "He grabbed them, held them close, and made everybody a part of it. He was so much fun to watch, he even got Kareem to smile once in a while. And when the big fella was happy, the Lakers won games."

Riley pored over tapes of Bird, pointing out specific tendencies to his team, such as Bird's preference to bring the ball up left-handed and his ability to split double teams by positioning his feet in between the trap. Yet all the technical tips, Riley knew, would not offset the true strength of Bird's game: his mental tenacity.

"You had to deal with his psyche first before you could even discuss the basketball aspect of it," Riley explained. "I always told my guys, 'You will never be able to beat Bird until you understand how much he wants to win and what he'll do to make sure he wins.'

"We had to be above and beyond him mentally, and I wasn't always sure it was possible."

Riley did have one unshakable weapon in his arsenal: Michael Cooper, the slender Lakers forward whose commitment to the defensive side of the game bordered on the obsessive. Cooper watched tapes of Bird while lying in bed with his wife Wanda before he went to sleep. He watched tapes of Bird in the morning while he was brushing his teeth. The tapes went everywhere with him, even on vacation.

"My goal was simply to make every single thing he did more difficult," Cooper said.

While Cooper was analyzing Bird, the Celtics forward was playing and rewinding and playing films of Cooper, looking for clues as to why this one player had been so successful in disrupting his offensive flow.

As Bird watched the film again and again, he looked to see where

Cooper was when he got the ball. Was he trying to shade Bird in one particular direction? Who did the Lakers have coming up behind him to double-team? What other defensive shifts were they using?

Bird consulted with D.J., who believed Bird should rely on his backdoor cuts a little more. He also suggested using quicker pick-and-rolls to keep Cooper off balance.

"But the key," D.J. told Bird, "is to get him in the post. He can't do anything once you've posted him up."

Magic's ability to see over the defense and connect with Abdul-Jabbar for easy baskets made him the focus of Boston's defensive schemes. His superior rebounding skills were also a major concern. Few point guards crashed the glass with his gusto. It enabled Magic to start the break himself, and his teammates soon learned to release as soon as Johnson moved toward the ball off an opponent's miss. Magic also posed unique problems because he was so physical and had learned to use his body to his advantage when muscling out smaller guards.

Because the Celtics had won 62 games during the regular season, the 1984 Finals would begin on their home floor, the hallowed parquet notorious for its dead spots. As the Lakers departed for Boston, Magic made a point of approaching Jerry West, who refused to travel to the Garden and would watch the games at home. He grabbed his boss's arm and told him, "Don't worry. We're going to make this right. We're the better team. I'm sure of it."

When the Lakers landed at Logan Airport on May 26, they waited nearly an hour for their bags, emblazoned with the purple-and-gold Lakers emblem. When the luggage finally appeared on the conveyer belt, many of them were unzipped. Nothing was missing, according to Magic, "but the message was clear. It was just Boston's way of letting us know we shouldn't get comfortable here."

The airport was crawling with Celtics fans who had braved the city's choked traffic on the Central Artery for the singular purpose of harassing Boston's next opponent. As Johnson scooped up his bag, a teenager displaying a shamrock logo on his kelly-green T-shirt waved enthusiastically to him. Magic slowed, expecting to fulfill an autograph request. "Hey, Magic, Larry is going to make you disappear!" he taunted.

Johnson advanced a few more steps before another pocket of "green people" (the generic name bestowed on the passionate group of fans who stalked the Celtics) surrounded him. "Larry's going to eat you up, Magic," a woman outfitted from hat to sneakers in Celtics memorabilia announced. Johnson smiled politely and picked up his pace. He was relieved to finally reach the team bus — until he noticed the driver was wearing a Celtics shirt. When he stepped up to the counter at the team hotel to check in, the manager who assisted him also proudly wore Celtics colors.

"Even the curtains in my room were green," Magic said.

The city was thirsty for a championship — specifically one over Magic and the Lakers. In the moments before Game 1 began, Bird took a moment to glance into the stands and was heartened to see fans walking through the aisles dressed in white sheets to signify the ghosts of Lakers past.

"It didn't have any bearing on the game," Bird said, "but I loved it when they pulled out those sheets."

Magic noticed the "ghosts" too and briefly harkened back to the heartache West had endured in his prime. "That won't be me," Johnson told himself. "We're taking these guys down."

The last Lakers player to take the floor for Game 1 was the 37-year-old Abdul-Jabbar, who had woken up that morning with a searing migraine, an affliction that plagued him throughout his career. Although the pain was crippling and usually induced acute nausea and vomiting, Kareem demonstrated an odd tendency to excel when he was suffering.

Game 1 was no exception. Abdul-Jabbar was brilliant (32 points, 8 rebounds, 5 assists, 2 blocks) in a stunning 115–109 Lakers win, his patent skyhook clearly flummoxing Boston center Robert Parish, who looked unprepared and overmatched. Bird finished with 24 points and 14 rebounds, but the resolute Cooper had clearly affected his shooting (7 of 17 from the floor). And although Abdul-Jabbar had rightfully stolen the headlines, it was Magic who left him concerned.

"Magic picked us apart that night," Bird said. "He got his guys easy baskets. I didn't like what I saw."

K. C. Jones chose to start the 6-foot-2 Gerald Henderson on the 6-foot-9 Magic because he felt Henderson would be able to utilize his speed to keep up with Johnson when he filled the lane in transition. It was a decision that deeply wounded D.J., who had been gearing up all week for a matchup with Johnson.

"I wanted a chance at him," D.J. said, "but I told myself, 'Be patient.' The last thing I needed was to be called a troublemaker again."

Magic was equally surprised and pleased to learn Henderson was guarding him. D.J.'s physical style often made it problematic for Magic to establish tempo because he was so preoccupied with the possibility that D.J. would swat the ball free. With the smaller Henderson on him, Johnson felt he'd have better success finding Abdul-Jabbar in the post and would be able to generate more offensive opportunities for himself.

He was correct on both counts. Magic scored 14 points by the end of the first quarter in Game 2, and his confidence was soaring. He was on the verge of leading the Lakers to victory when a seemingly minor miscue in the final seconds led to a series of gaffes that haunted him for the remainder of the series.

The Lakers held a 113–111 lead with 20 seconds to play when McHale, a 78 percent free throw shooter, was fouled and stepped up to the line. The young forward, his knees wobbling, missed them both.

Magic snared the rebound on the second miss and had victory in his hands. All he had to do was turn, take the ball up the floor, and run out the clock to preserve a 2–0 series lead for the Lakers. Instead, he inexplicably called time-out, enabling Boston to set its defense against the ensuing inbounds play.

Pat Riley had instructed Johnson to call time-out if McHale made both free throws to tie the game. He had not given the same instructions in the event McHale missed.

"I'm to blame," Riley said. "It was the biggest mistake of my career. I was so busy on the sidelines talking to my players and preparing for the final seconds, I never even looked up to see if McHale made the free throws.

"I just assumed he did. Earvin did what he was told. It was my fault. I should have been more conscious of what was unfolding. My best player had rebounded the ball, and all he had to do was run up the floor and the game would have been over."

Instead, Boston's defenders utilized the time-out to face-guard each Laker on the floor. Magic had to find someone who was open — quickly. He chose his whippet forward, Worthy, who had already scored 29 points in the game on 11-of-12 shooting. But Worthy floated a sloppy crosscourt pass to Byron Scott, and Henderson intercepted it. He streaked in for a lay-up to tie the game — and permanently cement himself in Boston's sports annals as a true Celtics postseason hero.

Worthy instantly identified who was about to be labeled the goat. He had played for North Carolina in the 1982 NCAA Final against Georgetown. In the final seconds of that epic game, Georgetown guard Fred Brown threw a pass right into Worthy's hands and cost his Hoyas the championship.

"It wasn't until that day in Boston Garden that I truly understood how Fred felt," Worthy said. "It's the most humiliating feeling in the world."

The Garden crowd, despondent just moments earlier, was now on its feet. Their ardent cheers of "Let's go, Celtics!" drowned out most of what Riley attempted to tell his players in the huddle, which was that LA still had a chance to pull out the win. They had the ball, their redoubtable center, their charismatic point guard, and 13 seconds to regain the momentum.

But Magic's swagger had dissipated. There was too much noise, too much pressure, too many scenarios to consider. He carefully dribbled the ball up the floor, searching for the open man, but Worthy was covered. He looked to Kareem, but Parish was denying Kareem the ball. With three seconds left in the game, Magic realized with horror that he was almost out of time. He quickly fired the ball to Bob McAdoo, but McHale, his long, gangly arms outstretched, prevented McAdoo from getting a shot off.

"Magic had a brain freeze," Carr said. "It happens. The place is loud. Everyone is yelling to you, and at you. And Magic was only a kid. He was still learning."

The Boston crowd was incredulous. Thirteen seconds to go and Magic couldn't deliver a shot for his team? The jeering began in earnest. The mistake was further magnified when a Scott Wedman baseline jumper sealed the win for the Celtics in overtime and knotted the series 1–1.

As the Lakers collected their warm-ups, Worthy patted his young point guard on the back. There would be two Laker goats on this night, not just one.

"I'll never forget the look on Magic's face," Buckner said. "It was one of absolute disbelief. He had never messed up before."

"When a player of that caliber does something so uncharacteristic, you know you are lucky," Ainge said. "You also anticipate that star will make up for it — in the next play, or the next game."

Bird contends that Magic may have been a victim of a Celtics home-court advantage. In 1984, the shot clocks atop the baskets were not four-sided or digital, as they are today. Bird found them to be unreliable, and when they were broken Boston placed electronic boxes on the floor displaying how much time was left. There were also game clocks suspended in the corners of the Garden, but often they were obstructed by a fan's jacket or sweatshirt.

"It seemed like someone was blocking them clocks," Bird said. "I bet Magic couldn't even see how much time was left. I never could. What I used to do was check the time during the time-out, then count down in my head."

In the aftermath of the loss, Magic reminded anyone who would listen that the Lakers had accomplished what they had set out to do: win a game in Boston. No one was interested in that angle. They were too focused on the mismanagement of the clock in the final seconds.

Johnson was vilified in the Los Angeles and Boston media for the glaring error, but he never said anything about his coach instructing him to call the time-out. He absorbed the worst public flogging of his young career in silence.

"I just felt, being one of the leaders of the team, I had to take the criticism," Magic said. "You don't want a situation where you are contradicting your teammates or your coach. We had to stick together."

The Lakers flew home to Los Angeles with their humbled point guard in unfamiliar territory. For the first time in his career, Magic found himself — and others — dwelling on his mistakes. The night before Game 3, the man who had fashioned a career out of positive self-talk had to keep pushing images of his mistakes out of his mind. It didn't help that Bird, his nemesis, was emerging as the catalyst of the Celtics.

Riley, recognizing that his floor leader was shaken, instructed him to push the ball on every miss. "Let's take them out of their game," he said to Johnson.

The Lakers began with an 18–4 run and demolished Boston 137–104 in Game 3. Their 51 fast-break chances pinned the Celtics with their largest playoff defeat in history. Magic was dazzling, dishing out 21 assists and completely controlling the tempo. Bird had 30 points and 12 free throws in the game, but sensing the series was slipping away, verbally assaulted his team with the aim of spurring them on.

"Until we get our heads where they belong, we're in trouble," Bird declared after Game 3. "We're a team that plays with heart and soul, and today the heart wasn't there. I can't believe a team like this would let LA come out and push us around like they did. We played like sissies."

His anger was neither contrived nor fleeting. Bird could see yet another chance at a ring faltering and he wasn't going to stand idly by and allow it to happen.

"I wanted to fight every teammate I had after Game 3," Bird said. "I did everything I could in the papers to get them fired up. I knew if something didn't change, we were going to lose. So I called them sissies, told them they played like girls. I didn't know if there would be some backlash, but I didn't care.

"I was not going to watch Magic celebrating in front of me again."

When reporters relayed Bird's rant to his coach, Jones suppressed a smile. Although he did not publicly condone or condemn Bird's remarks, he was privately thrilled that his best player had challenged the team.

"It was needed," Jones said, "and it was done by the only guy who could get away with it."

Although the insults may have been shocking to the public, Bird's outburst was nothing his teammates hadn't heard before. From the moment he slipped on his Celtics jersey, Bird had demanded excellence — of himself and of those around him.

"Larry was always saying stuff like that to us," Ainge shrugged. "We knew we played like garbage. Larry's comments usually reflected how we felt as a team."

When Bird returned to his Los Angeles hotel room, the message light on his phone was blinking. He wasn't in the mood to talk to anyone and didn't bother to check his messages. Later that night, his phone rang. Steve Riley, Bird's friend and the vice president of sales for the Celtics, was on the line.

"You guys are done. It's over," Riley said.

"Bullshit!" Bird retorted. "We're a long way from that."

The morning after Game 3, Magic was picking up some dry cleaning in his Culver City neighborhood when a fan asked him if he thought James Worthy would be the MVP of the series once the Lakers "wrapped things up." The Lakers' floor general winced. He had read Bird's "sissies" comments and understood the psychology behind it. The series, he knew, was far from over.

While Johnson was running errands, K. C. Jones was ushering Bird and his teammates into the visitors' locker room at the Forum. He shut the door, turned down the lights, and plugged in the projector.

"Watch," Jones said, then fell silent. Assistant coach Chris Ford started rolling the game film, with repeated clips of the Celtics getting beaten down the floor by the Lakers. The players said little. The images of Scott stroking pull-up jumpers on the wing untouched, Worthy streaking to the basket unscathed, and Magic, alone in the open floor, hitting his teammates with no-look passes, said it all.

"That was K.C.'s style," Ford said. "Watch the film. See the embarrassment. Do something about it."

Jones turned the lights back up, faced his team, and said calmly, "No more lay-ups."

As the players migrated to the Forum court to begin practice, McHale turned to Ainge, his closest friend on the team, and said, "We've got to foul someone hard."

Ainge rolled his eyes. He had played the role of the irksome antagonist since the day he joined the Celtics. As the last line of defense on transition defense, he was the one who usually grabbed Magic or some other opposing superstar on the way to the basket and endured the wrath of the opposition for it.

"Kevin, when have you ever hit anybody?" Ainge said.

McHale chuckled, but he was not amused.

"We were a bunch of pretty surly guys at that point," Ainge said.

Before Game 4, Jones switched D.J.'s assignment. He would be responsible for shadowing Magic the rest of the series. Only then did D.J. reveal to his coach how disappointed he had been not to assume that role in the first place. "I wish D.J. had said something to me sooner," Jones said. "If he had, I would have let him take Magic."

Although D.J. did have success tempering Magic's success, the Lakers still held a 76–70 advantage in the third quarter when Rambis, LA's version of a blue-collar grinder, streaked to the basket in transition. McHale, hustling to get back, remembered the edict from his coach: no easy lay-ups. As Rambis continued to the basket, Carr goaded McHale, "Hit him!!"

Rambis approached the basket at a sharp angle. McHale had already made up his mind to grab the Lakers forward and throw him down, which was a common (and accepted) tactic in the mid-eighties on a breakaway play. But Rambis was farther from the basket than McHale had estimated, and when the Celtics forward delivered the hit, he wasn't able to cushion Rambis's fall the way he'd planned.

Although Rambis knew a Boston player was coming for him, he couldn't initially identify the culprit. It appeared to him the player was coming for him at considerable speed, so he concentrated on holding on to the ball and bracing himself for contact. The last thing he saw before he absorbed the hit was his own foot, which seemed to be almost as high as the rim.

"Man, this is going to hurt," Rambis thought as McHale clotheslined him, sending him sprawling.

"Oh, there's going to be a fight now," McHale said to himself once he realized how badly he had flattened Rambis.

The Los Angeles forward was fortunate that instead of landing on his head, as he feared, his rear end absorbed most of the blow. When his body banged onto the floor, his first thought was, "Nothing hurts." His second was, "Where's McHale?" He popped up and charged toward the Celtics forward, but came at McHale from behind Worthy, who felt the presence of a moving body coming at him and wheeled around to defend himself. He shoved Rambis into referee Jess Kersey and a group of court-side reporters, unaware that it was his own teammate he was manhandling. Cooper, weary of Carr's verbal attacks from the bench, lunged at him, and both benches emptied. Although no actual punches landed, the psychological blow delivered by the Celtics was apparent.

McHale watched the proceedings with part awe and part elation. The flagrant foul was so contrary to anything he had ever done in his career that even his own coach would admit later he was flabbergasted by it.

"People say it was planned," McHale said. "It wasn't. If I thought about it ahead of time, I would have done it to Magic or Kareem or Worthy. They were a helluva lot more important than Rambis."

The brawl ignited chaos on the floor and turmoil in the stands. The Lakers, on the verge of putting the series away, lost their composure. They blew a five-point lead with under a minute to play behind a pair of free throws from Bird and a three-point play from Parish.

Predictably, the game came down to the final minute of overtime after D.J. missed a double-clutch shot in the key and Magic rebounded the ball. Johnson galloped down the floor on what would have been a 3-on-1 fast break and an easy Lakers basket, but the officials had already whistled D.J. for reaching in after his miss.

Magic went to the line with 35 seconds on the clock. Normally, his concentration when shooting free throws was flawless, but now he was second-guessing each move he made on the court.

His first free throw hit the back rim. His second did the same. On the Lakers bench, Abdul-Jabbar, who had fouled out, looked away. Bird grabbed the rebound on the second miss, and the Celtics called time-out.

"That's when I knew we had 'em," Bird said.

Magic, his trademark smile long gone, walked to his bench both bewildered and embarrassed. Having overshot the free throws because he was too hyped up, he left his team precariously close to blowing the game.

Boston emerged from their huddle with one plan in mind: locate Bird for the shot. Maxwell and Parish each set a pick on Cooper, who slipped trying to fight through the double screen, forcing Magic to switch over and cover his rival.

Once Bird realized he had Johnson guarding him, he waved madly for the ball. It was what he had been waiting for: the Celtics trailing 2–1 in the series, on Magic's court, and the two of them in the trenches to decide the game. It was Bird's chance for redemption from 1979, when Johnson had shattered his dreams in the NCAA championship. Maybe now he could begin to return the favor.

"At that moment," Bird said, "I knew I had to make that shot."

He did, lofting a soft fallaway jumper over Magic's head that dropped through the strings without a ripple, giving Boston the 125–123 lead with 16 seconds left.

Though the game was far from over, the momentum had clearly shifted. When Worthy stepped to the free throw line with a chance to tie the game, Carr, in a low voice, delivered a message.

"You're gonna miss," Carr said.

Worthy's first free throw clanged short, and Maxwell strolled across the key and flashed him the choke sign. Riley, watching from the Lakers bench, was apoplectic, yet his players did not seem to share in his outrage. The Celtics won, and the Lakers lost more than just a game. They lost control of the series.

In postgame interviews, Riley derided Boston as "a bunch of thugs." Maxwell and Carr mocked the Lakers for being unable to finish the job. McHale's takedown of Rambis was identified as the turning point of the game — and, in retrospect, the Finals.

"Before McHale hit Rambis, the Lakers were just running across the street whenever they wanted," Maxwell chortled. "Now they stop at the corner, push the button, wait for the light, and look both ways."

As the Celtics boarded their team bus and headed to the airport to fly home to Boston, an elated Bird plopped down next to D.J. and said, "Can you believe we're still in this? They're trying to *give* us the championship."

D.J. nodded in agreement. He scored 22 points in Game 4 and would go on to average 21.5 points a game over the final four games of the series. It was no accident that production coincided with his new defensive assignment. Magic inspired him like no other opponent.

"D.J. was the smartest guy who ever guarded me," Magic said. "He knew how to make adjustments. If I was rolling with a certain move, D.J. would say, 'You got away with that in the last quarter. Not this one.' It might take Gerald Henderson a whole game to figure out what I was doing. Sometimes he wouldn't even realize it until the film session the next day."

The venue for Game 5 was the antiquated Boston Garden, the site of so many past colossal Laker disappointments. Boston was in the midst of a heat wave, and there was no air conditioning in the building, so temperatures hovered at close to 100 degrees on the court by game time. A Lakers official brought an oscillating fan into the suffocating visitors' locker room, but it provided little relief.

"It was miserable in there," Magic said. "I had already sweated through my uniform before we had even had our pregame talk."

Although the Celtics locker room was larger, it was equally oppressive. Yet Bird was upbeat in the hours leading up to Game 5. He had slept fitfully the previous night, rehashing the action through the first four games of the Finals, and woke up exhausted. "I was concerned how we were going to stop Magic from controlling the tempo," he said.

By the time he drove down Causeway Street to the Garden, the exhaustion had been replaced by adrenaline. He was unconcerned with the heat and humidity; it was no more stifling than the summer heat of French Lick. When he arrived at the Garden, he was relieved to discover that his teammates were not about to be deterred by the oppressive temperatures either.

"We were the 'dirty' team," Maxwell said. "We weren't used to playing in luxury like the Lakers. We were a no-frills operation. When that game got hotter and hotter and hotter, we were like, 'All right, bring it on.'"

With a sizable portion of America watching on television, Bird delivered one of the finest performances of his young career, scoring 34 points on 15-of-20 shooting and grabbing 17 rebounds. He hit long perimeter shots, drives to the basket with his opposite hand, post-up jump shots, and put-backs in traffic.

"I was hitting everything," Bird said. "I had that rhythm you dream of. It was a tremendous feeling. And our crowd was fantastic. I felt after Game 5 we had it."

As Jones watched Bird take over the game, he expected at least a hint of exuberance from his forward over his remarkable performance. Yet Bird's demeanor was unchanged.

"When you are having a game like that, you figure the guy is going to be jumping up and down," K.C. said. "Not Larry. He did it without flair.

"In that regard, he was the exact opposite of Magic."

The lasting image of that 119–108 victory was Abdul-Jabbar slumped on the Lakers bench, sucking in oxygen through a small mask attached to a tank. The big man shot 7 of 25 from the floor and had wilted in New England's sweltering summer heat. Yet the Celtics knew better than to discount the fiercely competitive Hall of Famer, who still had the most lethal weapon in the series: the unstoppable skyhook.

Magic kept clear of his center in the aftermath of the loss. By the time the Lakers returned home, which required another flight across the country for both clubs, Abdul-Jabbar was suffering from another migraine. He vomited in the locker room before Game 6, then went out and scored 30 points and grabbed 10 rebounds. Worthy, in an attempt to quell some of the growing chatter that the Lakers were soft, shoved Maxwell into the backstop. The Celtics were unimpressed with LA's attempt at Eastern Conference physicality. They were convinced they had rattled Magic's confidence, and Carr spent the majority of Game 6 baiting him with the goal of breaking Johnson's concentration.

"C'mon, Cheese-o," Carr heckled. "Give us one of your cheesy smiles."

"Hey, Magic," Carr said the next time Johnson ran past Boston's bench. "Are you going to call time-out?"

The normally unflappable Johnson grew so agitated by Carr's antics that he approached the Celtics bench in the waning minutes of the third quarter. "Okay, Cheese-o, come get me. I'm ready," Carr coaxed him.

Referee Darrell Garretson walked over and pointed directly at Carr. "If you don't sit down and be quiet, I'm throwing you out of this game," Garretson warned.

"What do I care?" Carr retorted. "I'm not playing anyway."

The Celtics were so comfortable with their 65–59 halftime lead that they began encasing their lockers in plastic in anticipation of the champagne-soaked celebration they were sure would occur following the game. As late as the fourth quarter, Maxwell was still convinced Boston was about to wrap up the title. "We've got this," he said to Carr on the bench.

Riley needed a spark, and he turned to the kid, Byron Scott, who had spent an entire season auditioning for his Laker teammates. He hit four clutch jumpers to kick-start one final Los Angeles rally.

"Who the hell is Byron Scott?" asked Maxwell incredulously as he watched Scott steal a win for the Lakers and keep their championship hopes alive.

Bird checked out with 28 points on 8-of-11 shooting and left the Forum frustrated with his lack of touches in the final minutes. He wanted the ball — and he desperately wanted to end the series in Los Angeles. But Magic, who scored 21 points, dished out 10 assists, and grabbed 6 rebounds, had other ideas. He didn't want Bird gloating in his building.

"Not in our house!" Johnson urged his teammates.

As the Celtics left the Forum floor, they were pelted with debris from the hostile LA crowd. Carr was struck in the eye by a cup loaded with a concoction of mustard, beer, and chewed-up hot dogs.

In the wee hours the following morning, after the Celtics had taken a red-eye to LaGuardia and were waiting for a shuttle flight back to Boston, Auerbach sidled over to Bird to try to gauge his mood.

"What do you think?" Auerbach asked.

"No question we'll win this one," Bird answered. "We should have won it on their floor. I'm ticked we let it get away. We won't let this one go."

Lakers owner Jerry Buss engaged in a similar conversation with his own young superstar as they traveled back to Boston. Even though LA had won convincingly in Game 6, Buss sensed that Magic seemed distracted, a little down. It was a side of Johnson that Buss had never seen before on the court, and it worried him.

"Usually Earvin shook off mistakes pretty well," Buss said. "But this was different."

Buss was right. It *was* different. Magic had always been a winner — in high school, in college, in his first season as a professional. He was frustrated by his uneven results, which were further exacerbated in his mind by the clutch plays Bird had made. It was bad enough that the Lakers had faltered in a series they should have already won, but to blow it to the Celtics and Larry Bird in their first-ever head-to-head Finals was an unbearable notion.

The Celtics had never lost a championship series clincher on their home floor. K. C. Jones reminded his team of that before Game 7 — and so did Riley.

Carr emerged from the locker room for pregame warm-ups wearing goggles. While Boston's public relations staff claimed it was protection for his injured eye, most of the 14,890 Celtic loyalists in attendance knew the real reason: he was mocking Kareem, who was donning similar eye gear.

In the Lakers huddle just before tip-off, Magic surveyed the faces of his Lakers teammates. Kareem, as always, was a blank page, impossible to read. Yet when Johnson looked into the eyes of the rest of the starters, he saw the one thing he dreaded most: doubt.

"We had lost our edge," Magic said. "That takedown of Rambis had totally changed the complexion of the series."

Ninety-four feet away in Boston's huddle, Bird took a mental inventory of his team. What he saw was a group of veterans who were loose and confident. Moments earlier, as K. C. reviewed their game plan, the ever-cocky Maxwell announced, "Jump on my back, boys."

Maxwell backed up his bravado. He was electric on both ends of the floor, scoring 24 points with 8 rebounds and 8 assists. He also shot 14 of 17 from the line. Boston reverted to doing what it did best — punishing teams in the paint — and finished with a staggering 52–33 advantage on the boards.

Bird submitted 20 points on another mediocre night of shooting (6 of 18), but he was a perfect 8 for 8 from the line and hauled in 12 rebounds.

LA mounted a last-gasp run and had a chance to cut the deficit to one in the final minute, but D.J., who had stalked Magic from end line to end line throughout the night, stole the ball from his friend, then clinched the championship with a pair of free throws.

As Bird and his teammates mobbed one another at center court, Magic jogged to the same tiny visitors' locker room that Jerry West had occupied two decades earlier. Just as his general manager had done after a crushing defeat to Boston, Johnson sat in full uniform for several minutes, trying to fathom how it all had gone wrong.

"The Lakers, I felt, showed their true colors," Bird said. "I always thought they were soft, and they were that season."

While the Celtics celebrated madly down the hall, Magic lingered in the shower. He was normally the most accommodating star when it came to dealing with the media, but on this day he could barely face his teammates, never mind the national press. He remained sitting on the floor of the shower next to Cooper for the better part of a half-hour with the water spilling over him.

"All the water in the world wasn't going to wash away that pain," Riley said.

The coach finally sent Aguirre and Thomas in to retrieve him.

"I don't think I ever recovered from Game 2," Magic conceded. "I never felt in control after that. It was the first time I failed in a big situation. I'm used to coming through, and I didn't, and I handled it the wrong way.

"Instead of just saying, 'That was one game, I'm moving on,' I kept thinking about it. I couldn't let it go, and it carried through the whole series."

As the Lakers filed quietly onto their team bus, the Celtics fans partied wildly in the street. Within minutes, they identified the inhabitants of the luxury bus near the loading dock of the Garden.

A gang of more than 100 people surrounded the bus and began rocking it back and forth. The driver radioed for help; the Lakers slunk low in their seats as fans began throwing debris at the windows.

"It was frightening," Magic said. "Our nerves were shot to begin with because of this devastating loss, and now everyone is freaking out because we were surrounded and we couldn't go anywhere.

"We had no choice. We had to sit there and take it."

After several minutes, the police had dispersed the crowd. The bus finally crawled back to the Sheraton Hotel, a handful of "green people" in pursuit. Magic opened the door to his hotel room and dropped his boom box on the dresser. It was turned off, silent since that morning. Aguirre and Thomas trailed behind him, and while Magic appreciated their friendship, he desperately wanted to be alone.

"When they finally left, I cried like a baby," Magic said.

Ten miles away in Winchester, a Boston suburb, the Celtics had moved their celebration from Chelsea's to the home of team marketing director Mike Cole. Bird stayed until the sun came up, basking in the thrill of eliminating the "Fakers."

"It was one of those nights that you wished would never end," Bird said.

The forward, still feeling the effects of the victory celebration, did a live interview with a morning radio program. The team was departing shortly to visit President Reagan at the White House, and Bird announced he wasn't going.

"If the president wants to see me, he knows where to find me," Bird chuckled.

On the morning of June 13, Magic Johnson stood in the lobby with his bags packed. It was 6 A.M., but he was wide awake. In fact, like Bird, he never really went to sleep.

"It was the worst night of my life," Magic said. "I told myself, 'Don't ever forget how you feel right now.'"

The morning after Boston's celebration, Bird finally went home for a little shuteye. Around midafternoon, Buckner, who was experiencing his first-ever NBA title, drove to Bird's Brookline home with the hope of celebrating all over again. Dinah informed Buckner that Larry wasn't there.

"He was out running," Buckner said. "When he got back, I said to him, 'Man, what are you doing?'"

Bird looked at him quizzically before he answered.

"I'm getting ready for next year," he said.

6

★ ★ ★

SEPTEMBER 26, 1984

Palm Springs, California

NO LAY-UPS!" Lakers coach Pat Riley declared.

Magic Johnson wasn't completely sure what he meant, but Riley was already agitated, and it was only the first day of training camp. That was understandable. The Lakers had been mired in a perpetual state of gloom since the Celtics swiped the 1984 championship away from them the previous June. Overnight their reputation as a sleek, hip, dynamic team on the rise had deteriorated into a soft collection of underachieving chokers.

Magic, the embodiment of Showtime, absorbed most of the blame for the implosion of his Los Angeles team. After his uneven performance in the 1984 Finals, he returned to his Culver City apartment and squirreled himself away for three days. When he ventured outside, usually for milk or movie rentals, the vibes were as bad as he feared.

"Fakers!" a disappointed fan sneered from his convertible as he drove past the Lakers star.

The message was delivered more gently when he went home to

Michigan to commiserate with his family. Yet even tucked away inside his Lansing cocoon, his brethren wanted answers.

"Hey, the Celtics beat you," his puzzled friends queried him. "What happened to you?"

Johnson's angst was further compounded by the accolades showered upon Larry Bird. The Celtics star emerged from the Finals as clutch and fearless, adjectives previously associated with Magic. The young Lakers star was not accustomed to failure and even less equipped to handle the personal attacks that dogged him. Magic's self-esteem was built around positive self-talk, and for the first time in his career he couldn't conjure up a single thought to make himself feel better, so he spent the summer wallowing in his own misery.

"Looking back, it was the best thing that happened to Earvin," Riley said. "He stewed. He wanted to get back and save face. We all felt the same way. We wanted the opportunity to purge the ghosts."

Riley waited a month, then took the unusual step of writing a letter to each of the players. His note to Magic was a tome of forgiveness. He urged his point guard to grow and learn from his mistakes, just as the coach planned to do. "I respect you and I love you," Riley wrote. "We are warriors. We will not be defeated by this. Great warriors come back stronger than ever. I know you will too."

In midsummer a second letter arrived ordering Magic to find closure. "It's time," Riley wrote, "for us to stop being victims." His coach also made it clear that he expected Johnson to arrive at camp in the best shape of his life and suggested a playing weight of between 216 and 219 pounds. Magic showed up at 212 pounds to prove that he too was serious about redemption.

The third letter, received a week before training camp, was a call to action. "Get ready to work," Riley advised him. "I will push you like never before. You better have worked on your outside shot. And you better have been working on your conditioning, because I'm going to run your rear end off."

Magic was ready for it. He spent the summer training with Aguirre and Thomas, incorporating conditioning techniques with basketball drills that left him so exhausted at night that he literally fell into bed.

LA was in the midst of a routine training camp session until forward James Worthy glided through the lane uncontested for a jam. Riley stopped play, his jaw clenched.

"No lay-ups!" the coach barked. "From now on, if you don't take the man out who is going to the basket, if you don't put him on his *ass*, then you are going to be fined."

His edict was the residual of how badly the Celtics manhandled the Lakers in the Finals. Magic and his boys had failed to respond to Boston's physicality the previous June, and Riley was sounding the alarm that it was time for LA to finally push back. He instituted a new box-out drill that required the defender to hold off the rebounder for 24 seconds — or the equivalent of three NBA lifetimes. The drill became so physical and contested that Lakers teammates turned on one another, trading expletives — and occasionally punches.

Michael Cooper guarded Magic in the scrimmages and purposely hacked Johnson when he tried to penetrate. Johnson shoved his friend away; Cooper merely hit him harder. Riley was relentless, driving his team to the point of exhaustion. He created an atmosphere of edginess and uneasiness and celebrated when his cranky team stomped off the floor after yet another rugged practice.

"It was important," Byron Scott explained, "for us to stay angry."

Riley's call to arms was aided by the return of Mitch Kupchak, who had played in only 34 games the previous season because of a knee injury. Kupchak had undergone multiple surgeries to prolong his career and was undeterred by contact underneath. During the 1984 training camp he took an elbow to his face, and instead of attending to the cut, which was bleeding profusely, he slapped a Band-Aid across his brow and played for another hour and a half before getting stitched up by the team doctor.

While "no lay-ups" became the battle cry in Palm Springs, the champion Celtics gathered at Hellenic College in Brookline, Massachusetts, with a mantra of "no letdown."

The players took inventory in training camp and noted one significant absence. Cedric Maxwell, whose inspired Game 7 performance in 1984 had been so critical in propelling Boston to the championship, was a holdout as he haggled with Auerbach over a new deal.

Gerald Henderson, who had engaged in his own contract squabble the previous season, was traded on October 16 to Seattle for a future first-round draft pick. M. L. Carr had every intention of retiring, but Auerbach coerced him into one more tour of duty. Carr complied but second-guessed his decision almost immediately.

"In retrospect," Carr said, "I probably shouldn't have done it. I couldn't give my all anymore, and for guys like Larry, who still could, it was probably unfair I was still out there. I think it altered our chemistry."

Bird sensed an aura of contentment among his teammates that troubled him. Boston's margin for error against the Lakers was too small; they needed to remain driven if they wanted to repeat as champions. While Boston's players still put in long hours, "winning no longer felt like life and death — except for Larry," Carr observed.

Yet Boston remained the favorite in the Eastern Conference again, and with good reason. Kevin McHale was coming into his own, proving to be virtually unguardable in the post with his array of windmill fakes and up-and-under post moves. He became the model for all high school coaches who taught their young players to keep the ball high over their heads when they rebounded. Parish had established himself as a blue-chip center who ran the floor with the grace of a small forward. Bird was 28 years old and at the peak of his game.

Boston won 15 of its first 16. Bird perused the standings and noted that the Lakers lost 5 of their first 8. He knew, however, that it was far too early to draw conclusions about their rivals out west.

Riley had become obsessed with beating the Celtics and holed up in his office behind his Brentwood home to break down film of Boston's favorite son, searching for cracks in Bird's seemingly impenetrable armor. Riley's defensive assignments were designed with the moves of Bird, Parish, and McHale in mind. His offensive sets were created to exploit the weaknesses of the Celtics. Although the Lakers publicly feigned indifference about the fortunes of their East Coast enemy, privately it was another matter.

On the eve of the Lakers' season opener, Riley reviewed the team objectives with his point guard.

"Let's be clear about this," Riley informed Magic Johnson. "Our goal is not to just get back to the Finals. It is to beat the Celtics."

The 1984–85 season was the pilot for Pat Riley's "Career Best Effort" project. The Lakers coach recorded data from basic categories on the stat sheet, applied a plus or a minus to each column, and then divided the total by minutes played. He calculated a rating for each player and asked them to improve their output by at least 1 percent over the course of the season. If they succeeded, it became a CBE, or Career Best Effort. For Kareem and Magic, it was a significant challenge because they were already operating at such a high level.

"But if the other 12 players did it, we felt we had a chance to win it all," Riley said.

Riley's system was simplistic, but it was how the coach manipulated the data that made it so effective. He routinely recorded the performances of every NBA player and highlighted the success rates of Bird and Michael Jordan in particular. Solid, reliable players generally rated a score in the 600s, while elite players scored at least 800. Magic, who submitted 138 triple-doubles in his career, often scored over 1,000. Riley trumpeted the top performers in the league in bold lettering on the blackboard each week and measured them against the corresponding players on his own roster.

Some players ignored Riley's transparent motivational ploy, but not Magic. He became preoccupied with generating the highest score — not just on the Lakers but in the entire NBA.

Johnson was usually the lone player in the locker room while Riley and assistant coach Bill Bertka wrote the pregame directives on the blackboard. Riley often used that quiet time to tweak his star with his statistical ammunition.

"Earvin," Riley would say, "you've got great numbers for a point guard, but look at what your boy Bird did this week. He croaked you."

Johnson would remain silent.

"You had a bad week, Buck," Riley would continue. "Look at what numbers Michael put up."

Still, Magic would say nothing. There wasn't anything subtle about what Riley was doing, yet Johnson couldn't help but fall into the trap. He resented having his numbers up on the blackboard trailing the league's top stars for his teammates' viewing pleasure. He plotted to usurp both Bird and Jordan the next time his coach's "ratings" were revealed, just as his coach had hoped.

Riley was correct about Bird — the Boston forward was putting up big numbers and would go on to win a second consecutive Most Valuable Player Award in 1985. Yet Bird wasn't interested in repeating as the league's best player. He was gunning for back-to-back championships, and he grimaced when Maxwell finally showed up to camp with a new contract and gleefully announced, "Career's over, boys. Slam the books. I got my money."

Maxwell was clearly not a candidate for a Career Best Effort. His holdout had left him substandard, both in timing and conditioning. When the Celtics played the struggling Cleveland Cavaliers, Maxwell chortled before the game, "You're on your own, fellas. I don't do JV games. I'm saving myself for the varsity."

"It was supposed to be a joke," said Ainge, "but nobody thought it was that funny."

Bird was not amused. There were so many variables required to be successful in an NBA season, and he was in no mood to jeopardize Boston's chances because one of his teammates didn't feel like playing. One morning in practice, Maxwell put out his leg and said, "Someone jump on my knee and put me out for six weeks."

"Put that son of a bitch right here, I'll snap it in half for you," Bird growled.

"That kind of negativity really bothered me," Bird said. "We were trying to win back to back, something no one had done in over 15 years, and Max is talking about lying down on us."

Ironically, Maxwell suffered a cartilage tear in his knee in February. He tried to play through it, but the flap inside his knee kept grabbing, and the pain jolted him awake at night, leaving him popping pain relievers around the clock. After Boston's loss to the Lakers on February 17, Maxwell underwent arthroscopic surgery. McHale replaced him in the starting lineup and would remain there for the balance of his career.

When Maxwell returned, it was in a new role as a bench player. The veteran was unhappy with his reduced status, but his allies in the locker room were dwindling and his complaints went unheeded.

"Max was out of shape when he came back," Bird said. "He didn't do the rehab the way they asked. I was so pissed at him, because he was so good. He was a helluva player when he felt like it. But all that talk . . . it could bring you down.

"He got his money, and he quit. I like Max, but that's the bottom line. What he doesn't understand is, we helped him get that money, just like he helped me get mine. We were all accountable to each other.

"It was just a waste, that's all. We could have won in '83, but we didn't because of all the bullshit with Bill Fitch. Then we could have won again in '85, but we didn't because of more bullshit. There are two years, right there, where we were young and together and healthy, and we didn't capitalize on it. Looking back, it just kills you.

"I'm not going to lay all the blame on Max. It was more than just him, but we couldn't afford that kind of stuff, and he just didn't seem to get that."

Maxwell never denied he made joking references to his contract. He realized too late, he said, that his constant chatter proved to be a source of friction with Bird.

"We all used to tease and laugh about stuff," Maxwell said. "I think Larry fed into what Red Auerbach was hearing from [*Boston Globe* reporter] Will McDonough. He was talking to Red every day and saying I wasn't busting my hump.

"And when I did get hurt, Larry didn't believe it. He thought everyone should play through pain the way he did."

Bird's legacy was flush with examples of valiant performances while fighting through injuries, including persistent elbow troubles, double bone spurs in his heels (which eventually required surgery), and a chronic back condition that plagued him in the final six seasons of his career.

In 1982, while Bird was vying for a rebound against Milwaukee, he was elbowed by big man Harvey Catchings on the side of his cheek. The pain in his face and his jaw was excruciating. His skull had been depressed by the blow, but Bird refused to come out and finished the game. Afterward, Dr. Silva sent him to the hospital, where doctors drilled a hole in the side of his head and inserted a medical apparatus to pop his zygotic arch back out.

Bird hated sitting out so much that he often didn't tell his coaches when he suffered an injury. When Dell Curry tagged him with an elbow and fractured his eye orbiter in the mid-eighties, Bird ran around in the second half with double vision.

"I was seeing two baskets," he confessed. "I had to guess which one to shoot at."

After the game, when he noticed blood dripping from his nostril, he blew his nose, causing his eye to protrude grotesquely.

Year after year, he pushed his threshold of pain to new limits. In the deciding Game 5 of the opening round of the 1991 playoffs, Bird dove for a loose ball against the Indiana Pacers and knocked himself momentarily unconscious by violently slamming his head on the parquet. He had been questionable for the game to begin with because his back had seized up on him. (Days earlier, he had spent a night at New England Baptist Hospital in traction to stabilize his back.)

When he banged his head in the second quarter, he was carted off to the locker room and examined by team physician Dr. Arnold Scheller. It was clear to Scheller that Bird had suffered a concussion and was too woozy to take the floor to start the third quarter.

Bird's temple was throbbing, and his back was locked up again, but he could hear the crowd groaning on the television monitor as

Boston's lead slipped away. Midway through the third quarter, Bird started fidgeting.

"Doc, should I go back in?" Bird asked.

"Larry, I think you've done enough," answered Scheller.

"Ah, hell," said Bird, who popped off the table and ran back onto the court to a thunderous ovation. The Celtics, down three at the time, ripped off a 33–14 run and won the game.

Joe Bird would have been proud. Larry Bird vividly recalls his father Joe hobbling home one night with a horribly swollen and discolored ankle from an accident at work. The next morning the ankle was twice its normal size, but Bird's father loosened the laces on his boot, jammed his foot in, and limped back to his job. The moment left an indelible impression on his son, who concluded it was heresy to lie down on the job, no matter how much he was hurting.

That's why, during the 1985 season, Bird ignored the searing pain in his toe for nearly three weeks. When he finally allowed Dr. Silva to examine him, the team physician said, "You've got a serious infection between your two toes. This could lead to a dangerous situation.

"We'll give a shot of Novocain for that because I'm going to have to cut you."

"Nah," Bird said, "just give me one of those beers over there."

Silva administered a two-and-a-half-inch cut to allow the infection to drain. Then he wrapped it up. Bird played that night with considerable discomfort, and when he took his shoe off after the game, his sock was soaked in blood.

"I swear to God, they carved him up like he was John Wayne," Carr said. "Toughest guy I've ever seen.

"But what Larry doesn't understand [is that] other people don't have the same threshold for pain that he has."

Bird grappled throughout his career with separating his own lofty standards from the more pedestrian goals of his teammates. He had little tolerance for players who were unwilling or unable to demonstrate the mettle required to flourish in the NBA.

He was critical by nature, which contributed to his uncommon drive. Danny Ainge appreciated Bird's discerning basketball eye, but conceded, "If you were on the wrong end of it, it could be very tough."

Bird's smoldering intensity was a regular topic of conversation among his teammates. McHale admired his relentless pursuit of excellence, but Bird occasionally displayed an edge that McHale didn't totally understand — or condone. Thus, when Bird verbally harangued a teammate for not filling the lane or manning up properly, McHale cringed.

Conversely, Bird viewed McHale as an exceptional player who could have reached enormous heights but chose not to wring the most out of his considerable abilities. During one game against Sacramento, McHale was benefiting from an obvious mismatch and scoring at will. After the ball went to him on seven consecutive possessions, he told Bird, "Hey, spread it around. I've scored enough for one night."

While Bird was almost maniacal in his pursuit of the perfect game, McHale was content to contribute 15 points and 10 rebounds and call it a day. He refused to allow basketball to consume him; Bird refused to allow distractions to penetrate his basketball concentration.

Their contrasting approaches to the game made for an odd team dynamic. Bird respected McHale's game so much that he rarely criticized him for not possessing the killer instinct that, in Bird's mind, could have spurred McHale on to a league MVP trophy.

McHale was so taken with Bird's work ethic that he rarely challenged his teammate when he became moody or difficult after a tough loss. "Aw, that's just Birdie," McHale would say.

Their unusual relationship accounted for some comical on-the-court interactions with Ainge, who was friendly with both stars and became their floor conduit.

When Bird wanted McHale to do something, instead of approaching him and barking out instructions like he did with his other teammates, he'd motion Ainge over and say, "Tell Kevin to set a high screen for D.J., then roll to the basket." Moments later,

McHale would pull Ainge aside and whisper, "Tell Larry to pop out on the baseline and I'll flash through the key."

"It was kind of funny," Ainge said. "They were very careful about what they said to each other. Larry had no problem chewing me out, but he would never flat-out yell at Kevin. He just thought too much of him."

McHale's and Bird's contrasting ideals were accented in a span of nine days during the 1984–85 season. On March 3, McHale set about destroying the Detroit Pistons with his expanding ensemble of post moves. By the third quarter, when it became apparent this could be a historic day, the other Celtics — including Bird — abandoned their offense and fed their amiable forward a steady diet of passes on the block. When it was over, McHale had set a new Celtics single-game scoring record with 56 points. He was so exhausted by his milestone that he waved to Coach K. C. Jones to remove him in the final minutes of play, even as his teammates urged him to remain on the floor and add to his total.

It was a landmark performance made possible, in part, by Bird, who registered a triple-double that day directing most of his passes toward number 32. There were congratulations all around for McHale, who so often played second fiddle to his more celebrated teammate without complaint. Bird gushed about McHale's feat but couldn't resist chiding him. "You should have stayed out there," he said. "You should have tried for 60."

"We talked about it afterwards," Dennis Johnson said. "Larry didn't understand why Kevin didn't go for it. When Larry had his foot on someone's throat, he crushed them. Kevin was the kind of person who would say, 'Aw, he's already down. No need to hurt the guy.'"

Nine days later in New Orleans, Bird showed McHale how it was done. He went on his own tear against the Atlanta Hawks, hitting 22 of 36 shots, including improbable fadeaways, stop-and-pop jumpers, and twisting drives in the lane. His most spectacular basket was one that didn't count: an off-balance three-pointer in front of the Hawks bench that had the Atlanta players literally falling off their seats in disbelief. Just as they had done for McHale, the Celtics fed Bird the ball down the stretch, even intentionally fouling the Hawks to regain possession. Bird topped off at 60 points, nailing a jumper at the buzzer and breaking the team record set just a week and a half earlier by his front-court mate.

The most absurd component of Bird's feat was that he almost sat out the game against Atlanta. The day before the game Bird woke up and decided to run in a five-mile road race, something he and teammate Scott Wedman occasionally did together during the season. But Bird hadn't run on asphalt for a few months, and the morning after the race his legs were heavy and sore and his hamstrings were throbbing. Bird limped through the team shoot-around before he finally went to see his coach.

"K.C., I'm not sure I can go tonight," Bird said.

"Larry, you ran in another one of those races, didn't you?" Jones admonished him.

Bird went to the arena a half-hour earlier than normal to do some laps. As he started jogging, his lower legs loosened up, but his hamstrings were still tight and painful.

"I was hurting real bad when the game started, but for some reason I was making shots," Bird said. "There wasn't a whole lot of defense being played. My legs were killing me, but I figured, 'I gotta tough it out.'"

When he accepted handshakes in the locker room after his scoring barrage, he walked over to McHale's locker and said, "See, Kevin? I told you to go for 60."

McHale merely shrugged.

"Honest to God, Birdie, I really don't care," he replied.

"You will someday," Bird shot back.

Magic Johnson followed McHale and Bird's dueling scoring outbursts with amusement. He identified with Bird's competitive streak since he too turned everything into a contest, whether it was betting on which song would come on the radio next or counting who could bank in more free throws.

The Lakers usually ended their workouts playing 5-on-5 with Cooper and Magic guarding each other. One day, after Cooper hit the winning jumper, Riley said, "Okay, let's bring it in."

"No," Magic said. "One more."

His teammates groaned. They'd been practicing for more than two hours, but they knew Johnson wouldn't quit until he got the last word. When Magic drilled the game winner in the next game, they sprinted for the exits as Cooper hollered after them, "Wait! We're not done yet!"

During a long road trip, Scott and Magic played Tonk, a popular card game among NBA players, on the airplane. Scott took most of Johnson's money, and when the Lakers landed, Magic said, "Let's keep playing."

Scott fleeced his friend for a few more dollars on the bus ride to the hotel. When they checked in and hopped on the elevator, Magic said, "Meet me in my room. We've got to finish this."

"Finish this?" Scott said incredulously. "Buck, we've been playing for four hours!"

Defeat was not a palatable option for Magic, regardless of the nature of the competition — or the opponent. Longtime Lakers trainer Gary Vitti used to tease Johnson that if he played tiddlywinks with Vitti's two young daughters, Rachel and Amelia, whom Johnson adored, he would still need to win.

"He'd find a way to outwit them, outwork them, out-luck them, or out and out cheat them," said Vitti. "He's the worst loser I've ever seen."

Despite his impressive start to the 1984–85 season, Magic could not completely erase the disappointment of the 1984 Finals. The defeat lingered in his psyche, and as winter approached and the annual All-Star Game loomed, he brooded about seeing Bird again. He anticipated that the All-Star buzz would center on a possible rematch between the Lakers and Celtics — and by extension a rematch between Bird and himself — but the story line veered elsewhere.

Rookie Michael Jordan was making his All-Star debut and stole the spotlight when he irritated some of his peers by wearing Nike gear instead of the league-mandated apparel.

Jordan was a phenomenal talent with unparalleled athleticism. His jump shot as a North Carolina sophomore clinched the NCAA championship for the Tar Heels, and he went pro shortly after that. His court sense and his ability to control play above the rim was the talk of the league. The kid had talent, charisma, charm — and a staggering endorsement portfolio for an NBA rookie.

Everyone anticipated a big offensive night from number 23, yet Jordan took only 9 shots in 22 minutes of All-Star play, leading to whispers that he was "frozen out" by East point guard Isiah Thomas. Magic, because of his close association with Isiah, was also suspected of being involved in snubbing the league's newest sensation. After the game, media reports citing sources close to Thomas and Johnson claimed the two conspired to keep the ball away from Jordan because they were jealous of his endorsements and his rapidly expanding, worldwide appeal.

The story gathered steam when Jordan did not publicly refute the conspiracy theory.

Magic maintained he did not learn of the controversy until two days after the game when television personality Ahmad Rashad, a mutual friend of both Johnson and Jordan, called and asked him, "Earvin, what's going on with this?"

"Are you kidding me, Ahmad?" Johnson said. "Do you really believe I'm going to an All-Star Game thinking I don't want to let Michael Jordan have the ball? First of all, why should I care? What does that do for me? I don't have anything against him. I barely know him.

"That's just stupid. If I was going to come up with a conspiracy to freeze someone out, I would have done it a long time ago — to Larry Bird."

As a teenager growing up in North Carolina, Jordan was a Magic Johnson disciple. He even drove a 1975 Grand Prix with the license plate MAGIC MIKE on the front. Yet the young Bulls player was wounded by the events of All-Star weekend, and whether it was real or imagined, Jordan felt snubbed by both Thomas and his child-hood idol Magic.

Nearly 25 years after the fact, Jordan confirmed that the incident strained his relationship with Magic for years.

"It kind of split us," Jordan said. "I felt Magic didn't like me. He and Isiah were freezing me out. I had some endorsements and a good agent [David Falk]. I was taking advantage of some situations that Magic could have had too, with the right representation.

"I felt there was some envy between the two of us. But I took it with a grain of salt.

"I just didn't spend time with him. I respected his game and left it at that."

Although both paid each other the proper homage publicly, there was little interaction between Johnson and Jordan outside of the game. Their differences were exaggerated by the silence between them. Although Michael and Magic evolved into two of the game's biggest icons, their "relationship" lacked any genuine substance.

"We never got a chance to talk about it," Magic said. "It was Magic against Michael. That's why we never became friends. It's too bad we never spent any time together. People ask me all the time why I didn't do more projects with Michael. I don't even know what to tell them. It [the freeze-out] was a misunderstanding, and neither one of us ever reached out and tried to smooth things over. So the next thing you know, the years go by and there's this distance between us, and it all could have been avoided if either one of us just made the first move. But we didn't.

"That was a big reason why, even today, Michael and I don't know each other as well as we should."

Although Jordan captivated a new generation of NBA fans, his Chicago team was not yet ready for prime time in 1985. The Bulls were eliminated by the Milwaukee Bucks in the opening round of the playoffs, and Boston and Los Angeles appeared headed for another collision in the Finals.

Boston rolled over Cleveland, Detroit, and Philadelphia (whose window of opportunity finally closed as Julius Erving approached retirement), while Los Angeles blew past Phoenix, Portland, and Denver.

Kareem remained LA's primary offensive weapon, but Magic, driven by echoes of "Tragic" (which the Boston fans delighted in chanting during his lone visit to the Garden during the regular season) and "Fakers," tried to post his own Career Best Effort every night. When he was tired or worn down by the travel, all Magic had to do was close his eyes and visualize the celebration in the streets after the Celtics clinched the title.

The Lakers liked their odds. They were quicker and deeper than Boston, which often shortened its rotation to seven players. Kupchak and veteran Bob McAdoo supplied the muscle that had been missing the previous year, and Riley painstakingly prepared each of them for their chance at redemption.

When it became clear the Lakers would be playing the Celtics in the Finals, Riley called ahead to the Boston hotel that would be hosting them and made it clear that he did not expect to see Celtics banners hanging in the lobby or employees wearing shamrock shirts checking them in. He made sure his players checked in under assumed names and told them to take the phone off the hook when they went to bed to prevent any crank calls in the middle of the night.

All year long Riley harped on treating each possession like it was a rare jewel, even during 25-point blowouts. Magic adopted that philosophy, and the byproduct was a more patient and diligent point guard. As Johnson warmed up before Game 1 in Boston Garden, the site of his lowest moment as a pro, he turned to Cooper and quietly announced, "It's Showtime."

The debacle that followed was equally stunning and inexplicable. Boston mugged LA 148–114 on a night when everything went right for the Celtics, including Scott Wedman's perfect 11-of-11 shooting from the floor. Kareem appeared weary and sluggish and was repeatedly beaten down the court by Parish. Within hours, the obituaries for the Lakers captain and his team were distributed. The beating was forever dubbed the Memorial Day Massacre.

Riley was flabbergasted by his team's meltdown. For 11 months he had harped on the pride of the Lakers franchise and the indignities they had suffered at the hands of the Celtics. He cursed the arrogance of Auerbach, the irreverence of Maxwell, and the swagger of Bird on a daily basis, systematically constructing a hatred for the Boston franchise that he fervently believed would withstand any challenge.

He had pushed his Lakers team to the brink, from the no-lay-up rule to the Career Best Effort campaign to hours and hours of film on the Celtics and their tendencies.

And the best his center could do in response was 12 points and 3 rebounds? Magic had scored 19 points with 12 assists, but he had come away with only 1 rebound, thereby limiting the Lakers' transition chances.

"You call yourself a fucking Hall of Famer?" Riley challenged Kareem afterward. "That guy kicked your ass. Parish embarrassed the hell out of you. Look at this pathetic stat line. Three rebounds? Three rebounds for a Hall of Famer?"

"And you," he said, turning to Magic. "You're supposed to be one of the best players in this league. You got dominated today. Fucking dominated. One rebound? You think that's going to get it done against this team, against your boy Larry?

"Where's the fucking leadership? This is supposed to be your team!"

Riley then turned his wrath toward Worthy, who had missed 11 of his 19 shots, but by then Magic had stopped listening. He was still smarting from his coach's assault on his game.

"He got me with the leadership thing," Johnson said. "That hurt. But I didn't say anything. When Pat got into his little zone, if you knew what was good for you, then you just sat there and took it."

As his coach railed on about their lack of concentration and professionalism and heart, Magic started recalling their final practice before Game 1. The Lakers had been loose, confident. They played H-O-R-S-E, took wild shots from half-court, had a few laughs. In retrospect, they had lacked the proper focus and purpose.

"We paid the price for that," Magic said.

The next morning, humiliated by his poor showing and portrayed in the Boston papers as an old man whose time had passed, the 38-year-old Abdul-Jabbar vacated his customary seat in the back row of Riley's film sessions and sat in the front.

Riley treated his players to a three-hour horror film. The Lakers relived their Game 1 mistakes in slow motion with profane prose accompanying each error. As they watched Wedman sink shot after shot, their coach became enraged all over again. "Who the fuck is Scott Wedman?" Riley screamed. "This guy can only shoot when he's open. And we left him open all damn night!"

Kareem apologized for his play and promised a different outcome in Game 2. As the Lakers walked out to the practice floor, Riley announced, "Today there will be no fouls. I don't want to hear shit in this gym. I better not hear any complaining. You got me?"

Silence.

The practice was a free-for-all. The forwards knocked each other to the floor. Cooper manhandled Magic, holding him and bumping him and chopping his arms. "That's a foul," Magic moaned. "Get off me."

"Quit crying," Cooper snapped. "I'm doing exactly what D.J. is going to do to you tomorrow night."

When Riley finally ended the workout, the players dropped the balls, walked to the bus without speaking, then scattered to their hotel rooms. It was the first time Magic could remember not making plans for supper with Cooper and Byron Scott. The trio had become inseparable, dubbing themselves "the Three Musketeers," yet on this night the swashbucklers had gone solo.

Magic padded around his hotel room. One hour passed, then another. Finally, he placed two phone calls. "Coop, Byron," he said. "We can't do this. Let's grab something to eat."

They spent a solemn evening analyzing Riley's criticisms. The coach didn't care if they united against him as long as they were united, yet his biting words had troubled Magic. Riley was no longer a hesitant assistant thrust into the driver's seat. He was in charge, demanding accountability, and Magic knew he needed to deliver.

In a quiet moment before Game 2, Riley pulled Johnson aside.

"You need to control the tempo of this game," he said. "It's paramount that we establish early that we've come to play. That's up to you."

Magic nodded. The Lakers had made some mild adjustments defensively; he now had the assignment of guarding Danny Ainge to start the game, with the expectation he would drop down and double-team Boston's front line when needed.

On the other end, his job description was the same: find the big fella in the post and create fast-break opportunities.

The first few minutes of Game 2, Magic knew, were critical. So, on the opening possession, Magic dropped the ball into Kareem in the post. He set his team in motion after a Boston miss, driving through the paint, waiting for the inevitable crowd of defenders to gravitate toward him, then dishing off to a wide-open Kurt Rambis underneath for a lay-up. The next time, on a textbook 3-on-2 fast break, he found Worthy on the wing and set him up for a transition jam.

After his team crafted an early 13–6 lead, Magic was on the move again, ambling up the floor on another 3-on-2 fast break. His instinct was always to pass, but as he penetrated the key, he saw number 33 in a white jersey coming over to help. Johnson couldn't resist. Instead of dishing off, he went right at Larry Bird, knocking in the lay-up over his rival's outstretched arms.

"Now that's what I'm talkin' about!" exulted Magic when the Celtics called time-out.

Once safely ensconced in his huddle, Magic clapped his hands and encouraged his guys, "Let's go now! Let's go for the kill!"

The Lakers' primary weapon of choice was Abdul-Jabbar, who was reborn in Game 2, scoring 30 points, grabbing 17 rebounds, dishing off 8 assists, and blocking 3 shots so the Lakers could wrestle the home-court advantage away from the Celtics.

Bird, who had been battling a balky elbow, scored 30 points but shot 9 of 21 from the floor. As LA walked off with the victory, Larry told D.J., "We're screwed if we don't start shooting better."

When Bird's aim (8 of 21) did not improve in Game 3 and LA thrashed Boston 136–111 at the Forum, speculation centered on whether it was Michael Cooper's redoubtable defense or Bird's sore elbow that hampered the forward.

"Mostly Cooper," Bird said. "But truthfully, a little of both."

Bird's elbow had been nagging him since the end of March. He had it drained, even looked into having surgery at one point, but when the doctors explained it was a sensitive area and there was risk of permanent nerve damage if they operated, Bird decided to play through it. He spent the tail end of the regular season coming off the bench in a few games to economize his minutes, but the elbow often locked up without warning. He missed a playoff game against Cleveland that spring when he woke up and was unable to bend his arm. After some physical therapy, it would eventually loosen up, but that was a temporary fix that could fail him at any time.

"Most days I couldn't extend my elbow its full length," Bird explained. "Once the game started, I didn't think that much about it, but it was hard to get the proper rotation and height on my shot. No question, I was struggling."

Cooper added to his woes by bodying up to him whenever he received the ball and taking away his lanes to the basket. Bird was able to drive past most other defenders, but Cooper's quickness and his deceptive strength prevented Bird from enjoying his usual spacing. "I knew when he was on me to make every open shot count, because there weren't going to be many," Bird said.

Bird wasn't the only Celtic out of sync. Parish's play was up and down. The bench wasn't deep, and the Boston starters had logged too many minutes. When Boston called a team meeting, half the guys mistakenly went to the Forum and the other half met at the team hotel.

A Dennis Johnson jumper at the buzzer knotted the series 2–2 in Game 4, but Abdul-Jabbar answered again in Game 5 with 36 points and another Lakers victory. As the action shifted back to Boston with LA ahead 3–2, the Lakers were poised to win a title in the same city where their dreams had been annihilated a year before.

The aura of Auerbach's cigars, the booby-trapped parquet, and the plethora of championship banners was not quite so daunting the second time around. Riley ordered high-powered fans to cool off the locker room in case another heat wave settled into the visitors' area.

"The Celtics mystique definitely bothered us in 1984," said Worthy, "but by 1985 it was old news."

In Game 6, the Celtics shortened their rotation further. Riley instructed Magic, "Run them off the floor." Johnson pushed tempo and fed Kareem for 29 points, but also sprinkled in some key baskets of his own. He managed the game so thoroughly that it appeared as though he could score at any time but chose to only when absolutely necessary. Magic checked out with a triple-double — 14 points, 14 assists, and 10 rebounds — and the Lakers posted a Career Best Effort against the team that had tormented their franchise for decades. They had done something no other team in history had accomplished: clinched an NBA championship on the Garden floor.

While Abdul-Jabbar fittingly was awarded the Finals MVP trophy, Riley grabbed his point guard and whispered in his ear, "We couldn't have won this without you."

"Magic's purpose was written all over his face in Game 6," Riley said. "It was, 'Atone for 1984.' It was life or death for him."

Bird scuffed his way through another poor shooting night (12 for 29), which left him shooting 44.9 percent for the series. As he headed to his locker room, Bird noted that the normally frenzied Celtics fans were silent, numb with shock. He felt the same way.

For Riley, whose career had been marred by a series of crushing losses to the Celtics, the championship was a dream fulfilled. For Jerry West, who watched from his living room in California, shouting instructions at his television set, it was payback — finally.

And for Earvin Johnson, who reversed his fortunes from Tragic back to Magic, it was redemption of the sweetest kind. He celebrated the win over the Celtics in the name of West and Chamberlain and Baylor and every other Lakers loyalist who had wondered if this day would ever come.

He gently corralled Kareem court-side, a far less demonstrative hug than when he leaped into his arms five years earlier as a rookie, yet far more heartfelt. This time the embrace truly meant something.

In the cluttered visitors' locker room, the Lakers gathered in a circle and chanted "LA! LA!" in unison. Their owner, Jerry Buss, accepted the championship trophy from David Stern and declared, "This has removed the most odious sentence in the English language. It can never again be said the Lakers have not beaten the Celtics."

After Riley proclaimed that "all the skeletons are cleared out of our closet," a subdued Magic admitted, "It's been a long, long wait for this moment."

Johnson's sense of relief was overwhelming. Since his performance in the Finals the previous season, he had carried a burden that weighed him down in ways he didn't realize — until he and the Lakers finally turned the tables on the Celtics. This time, as he let the cold water from the antiquated shower in Boston Garden pour over him, he reveled in the moment.

"I'll never forget this moment for the rest of my life," he told Michael Cooper.

During the long, regretful summer that followed, Celtics coach K. C. Jones dissected the game film for clues to how his team could have played Magic differently. There were instances when they should have shaded him left, or doubled him off the glass, but, Jones conceded, "I honestly don't know if it would have made any difference. Magic's mindset was just like Larry's, which was, 'I'll do whatever it takes.' He'd rebound, he'd take a charge, he'd dive for a loose ball.

"How many superstars do that? That's what separates Magic and Larry from the rest, and always will."

Shortly after the Lakers' championship parade, Riley took his wife Chris on vacation to the Bahamas. They were sitting on a sand dune in Nassau, sipping on some island cocktails, when Riley looked down the beach and saw a crowd forming. There were some shouts and excited chatter, and his curiosity got the best of him.

"I wonder if someone is drowning," Riley said, squinting into the sun.

It was then that he recognized the unmistakable gait of a large man strolling down the beach with a trail of people following in his wake. It was Earvin Johnson.

Riley sprinted toward him and hid behind one of the palm trees. As Magic walked by, he whistled twice. Johnson stopped and wheeled around. He knew that whistle. Coach Riley never used a real one; he had his own, distinct ability to stop the Lakers in their tracks.

"Coach," Magic said, peering into the palms, "is that you?"

While Riley was ecstatic about the chance encounter with his superstar, Magic, who had come to the island to sleep and replenish, was mildly disappointed. He truly wanted time alone.

"I was thinking, 'Oh, no, of all people, I do not want to see Pat Riley right now,'" Magic confessed. "I had gone to the Bahamas to get away from basketball. I had been working and training and fighting with the Lakers for eight months. I was wiped out. I just wanted a break."

He sat with his coach in the sand for three hours, rehashing everything from holding the ball to the no-lay-up rule to the ultimate thrill of beating the Celtics on their own crooked, warped floor.

"You better believe Larry Bird came up in that conversation," Magic said. "We both knew we were going to see him again."

Bird wasn't lounging on the beach in the summer of 1985. He was shoveling gravel for drainage to protect the new basketball court he had just installed. Although he had the financial means (times ten) to hire someone to do the work, the Celtics star prided himself on doing his own chores.

He knew it had been a mistake, however, the minute he tried to get out of bed the following morning. He had done something to his back and was alarmed by his lack of mobility. He walked around, tried to shake the stiffness, but the pain was unbearable. He lay down and tried to rest, but the sharp jolts shooting down his leg were persistent. Something was wrong — seriously wrong. In subsequent years, Bird would learn that his back troubles were the result of a congenital condition. The canal in which the nerves led to his spinal cord was too narrow, which caused all that unbearable pain. It was truly remarkable, his surgeon told him after watching Bird play basketball, that he managed for as long as he did.

For the next three weeks, Bird did not play any basketball. Still, the back problems did not subside. Quinn Buckner called to see about working out with him in West Baden. He knew something was amiss when Larry declined.

"Quinn," he said, "I'm in trouble."

And so, quite suddenly, were the Boston Celtics.

7

★ ★ ★

SEPTEMBER 12, 1985

West Baden, Indiana

LARRY BIRD STEERED his Honda motorcycle into the parking lot of the Honey Dew convenience store in the center of West Baden, Indiana. It was a warm, sunny morning, so he left his Ford Bronco, the car presented to him for winning the 1984 NBA Finals' Most Valuable Player Award, back home in the garage.

The car was spotless, as pristine as the day he received it, and although he didn't articulate it when they handed him the keys, it amazed him that someone would reward him with a car for playing basketball. His mother held down two jobs and his father labored through 12-hour shifts in order to fill grocery carts each week for Bird and his five siblings, and still there was never enough money left for a family automobile.

Bird had just completed his morning workout, so he was wearing a T-shirt, shorts, and sneakers when he stiffly unfolded his 6-foot-9-inch frame off the cycle and began filling his own tank. His injured back had improved only slightly, and with training camp just weeks away, Larry was growing concerned. He'd refrained from pushing himself through his usual grueling off-season program in hopes that the rest would heal his injury. While the time off had helped, he was skeptical that he'd be able to play an entire NBA season unless he could find a way to alleviate the jarring pain.

As he shifted his weight while he pumped his own gas, three sleek black limousines glided past him on Sawmill Road.

"Well, they're here," he said, to no one in particular.

Inside the second limousine, Earvin Johnson sat perched by the window. He surveyed the landscape of the modest Indiana town adjacent to French Lick, the birthplace of his most ardent competitor. Magic was surprised to discover it stirred memories of his own midwestern roots.

"This reminds me of Lansing," he said to his agent, Charles Tucker, squinting through the tinted windows.

Johnson fidgeted in the back seat. He was uneasy. He had spent the balance of his young career aiming to establish the upper hand in this increasingly heated rivalry between himself and Bird, the Lakers and the Celtics, and yet now he was traveling to Bird's backyard to engage in a joint endorsement campaign for Converse sneakers.

He knew how his Lakers coach, Pat Riley, would feel about it. He would be enraged. Riley despised the Celtics and would undoubtedly chafe at the knowledge that his star player was knowingly and willingly embracing his nemesis.

As the limos snaked up Bird's gravel driveway, Johnson leaned back in his seat and closed his eyes.

"Maybe," he lamented, "I shouldn't be doing this."

Bird, trailing the caravan back to his house, was also having second thoughts. He regularly chastised Celtics teammates who fraternized with the opponent before big games, yet here he was, hosting the player who had proved to be his most worthy adversary.

Bird didn't like the commotion that three luxury vehicles kicking up dust on his town's main thoroughfare was bound to cause. As he watched the limos driving toward his house, he wondered to himself, "Why in hell did I say yes to this?"

* * *

The finished product took all of 28 carefully scripted seconds, but the tenor of the relationship between pro basketball's premier dueling superstars was altered permanently on that early fall afternoon when Magic and Larry came together to sell Lakers gold and purple and Celtics black Converse basketball sneakers.

Until that point, the interaction between the two had been limited to cursory small talk. That was by design. As Boston and Los Angeles emerged as the premier teams in the NBA, the inevitable animosity between the two franchises — and their main characters — began festering. Whenever queried on his partner in this East versus West dance, Bird was predictably restrained, making it clear he had no interest in developing a relationship with his rival.

"I admired the hell out of Magic," Bird said, "but I didn't care to know him."

Although the two players rarely engaged in banter on the court during their twice-a-year regular season meetings, it did not preclude them from issuing challenges away from the action. In Bird's and Magic's second season in the league, Johnson was sidelined with a knee injury when the Celtics made their annual pilgrimage to the Forum on February 11, 1981. Bird spotted Johnson sitting on the bench in street clothes and went over to shake his hand.

"Now you just sit there and relax. I'm going to put on a show for you," Bird said.

By the time Bird was done, his stat line encompassed a cornucopia of basketball delights: 36 points, 21 rebounds, 6 assists, 5 steals, 3 blocks. He also played all but one minute of the 105–91 Celtics win. All Magic could do was watch as Bird unveiled one spectacular play after the next, pointedly staring in Johnson's direction after each basket.

"Drove me crazy," Magic admitted. "He was sticking it right in my face."

No wonder, then, that there was hesitation from both men about letting down their competitive guard for the sake of an endorsement payday.

Converse hatched the idea of the "Choose Your Weapon" shoe campaign while chronicling the drama of the 1984 and 1985 Finals.

They approached Bird's and Johnson's representatives about a joint venture, and predictably, the initial response was negative.

"Forget about it," Magic said.

Bird was equally emphatic. Although his attorney, Bob Woolf, lobbied for him to do the commercial by pointing out the obvious financial benefits, Boston's forward was unmoved.

"Magic was the enemy," Bird explained. "And I had no interest in spending any time with the enemy."

Their individual contracts with Converse had required previous joint commitments at industry shows, company meetings, and occasional private corporate outings. Magic, Julius Erving, and Bird were commissioned to appear at a golf outing in Connecticut once and while Johnson didn't play, he toured the course in a cart with clients, regaling them with NBA anecdotes.

"Dr. J and I were chatting away, having fun," said Magic. "Larry was hitting the golf ball and ignoring us completely."

It was a time when athletic endorsements were still relatively rare, and savvy companies were just beginning to launch their new lines using sports personalities. During the 1984 Olympic Games in Los Angeles, for instance, Nike plastered the city with billboards of its shoes using five-time Pro Bowl safety Lester Hayes of the Oakland Raiders as the face of its product.

Three months into his job as Converse's advertising manager, Lou Nagy was sent to New York to oversee a commercial with Bird, Magic, and Dr. J at Manhattan College. It was a traditional shoot featuring the three stars discussing how the Converse Pro sneakers made them better players, and it was slated to run only in the top ten television markets in the country.

The trip was memorable to Nagy for one reason in particular. The night before the taping, Converse hosted a dinner at the Hyatt Regency in New York City for the players. Bird and a friend from French Lick showed up wearing jeans and windbreakers. The restaurant enforced a dress code that required a sport coat. Nagy assured Bird that he would find him a blazer, but as soon as he went inside to rustle one up, the Celtics star disappeared into the city streets.

"At least he showed up for the shoot the next day," said Nagy.

As Magic's and Bird's careers continued to blossom — and interconnect — Converse senior vice president Jack Green determined that the best way to capitalize on the rivalry was to accentuate their differences. The "Weapon" campaign would not be a commercial featuring two rivals walking arm in arm, he explained. Instead, Converse would highlight the fierce competition between the two.

"It wasn't going to be cutesy," Green said. "We wanted it to be unique, but a very basketball-oriented ad. That appealed to Larry in particular."

When presented with that story line, Johnson warmed to the idea. Bird, clearly the more reluctant of the two, finally agreed to tape the commercial, but only if Magic was willing to travel to Indiana to shoot it. That stipulation, he figured, would be a dealbreaker.

He was astonished to learn later that Johnson agreed to the terms.

"The more I thought about it, I just thought it would be something that could be great for both of us," Magic said. "Did I want to go all the way out to West Baden, Indiana? No. But it became pretty clear that was the only way it was going to get done."

The production crew descended on Bird's property a few days in advance of Magic's arrival to set up their equipment and frame the backdrop they wanted. The day before the commercial was to be shot, Converse executives received a phone call from Charles Tucker, Johnson's agent. Both Magic's and Larry's contracts were up, and he informed them that the two players had decided their compensation wasn't lucrative enough. The two were prepared to hold out for more money. Larry, who had a close relationship with Converse executive Al Harden, told him to take care of Magic immediately, and he'd trust Harden to pay his portion later. Their demands were not that exorbitant — about an extra $15,000 each — and with the shoot already running up a bill of $180,000 a day, Converse capitulated.

When Johnson and his cadre of limousines arrived at Bird's summer home, the first to greet him was Larry's mother, Georgia Bird.

She was a devoted basketball fan whose interests did not lie solely with her son's Celtics. Born and raised in Indiana, she faithfully chronicled the college game and her favorite player, Isiah Thomas, the former college star of Indiana University.

Two years after the taping of the Converse commercial, the Pistons lost in the Eastern Conference Finals to the Celtics in a thrilling seven-game series, prompting a bitter Thomas to remark that Bird's accomplishments were inflated by the media because of the color of his skin.

His words touched off a firestorm of criticism. Pistons forward Dennis Rodman, who initiated the dialogue by asserting that Bird was "overrated," was dismissed as an immature, loose-lipped rookie, but Thomas was a veteran who presumably knew better.

The incident left a permanent stain on Isiah's résumé. He was portrayed as the ultimate sore loser, unable to recover from the disappointment of Game 5 of the Conference Finals, when Bird picked off his floating inbounds pass in the final seconds of the game and relayed it to Celtics guard Dennis Johnson for the winning basket.

Yet none of it, not even Thomas's pointed criticism of her son, dissuaded Georgia Bird from abandoning her favorite point guard.

"Isiah was her number-one guy of all time," Bird said. "She followed him religiously when he was at IU. She felt that way even after '87. She told me, 'Oh, Larry. You two are out there working hard and things are going to be said.'

"You know who else she loved? Bill Laimbeer. He was at Notre Dame — another Indiana school. And she *knows* how much I hated that guy."

During the 1986 season, when the list of All-Stars had just been announced, Bird asked a group of Boston reporters if Laimbeer, who had been an All-Star the previous three years with the Pistons, had been selected again. Informed that Laimbeer had been left off the squad, Bird deadpanned, "Good. Now I won't have to worry about him getting on the bus and saying, 'Hi, Larry,' and me having to say, 'Fuck you, Bill.'"

Although Earvin Johnson had not played for one of the Hoosier state's finer institutions of learning, he was still a midwestern boy who played his college ball in close enough proximity for Georgia Bird to joyfully follow his career.

Georgia embraced Magic warmly, then fussed over her son's rival as if he were one of her own, offering him lemonade, iced tea, and a home-cooked meal that she had been planning for a week. By the time Bird arrived at the house and stiffly shook Magic's hand, Georgia Bird was already piling piece after piece of her signature fried chicken on his plate, adding gravy and mashed potatoes and green beans and corn.

She introduced Earvin to her own mother, Lizzie Kerns, who had baked one of her specialties, cherry pie, just for the occasion. Then she ushered Johnson over to say hello to Mark Bird, Larry's older brother, spouting statistics and highlights of Johnson's numerous basketball accomplishments in college and the pros. As his mother continued to fawn over Magic, Bird excused himself to take a shower.

"I think he was feeling a little uncomfortable," Mark Bird said. "Larry likes his privacy, and there were so many people around. It was a little awkward."

The camera crew had previously applied for permits to close Sawmill Road during taping, and the local newspaper had been contacted and asked to refrain from reporting the date the commercial would be shot in order to limit distractions. The crew had particular interest in shooting footage of a cornfield that was opposite Bird's property, so they contacted its caretaker, Ben Lindsey, for permission to film the area. Lindsey approached Bird and told him, "They want to drive my combine through the fields. Should I charge them for that?"

"Sure," Bird told him. "Get whatever you can."

"I think they wrote him a check for $5,000 just to drive by his own field," Bird said.

While the lighting crew pulled out their equipment and began setting up down at Bird's asphalt court, the Bird brothers pulled out their four-wheeler and offered Earvin Johnson a ride. Magic good-naturedly complied, jerking around the property like a newly minted cowboy on a bucking bronco.

"From the looks of it," Mark Bird said, "he had never been on one before."

After Georgia's carefully prepared feast, Bird shooed his family and the film crew away and disappeared with Johnson to the basement of the house.

Initially, the conversation was halting. Bird made a crack about Magic having the upper hand again in light of the Lakers '85 championship.

"The league is loving us," Johnson replied. "Do you know how much money they are making off you and me?"

"I'd like to see a little more of it coming our way," Bird said. "And how about what they're paying these rookies that are coming in? I can't wait until my contract is up."

The two superstars laughed. Each acknowledged that he had already earned more money in six years in the NBA than he had anticipated making in his entire lifetime.

As they began to discuss their upbringings, they were surprised by the similarities of their stories. Each grew up poor in the Midwest, raised by parents who stressed pride and self-discipline in spite of their challenging economic situations. They compared notes on being crammed into a tiny bedroom with their siblings. Bird had shared a room with his sister Linda, who did not subscribe to his obsession with orderliness and left him in daily fits of rage from her clothes slung about her bed and the floor. Magic shared tales of his brothers and sisters sprinting down the hall in a desperate attempt to be the first to reach the one and only bathroom in the house.

They swapped stories about their baseball exploits as teenagers and discovered they both had paper routes growing up. Magic and Larry also shared another childhood trait: each had spent most of his quiet moments dreaming of basketball greatness.

Johnson told Bird about the afternoon he saw a wealthy Lansing businessman drive through the town center in a sparkling new Mercedes. Earvin, who was dribbling a basketball at the time, promised himself that, once he made it big in the pros, a blue Mercedes would be one of his first purchases.

A luxury of that magnitude was foreign to Bird because nobody in French Lick or West Baden was driving much more than a station wagon or a pickup truck.

"When everybody else around you is the same way, you don't even realize you don't have money," Bird said.

That didn't prevent either young boy from occasionally longing for the finer things. Bird became fixated on a pair of suede tennis shoes one of his teammates wore to school. He was given two pairs of canvas Converse sneakers a year for being on the school basketball team, and knew they would have to last through the summer.

"But then I saw those suede shoes, and it was all I could think about," Bird said. "I couldn't imagine I would ever have a pair of them, but then I got lucky. I found a pair for 20 bucks. I was just so happy.

"I never would have asked my parents for anything like that."

In his senior year of high school, when Bird and his classmates received the flier for their high school rings, he looked at the picture for a long while, then folded it carefully and threw it away. Two or three months after graduation, Georgia Bird said to him, "Hey, where's your class ring? I don't remember paying for it."

"I didn't get one," Bird answered.

"What?" Georgia Bird shrieked. "Why not? I would have found a way to pay for it."

"I just didn't feel right asking," Bird shrugged.

Young Earvin Johnson's wish list had included a pair of Converse's special Dr. J leather shoes to replace the $2 sneakers that were his standard footwear, but he never was able to scrape up the money to buy them. He made do with his own canvas Cons by sprucing them up with red laces, the color of nearby Sexton High School, where he planned on being a star someday.

Magic owned two pairs of school pants and a suit to wear to church. The jacket was reversible, and he alternated his wardrobe weekly by turning that jacket inside out. What he really wanted was a pair of blue jeans, the ones the popular R&B singers (and a few lucky Lansing residents) wore.

"I wanted those jeans so badly," said Magic. "But my dad told me it wasn't in our budget. There were just too many of us."

Like Larry's father, Earvin Johnson Sr. had two full-time jobs to help defray the costs of raising ten active kids. He worked for General Motors for 30 years, many of them on the assembly-line late shift. Sometimes he came home pocked with burns from the sparks of the welding tools that seared through his T-shirt.

Magic's father finished his shift at three in the morning, took a nap, then reported to his job pumping gas at the Shell station. In later years, he started his own trash collection business and promptly put his sons to work. Some of Johnson's favorite memories were riding the garbage truck with his father.

The elder Johnson loved to watch professional basketball on television with young Earvin, who was nicknamed "June Bug" because he couldn't sit still. When the game ended, Magic pushed the couch aside, rolled up some socks, made a mark on the wall, and started shooting.

Earvin Sr. would not tolerate smoking or drinking in his home. He assigned chores to each of his children and expected them to be completed in short order. It was not a wise idea in the Johnson household to challenge this simple edict.

"We were going to earn our keep, like it or not," Magic said. "No Johnson child was ever going to be called lazy."

Joe Bird also stressed the importance of hard work — and always finishing the job. Larry's father was a gregarious man who was popular in town and loved to roughhouse with his kids. He had a quick wit and a generous nature, but he also had a darker side. Joe Bird returned home from the Korean War haunted by his experiences, and although he rarely talked about what he had seen, his family was often woken in the middle of the night by the blood-curdling screams of his many nightmares.

He worked a variety of jobs over the years — at a chicken farm, a piano company, a shoe factory. He would stay sober for months at a time, but once every few months Joe's wages never made it home, squandered on cigarettes and a few drinks with the guys after work.

The Bird family was constantly in financial peril. Larry moved 15 times in 16 years, sometimes because the rent went unpaid, or the electricity was turned off, or simply because his mother preferred a change of scenery.

Eventually, when Larry was 16, Georgia and Joe Bird divorced. On more than one occasion, Larry's father told him bluntly, "You'd all be better off without me."

His son disagreed. He loved his father and enjoyed many happy afternoons playing catch with him in the yard. As Larry's celebrity grew, so did the scrutiny regarding his family, and Joe Bird was often portrayed in a poor — and inaccurate — light. More than one publication claimed Joe Bird was physically abusive toward his wife Georgia. If that happened, Larry said, he never witnessed it.

"If something happened, it had to have been before I was born," Bird said. "All I can tell you is, I was with him for 18 years and I never once saw him hit my mother. I did see my mom chase my dad around the house and whack him with a broom, though."

Bird was 19 years old when the police visited Joe Bird and notified him he was behind in his support payments again. Because it was a small, tight-knit community, the officers knew Joe, so when he asked for a couple of hours to put his affairs in order before they hauled him off to the jail, they obliged.

Larry's father called Georgia, expressed his regrets, told her what he planned to do, then put the phone down and shot himself. Upon his death, his Social Security payments reverted to his cash-strapped — and deeply grieving — family.

Although Joe Bird's suicide was an incredibly traumatic event, it did not destroy his third son. In fact, Bird maintained, it only made him stronger.

"I never had an issue with it," Bird said. "I always felt my father did what he had to do. He made his own choices. The thing about it is, really, that he bailed out on us.

"In some ways, he couldn't help it. He had his own demons from the war and all that. But you've got to move on. It was hard, but I did it. There was nothing I could do about it.

"I don't look back much. Someone said to me once, 'Wouldn't you like your dad to be here to see all that you've accomplished?' I said, 'Well, I wish he would have stuck with us. I wish he hadn't given up so soon.'"

Bird was already obsessed with basketball when his father died, but after that it became a welcome escape from the sadness that enveloped his family.

From the start, the blond white kid in French Lick and the gangly African American from Lansing exhibited unusually disciplined work habits. While other boys were playing stickball, riding bikes, sipping a soda down at the drugstore, or lounging in the nearest swimming hole, Bird and Magic were on the court, outlasting whoever had joined them that morning to shoot a few hoops.

Bird's childhood friend Tony Clark recalled numerous times when his mother would drive him past the outdoor courts and Bird would be there alone, shooting in the rain. "He had this drive none of the rest of us had," Clark said.

When he was young, Bird would go along with his brothers and his mother to the grocery store at the start of the week. They would fill four baskets full of food, and Bird assumed they would eat like royalty for weeks. Instead, by Thursday, all that was left was some peanut butter and stray pieces of bread.

"If you got a piece of that bread on Friday, you were doing pretty good," Bird said.

He was in the fourth grade when the principal came in looking for volunteers to work in the cafeteria. Everybody raised their hands, but the principal picked Bird. He worked during most of the 45-minute recess for his neighbor, Phyllis Freeman, handing out milk, wiping tables, and busing the dishes. In return, he got a free lunch and a check for $5.50 every other week. Most days he'd catch only the last five minutes of recess. His friends asked him, "Where you been? You missed all the games."

"I felt bad about it until I got that check," Bird said.

He ran home with his pay stub and the refunded lunch money Mrs. Freeman gave him and proudly showed them to his mother. Georgia Bird congratulated her son on his hard work and let him keep the check, but took the lunch money back from him. "That's my hard-earned pay," she said. Later that evening, when Joe Bird came home, he scooped up the lunch money. "That's *my* hard-earned pay," he said.

While Bird exhibited a wry sense of humor like his father, he was also proud and stubborn like his mother. He occasionally had trouble containing his emotions and could be surly if he felt he was slighted.

Larry weighed only 130 pounds as a high school sophomore at Springs Valley High when he broke his ankle in practice with the junior varsity team. He knew immediately he had injured himself badly because he couldn't put any pressure on his foot. Coach Jim Jones, figuring it was a sprain, took the boy out back and taped up his ankle, right on the skin. Then he told the scrawny forward, "You'll be all right. Just get out there and move a little bit." Larry did what he was told. His foot swelled so badly that it took three weeks for it to calm down enough for the doctors to cast it.

"Jonesy cost me almost a month of playing time for that," he said.

He spent most of the season propped up on crutches, shooting free throws and working at Agan's Market in West Baden. When tournament time rolled around, Larry was healed but still limping slightly. Jones added him to the postseason roster anyway, and when the coach tapped him on the shoulder to go into his first varsity game, Bird galloped onto the court and promptly launched a 15-footer. It dropped through. He went on to win the playoff game for Springs Valley with two free throws from the line in the final seconds.

"That was it," said Jim Jones. "Larry was hooked."

Jones dropped by the outdoor courts each summer to see who was refining their skills. Jones told his players, "I'll be back to check on you." Sometimes he came back in 15 minutes. Sometimes he came back after 18 holes of golf. Each time his prized player was still there, working on his game.

As a 6-foot-7 senior in high school, Larry led Springs Valley to the regional finals, where they lost to Bedford. Bird went home with 25 points and a series of bruises on his upper thighs from the opposing player pinching him throughout the game.

The summer before his final year of high school, Larry went to visit his brother Mark, who was working at a steel mill in Gary, Indiana. In the evenings, Mark Bird played at Hobart High School, where most of the top college stars congregated. On the night Larry showed up, his brother marveled at how much taller and stronger he looked. When the college players started divvying up sides, Mark whispered to the guy who had picked him, "Take my brother. He's pretty good."

The Bird brothers played together for almost four hours and didn't lose a game. Larry dominated play, first with his passing, then with his shooting. Mark Bird was asked repeatedly, "Which college does your brother play for?"

"He's a high school kid," Mark answered.

One of the guys who inquired about Larry played for UCLA. "Within a week, Larry was getting letters from John Wooden," Mark said.

Earvin Johnson grew up chronicling the careers of all the UCLA Bruins, particularly center Lew Alcindor, who later changed his name to Kareem Abdul-Jabbar. When Magic was a teenager, he solicited the big man for an autograph following a Pistons game. While his future teammate did sign his scrap of paper, Alcindor was so dismissive that Johnson felt horribly slighted and brooded all the way back home to Lansing.

"When I make it big," Johnson vowed, "I'm going to smile at every single person that wants my autograph."

There was no doubt in Earvin Johnson's mind that he would be an NBA star someday. When he was in fifth grade and his teacher, Greta Dart, asked the kids what they wanted to be when they grew up, Johnson wrote "basketball player" in bold letters.

"Sure, Earvin," Dart said. "Get your education first."

Yet Dart couldn't help but notice there was something striking about Johnson's leadership capabilities, even as a 10-year-old. His ability to connect with his classmates and bring them together was remarkable. Dart was often the teacher on duty for recess when the kids traditionally played a spirited game of kickball. Magic, who was so much stronger and better than most of his friends, would choose Dart and two of the least athletic kids in the class to be on his team. Together, they'd go out and beat the top athletes in the school.

"He was an organizer," said Dart. "He was always the one who took the kids that weren't included and found a way to make them part of it."

Dart was a disciplinarian, and while she found Johnson to be charming, she also expected him to be responsible. In her first year as a teacher, she warned him that if he didn't finish one of his school assignments by Friday, she would not allow him to play in the big fifth-grade YMCA game the following day.

Magic made the mistake of calling Greta Dart's bluff. When the paper didn't land on her desk, she forbade him to dress for the game. His formerly undefeated team lost without him.

"The kids came in on Monday and said, 'Mrs. Dart, you should have let Earvin play,'" Dart said. "But Earvin didn't say a word."

Johnson couldn't wait until high school so he could wear the uniform of the Sexton "Big Reds." Before he got the chance, his street was redistricted and Magic and his siblings were bused to Everett High School instead. It was a crushing development for his older brothers Quincy, who played football, and Larry, a basketball player who also had longed for the day he'd wear a Sexton uniform. While Sexton's population was made up mostly of African American students, Everett was a mixed-race school, and Magic and his siblings were wary of their new surroundings. Quincy endured racial slurs and bruising fistfights. Larry became involved in a series of scrapes with white students and clashed with the high school basketball coach, George Fox.

Larry Johnson didn't like people telling him what to do. He showed up late for practice, and his effort was spotty. He was angry that he had to stay at Everett, and he took it out on everyone around him.

"I felt like all these white teachers and white coaches were looking down on me," Larry explained. "It seemed to me they treated me like I was nothing. It wasn't like that — but back then that's how I saw it."

Larry Johnson was riding the bench on a junior varsity team with a record of 1–6 when Fox called them together and said, "Do I have to call up that eighth-grader Earvin Johnson from the middle school to show you guys how to bring the ball up?"

Earvin, who was already 6-foot-4, dropped 48 points on the Oddo Eskimos, a crosstown middle school rival. He entertained a packed gymnasium with behind-the-back passes and full-court jams while his brother Larry sat court-side, urging him to smash the school record of 40 points. He did so in three quarters, then sat back and watched his teammates from the bench in the final minutes.

By the time Earvin was a ninth-grader, Larry Johnson had been bounced from the high school team because of his poor attitude. When he left, he angrily told Fox, "My brother Earvin will never play for you. I'll make sure of it."

When Magic finally arrived at Everett, his initial interaction with Fox and the players was awkward. He was fiercely loyal to his brother Larry, but he also ached to play.

"I've got to do this," he told his older brother, the anguish clear in his voice.

In the beginning, Johnson's older teammates resented his abilities and, ignoring him completely, pointedly passed the ball among themselves. Yet, over time, their stance softened. Magic was too talented, too unselfish, and too charismatic to dislike.

"What they figured out," said Larry Johnson, "was if they gave Earvin the ball, he was going to give it right back."

Magic's congeniality was a gift and a blessing to a school that was struggling to maintain order in the wake of the redistricting. There were incidents throughout Johnson's tenure at Everett between white and black students, yet the gifted young ballplayer defused much of the tension by coaxing his friends into becoming like him — colorblind.

He showed up at parties held by his white teammates, even though he and his friends were often the only blacks in attendance. He convinced his white friends to listen to his soul music and coaxed the principal into setting aside a room to dance during free study periods. He organized a protest when no African American cheerleaders were picked for the school's squad, even though their talents were undeniable.

"For all his basketball skills, the biggest contribution Earvin made to Everett was race relations," said Fox. "He helped us bridge two very different cultures. He ran with the white kids, but never turned his back on the black kids. He broke down so many barriers. He was so popular the students figured, 'Hey, if Earvin is hanging out with these guys, it must be okay.'"

It was an Everett tradition that after the first practice of the season, the players ran around the basketball court until the last teammate was standing. Two years in a row, that person was Earvin Johnson. The summer before his senior season, Johnson's teammate Randy Shumway informed Fox that he was out to beat Magic. The two ran around the court for more than a half-hour as their teammates dropped by the wayside. After 45 minutes, both players were panting, clearly exhausted, yet neither was willing to quit. Fox was contemplating how he should break the stalemate when he noticed Johnson whispering in Shumway's ear. The two did one more lap together before Magic announced, "That's it, Coach. We're calling it a draw."

"Earvin could have outlasted him," said Fox, "but he knew it would be better for team morale if he didn't."

Although Johnson was the hardest-working player Fox had ever seen, he was not above challenging his coach. In Magic's sophomore season, Everett played in a holiday tournament against Battle Creek Central; the players were told to be at the school at a designated hour, and not a minute later. As the team filed onto the bus, their best player, the notoriously tardy Earvin Johnson, was missing. Fox took a deep breath, then instructed the bus driver, "Let's go."

As the bus started pulling out of the parking lot, Fox tapped the driver on the shoulder.

"But drive real slow," he said.

As the bus turned the corner, a horn tooted behind them. It was Earvin Johnson Sr. with his son in the back seat. Magic hopped on board but moved to the back to sit alone. His signature smile was absent, and he would not talk to any of his teammates. He was still sulking before warm-ups when Fox called him over and told him, "Listen, big fella. It's time to get over it. Let's play ball."

"Okay, Coach," Johnson answered. "That sounds good."

He went out and submitted a triple-double, and Everett won easily.

"Earvin was awesome that night," Fox said. "Heck, he was awesome every night."

Johnson led Everett to the Class A state championship over Brother Rice in his final season by sharing the ball instead of scoring 45 to 50 points a game, which he could have done at any time. He worked tirelessly on his ball-handling and his rebounding with the advice Fox gave him imprinted on his mind: when you think you have done enough, do a little more, because someone out there is working harder than you.

Bird was told the same thing by coach Jim Jones. As he advanced from high school to the college game, he wasn't sure that "other person" truly existed.

"Not until I met Magic," Bird said.

As they sat in his basement in West Baden, Bird was not surprised to discover that Magic used to practice his fictional last-second shots against Russell and Chamberlain, just as he himself did. The two compared notes on their solitary workout regimens and their off-season conditioning programs.

Magic discovered that the man notorious for his stubbornness and frankness had a sharp sense of humor. Larry was an excellent storyteller, a loyal friend, protective of his family. He had a legitimate aversion to crowds and avoided mobs of autograph-seekers at all costs because of it. He told Magic he marveled at the way Johnson maneuvered through throngs of fans, touching each person and making them feel as though they'd been blessed.

"As I was sitting there listening to him," Johnson said, "I realized the Larry Bird that had been created in my mind through our battles, and the media, and my coaches and my teammates, was not the person I was talking with.

"He was somebody completely different. He was someone I could relate to completely. It was a little strange, in a way, to be sitting across from someone who had the exact same mindset about competition as I did. I had played with and against a lot of basketball players, and he was the first one I felt that way about."

When the two stars emerged from the house to continue filming the commercial, the Converse people were astonished at how easily the two collaborated. In previous joint appearances, Bird had seemed reticent, distant, unwilling to invest in any kind of interpersonal relationship.

"We could all see something had changed that day," Nagy said.

The original script called for Johnson and Bird to stand back to back, then turn quickly and face one another. That had to be scrapped because the two players convulsed with laughter each time they tried to turn and stare each other down.

Yet there was no evidence of their budding camaraderie in the finished product. With menacing music underscoring the opening scene, the commercial began with a black limousine gliding down a dirt road flanked by fields on either side. As the limo approached a clearing that featured a simple blacktop with a hoop, Bird stood glaring at the approaching vehicle, a basketball tucked under his arm.

The camera panned to the front of the limousine's license plate: *LA 32*. An agitated Bird slapped the ball between his two palms. At that moment, Magic Johnson, dressed in his full Lakers uniform, lowered the power window and said, "I hear Converse made a Bird shoe for last year's MVP."

"Yep," snapped Bird, looking down at his sneakers.

"Well, they made a pair of Magic shoes for this year's MVP!" retorted Magic, who, stepping out of the limo, snapped off his warm-ups and approached Bird.

"Okay, Magic," said Bird, whipping him the ball. "Show me what you got."

As Johnson leaned back to launch a fadeaway jumper, Bird, wearing shorts and a Converse T-shirt, lunged to stop him.

Cut to a black pair of Converse shoes, situated next to a pair of bright gold ones. The announcer growled, "The Bird Shoe. The Magic shoe. Choose your weapon. From Converse."

The commercial was an instant classic. Sales of both models skyrocketed, and Converse sneakers quickly ruled playgrounds from the East Coast to the West Coast. The black-and-white Weapons sold two-to-one over the gold ones, not because Bird was more beloved than Magic but because the neutral colors of his shoes were more appealing to the masses.

Converse sold 1.2 million pairs of the Weapon in its first year and an additional 600,000 pairs the next. "Those were extraordinary results," said Gib Ford, former Converse CEO. "And there's no doubt a major reason for our success was the Bird and Magic promotion."

The public's perception of the two players was altered once the spot hit the airwaves. Suddenly, they were viewed as respectful competitors, not bitter adversarial rivals.

"It wasn't until they did that Converse commercial that people started to realize they weren't enemies, just two very tough guys who hate to lose," said Lakers forward James Worthy. "They were both great assist men who enhanced everyone around them."

The Converse ad received mixed reviews from Johnson's Lakers teammates, who were stunned to learn he had flown to Indiana — more specifically, *to Bird's house* — to tape it. When Johnson returned to Los Angeles, he called up his friend Byron Scott and told him, "You know what? I've got a different feeling about Larry Bird now. He's a real down-to-earth guy. I think we could end up being friends one day."

"I couldn't believe what I was hearing," Scott said. "I was shocked. We *hated* Larry Bird and the Celtics."

Scott mercilessly taunted Johnson about his new Converse advertising partner. When Magic showed up for practice, Scott and Michael Cooper were waiting. Cooper played the role of Bird, complete with the hardened glare and the biting words. "Okay, Magic. Show me what you got!" Cooper shouted at Scott, who played the role of Magic. At that moment, Scott ripped off his warm-ups, just as Johnson had done in the spot.

While the skit usually left Magic's teammates doubled over with laughter, it did not amuse his coach. As Johnson suspected, Riley was furious when he learned of the commercial — and its location.

"I didn't like it," Riley said. "I didn't say anything about it, but I was not happy. We all knew the Magic-Bird thing transcended the Lakers versus the Celtics. It was between them as to how they handled that.

"I wanted to ask Earvin if he thought Bird would have filmed it if he had to come to Los Angeles. He wouldn't have. We all know that."

Riley hoped there were other reasons Magic had agreed to film the commercial. He had witnessed Johnson disarm many of his would-be adversaries with his dazzling smile and knew that while Bird considered fraternizing a sign of weakness, Johnson's charms were often too irresistible to ignore.

"The more I thought about it, maybe Earvin had a plan," Riley said. "He was such a competitor himself, maybe his idea was to catch Bird off-guard, to soften him up a bit."

Back in Boston, the commercial registered barely a blip in Celtics workouts. McHale occasionally serenaded Bird with a sudden outburst of "Choose your weapon!" but he soon grew bored with it and left Boston's franchise forward alone. If any of Larry's teammates resented his decision to film the ad alongside Magic, they didn't articulate it.

"There was none of that," said former Celtic Rick Carlisle. "Honestly, I think that just epitomizes the difference between the two personalities. Magic was probably concerned about what his teammates thought of him. Larry didn't really care."

Celtics coach K. C. Jones had no concerns at all about Magic and

Bird's time together and how it might alter the mental toughness of his star.

"Are you kidding?" Jones said. "Larry was the most competitive person alive — except for maybe Magic. I couldn't see how any commercial was going to change their approach.

"I never did understand what Pat Riley's problem was. It was a harmless thing. It was good for the league, good for their image, and good for both of our franchises."

Jones had an intimate knowledge of such rivalries, since he had played alongside Bill Russell during his epic battles with Wilt Chamberlain. When the Celtics played in Philadelphia, Russell often spent the day with Chamberlain — even took a nap in his bed — but when it was game time, all that hospitality was forgotten.

"We'd get on the court, and Russ would look through Wilt as if he wasn't there," Jones said. "I knew Larry would be the same way."

Following the commercial, Magic anticipated a more civil reunion when he saw Bird before their rare regular season meetings.

"I still wanted to beat the Celtics in the worst way," Magic said. "I still wanted to take away what Larry Bird had. But now, after the game, I found myself saying, 'Hey, let's go have a beer.'"

Bird's answer, however, did not change from previous years: thanks, but no thanks. Their relationship changed that afternoon in West Baden, but he still wasn't willing to socialize with the one player who stood in the way of every single basketball goal he'd set for himself and the Celtics.

"I could separate the guy who sat in my basement and told me all about his family from the guy who was wearing a Lakers jersey and trying to keep us from winning a championship," Bird said. "It was easy, to be honest."

The slogan "Choose Your Weapon" eventually became dated and politically incorrect. According to Jack Green, the name of a subsequent campaign for Phoenix Suns star Kevin Johnson, originally "Run and Gun," was scrapped and the campaign renamed "Run and Slam" after urban groups voiced their opposition. The "violent nature" of the wording ultimately killed the Weapon campaign.

Yet the success of the concept convinced Nike to invest millions in a young megastar they nicknamed Air Jordan. The spectacular young Bulls star turned the Oregon-based shoe company into a major player in the athletic industry.

Because their schedules were so busy and because they lived on different coasts, the karma between Magic and Larry on that beautiful fall afternoon was never again re-created on camera. Yet the residual effect of their time together was an unspoken, shared understanding of the blessings and burdens of carrying a franchise.

"I would have never guessed how it would turn out," Bird conceded. "If we had never done that commercial, I doubt we ever would have sat down and talked like we did. We may never have gotten to know each other."

The commercial aired throughout the 1985–86 season, which began with Bird continuing to labor through severe back pain. By the end of the exhibition season, Bird was contemplating shutting it down for the year. The pain was nauseating, and the stiffness limited every aspect of his game. Dr. Silva brought in a physical therapist named Dan Dyrek to examine him. Dyrek discussed surgery, an option Bird quickly dismissed. They talked about rest and treatment, and Bird agreed to half of that course of action.

"I'll do the treatment," he said, "but I'm not missing any games."

For the next three months, Dyrek worked on Bird's back, attempting to alleviate the pressure of the compressed nerves. After every practice, the forward would drive to Dyrek's office for an hour (or more) of treatment. He religiously did a series of exercises that helped his mobility, but shooting a basketball remained problematic for the first ten weeks of the season. By the New Year, however, the treatment finally paid dividends.

Once Bird regained his touch, the Boston Celtics were brimming with Career Best Efforts of their own. The Big Three of Bird, McHale, and Parish was in its prime, and D.J. and Ainge had established themselves as reliable fixtures in the backcourt.

Auerbach asked Maxwell to come early to rookie camp to reclaim his place in the team nucleus, but the veteran declined, citing the need to oversee construction of his new home. "Where the hell does he think he got the money for that new home?" Auerbach groused.

"The veterans never went to rookie camp," said Maxwell. "Why all of a sudden was it so important that I be there?"

Boston had previously been engaged in on-again, off-again talks with the Los Angeles Clippers about center Bill Walton, who was on the back side of his career and looking for a change of scenery. Walton contacted the Lakers first, but West was wary of his medical issues, so Walton placed a call to Red Auerbach, who ran it by Bird.

"Hey, if the guy's healthy, he'll help us," Bird said. "Let's go for it."

After Maxwell's refusal to attend rookie camp, Auerbach decided the former 1981 Finals MVP would be the bait to pry Walton away from the Clippers. When the deal was announced, Maxwell bitterly departed Boston believing Bird had angled to have him shipped out of town.

In later years, Bird would continue to laud Max as "one of the greatest teammates I've ever had," but their relationship had suffered irreparable harm. Bird thought Max quit on him, and in the end Max thought Bird did the same to him.

Walton's arrival connected Bird with a teammate who loved and respected the game as much as he did. The two became instant friends and verbal sparring partners. They played 1-on-1 for hours before and after practice, trash-talking to one another throughout. Their chemistry was electric, their camaraderie genuine. Walton, who had seriously considered quitting, was reborn.

"Larry didn't just give me my career back, he gave me my life back," said Walton.

The liberal mountain man, a disciple of the Grateful Dead and a passionate political pundit, provided his teammates with a plethora of material to use at his expense. After practice, Walton, McHale, and retired Celtic John Havlicek would adjourn to Bird's house for lunch so McHale could begin his interrogation in earnest.

"So, Bill," McHale would say, "what do mushrooms really taste like? And was that really Patty Hearst tied up in your basement?"

After McHale had worked Walton into a proper lather, he'd sit back and announce, "Richard Nixon was the best president we ever had, don't you agree, Bill?"

The big redhead, whose one regret was that he never made Nixon's infamous "enemies list," would screech in protest as his new teammates howled with laughter.

Walton was a student of basketball history who tried to emulate Bill Russell as a young player. He was so taken with Bird's game that he made a trip to his friend's Indiana home and bottled up some of the French Lick dirt as a souvenir.

Walton, Jerry Sichting, and Scott Wedman became Boston's primary weapons off the bench and dubbed themselves the Green Team. They prided themselves on pushing their more celebrated teammates to the limit. The starters, nicknamed the Stat Team, often logged 40-plus minutes a night, so it wasn't uncommon for the reserves, fresh from 10 minutes or less of playing time, to beat them in practice the day after a game. Regardless of the score, assistant coaches Jimmy Rodgers and Chris Ford rigged the results in the Stat Team's favor. One day Walton had seen enough.

"K.C.," Walton said, "how can you let this travesty of injustice unfold before your eyes?"

"Bill," Jones answered, "you know we can't let practice end until Larry's team wins."

Although injuries had taken their toll on his body, Walton was still a superb rebounder and a defensive presence. He was also a gifted passer, and there were nights when he and Bird deftly performed basketball poetry together. The former UCLA star with the West Coast roots became an instant folk hero, embraced by the normally discerning Boston fans as one of their own.

His arrival pushed Parish, the silent center nicknamed "Chief" — after the character in *One Flew over the Cuckoo's Nest* — further to the back of the public's consciousness. Walton was keenly aware of Parish's value to the team as well as the public's habit of overlooking him. The afternoon he arrived in Boston and was picked up at the airport by M. L. Carr, he asked to be taken to Parish's house, where he promised the Chief he had no aspirations other than being his backup.

With the physical therapist Dyrek a new (and permanent) member of Bird's inner circle, Larry was able to shake off his back woes and submit the most complete season of his career. He averaged 25.8 points, 9.8 rebounds, and 6.8 assists a night, picked off a career-high 166 steals, and led the league in free throw shooting with an .896 percentage.

The 1986 All-Star weekend featured a new event, the Three-Point Shootout. Bird walked into the locker room and asked, "Which one of you guys is going to finish second?" After he blew away the competition and was handed an oversized check for the victory, he cracked, "This check's had my name on it for weeks."

Bird's demeanor was emblematic of the Celtics team as a whole. They were young, loose, cocky, and together.

"It was the best time of my life," McHale said. "Of all the things we did, what stands out is how naturally we gave of ourselves to the team. No one person was bigger than the rest of us."

Although Bird was still the Celtics' headliner, his teammates garnered their share of praise. The Big Three was universally recognized as the most frightening front line in the league, and Walton's resurgence became one of the NBA's most endearing stories.

One night when Parish was sidelined with an ankle sprain, Walton arrived at the Garden three and a half hours ahead of time. He was about to make his first start ever for the Boston Celtics and wanted to be prepared. As he stretched on the parquet, Bird stood over him.

"Now, look," Bird said. "Just because you are starting instead of Chief, don't think for a minute his shots are yours. Those are my shots. You just get to the weak side and rebound the ball."

As his popularity increased, Bird was inundated with endorsement requests. Everyone wanted him to hawk their products, but he judiciously picked his spots. When Lay's potato chips made him a lucrative offer, Bird agreed to appear in a commercial with Kareem.

The ad began with Larry about to open a bag of chips.

"Betcha can't eat just one," Abdul-Jabbar deadpanned.

"Bet I can," replied the cocky forward, who popped the single chip into his mouth.

As the camera panned back around, Bird sat greedily eating the whole bag of Lay's — with a completely shaved head to match Kareem's bald pate.

Mindful that his success was tied directly to his teammates, Bird often tried to incorporate them into his good fortune. When a local eatery near the Garden asked Bird to be their spokesman, he agreed and quietly arranged to put his teammates' tab on his docket each time they joined him for a meal there.

The portfolio of three-time champion Earvin "Magic" Johnson also continued to overflow with financial opportunities. The combination of his unique athletic skills and his infectious personality led to new commercials, new business ventures outside of basketball, and lots of new friends. Johnson no longer needed to rely on Buss to score him an invitation to the hottest events in Hollywood. He was atop the A-list with actors, comedians, athletes, and entertainers.

Jackie and Jermaine Jackson from the Jackson Five became regulars at the Lakers games and invited Magic to Hayvenhurst, their gated mansion, where they tried to coerce him into dating their sister La Toya.

One night Johnson was hanging with Jackie when the singer said, "You should come on tour with us."

"What would I do?" Magic asked.

"Hang with the brothers!" Jackie answered.

Johnson joined the Jackson entourage for the "Triumph Tour" in 1980 and the "Victory Tour" in 1984. He ate with them, traveled on their tour bus, even sat onstage while they performed. He was overwhelmed by the number of fans, lined three deep, who clamored for a view of the musical idols.

The Jacksons had it all worked out. They sent out a pair of stretch white limousines with dark-tinted windows an hour or so before the show, and the fans went berserk in pursuit. Hundreds of girls sprinted after the vehicles, shrieking their undying devotion.

Ten minutes later, after most of the crowd had dispersed, a nondescript white van pulled out of the hotel with the legendary band of brothers and a future Hall of Fame basketball star inside.

Had Riley been aware that Magic was touring with Motown stars, he most certainly would have objected. Jerry Buss, meanwhile, thought Johnson's travels with the Jackson Five was a terrific opportunity.

"Nobody balanced loving the game and loving life better than Earvin," said Jerry Buss.

It was a juggling act his coach could not understand. Riley was not capable of doing anything in season except immersing himself in the Lakers. He often lectured Magic that there were two states of mind in competition: winning and misery.

Misery, it seemed, was always lurking. Even though the Lakers broke out of the 1985–86 season with a 27–3 mark, there were subtle warning signs that their team structure needed tweaking. Abdul-Jabbar was still the focal point of the Lakers, yet Magic could see evidence of fatigue, particularly after long road trips or back-to-back games. Kareem — finally — was showing his age.

The addition of Walton enabled the Celtics to tag-team Abdul-Jabbar with both Parish and the big redhead. It also afforded them the opportunity to play both big men side by side, a lineup that coach K. C. Jones implemented on occasion.

Boston breezed to the Finals, but not before the emerging Jordan provided them with a glimpse of the NBA's future in the first round. "His Airness" was spectacular in defeat, dropping 63 points on the Celtics in Game 2 of a three-game sweep. His otherworldly performance prompted Bird to remark, "That was God disguised as Michael Jordan."

Knowing he had witnessed the next marquee star, Bird felt even more urgency to seize another title while the Celtics were young and healthy. Jordan didn't yet have the complementary pieces he needed to contend for a championship, but it was clear to Bird that it was only a matter of time before he would.

"Early on, people were saying Michael didn't have a team mentality," Bird said. "That was because he didn't have a *team*."

Magic and Bird weren't the only ones checking each other's box scores in the eighties. Young Jordan took note every time Johnson recorded another triple-double or Bird submitted another 16-rebound effort. The two superstars became his standard of measurement.

"They had what I wanted — the respect of the entire league," Jordan explained.

The anticipated LA-Boston Final in the spring of 1986 did not materialize. LA was derailed by a Houston Rockets team that featured twin towers Akeem (later Hakeem) Olajuwon and Ralph Sampson, the object of Auerbach's desire five years earlier. It was Sampson who drove the final stake through LA when he nailed a 12-foot, blind, turnaround corkscrew jumper at the buzzer to eliminate Los Angeles in six games in the Western Conference Finals.

Again, Bird felt cheated. His 1986 team was one for the ages, and he was certain they could have beaten LA.

"I would have rather played the Lakers," Bird said. "I would have rather played the best."

The Rockets proved to be a suitable consolation prize. The series held extra meaning for Bird because he would be playing against his former coach and mentor, Bill Fitch, whom he still revered. It was paramount for him to perform admirably in front of his first NBA coach.

Very quickly, Ralph Sampson became the lightning rod of the series. The 7-foot-4 forward shot 1 of 13 from the floor in Game 1 and appeared to be genuinely spooked by Boston's formidable front line. No wonder. Bird, Parish, and McHale combined for 65 points in the Celtics win.

Coming into the Finals, national pundits were trumpeting Houston forward Rodney McCray as a potential Bird stopper, similar to how Robert Reid was portrayed three years earlier. Bird, who never felt anyone except Cooper had successfully stymied him, took offense and torched McCray by scorching him for 31 points on 12-

of-19 shooting in Game 2. It wasn't until Game 3 that Sampson discovered his comfort zone and submitted a monstrous game, with 24 points and 22 rebounds in a Rockets win.

Game 4 provided the backdrop for Walton's signature moment. With the score tied 101–101 late in the game, Walton wrestled away an offensive rebound and relayed it to Bird, who calmly swished a three-pointer. On the next possession, Walton converted a tip-in to put his team in front for good. He finished 5 of 5 from the floor.

In Game 5, with the Rockets trailing 3–1 in the series, Sampson demonstrated the collective frustration of his team when he tried to establish position in the post on a mismatch. Jerry Sichting, Boston's balding Charlie Brown look-alike who was 11 inches shorter than Houston's big man, grabbed on to Sampson on the block and wrestled with him until help arrived.

Sampson didn't appreciate the guard's hands-on tactics and reared back and punched Sichting. Dennis Johnson charged in to defend his teammate, and Walton administered an impressive open-field tackle to send Sampson sprawling to the ground. Predictably, both benches emptied.

Sampson was ejected and later fined $5,000. Houston rallied to win 111–96, but their big man was heading back to Boston as Public Enemy Number One.

Celtics fans were among the most knowledgeable in the NBA. They knew the names of the opposing coaches and trainers and were on a first-name basis with nearly every referee. They knew the strengths (and weaknesses) of the opponent and exploited them accordingly. Sampson became the sole target of their ire, and the slender giant was barraged with insults and crude references to his family.

"It was brutal," Bird said. "Some of the worst I've ever heard."

The catcalls were incessant. Sampson was a crybaby, a bully, a coward. A petite woman sat on the floor with a sign that announced SAMPSON IS A SISSY! on the front, and HEY, RALPH, I'M 5-FOOT-1, 90 POUNDS. DO YOU WANT TO FIGHT ME TOO?! on the back.

Sampson checked out at the half, having shot a dismal 1 for 8 from the floor. Houston was reeling from a 55–38 deficit, and Bird already had rung up 16 points, 8 rebounds, and 8 assists.

"I was so pumped up, I thought my heart was going to jump right out of my chest," Bird said.

At halftime, sensing victory was looming, Bird departed from his usual custom and changed his jersey. He wanted to have two souvenirs to commemorate what he knew was a historic team. After he capped off his evening with 29 points, 12 assists, 11 rebounds, and the Finals MVP trophy, Bird gave both jerseys to the team equipment manager and told him to tuck them away safely somewhere. The next day, when Larry went to retrieve his mementos, both jerseys were gone.

The Celtics convened to celebrate their championship at the downtown restaurant owned by K. C. Jones. Bird, while elated, was also exhausted. The days of bumming rides from fans on Storrow Drive and partying until the wee hours of the morning were behind him. He was home and in bed by 10:30 P.M. His phone rang throughout the evening, but he ignored it. All he wanted to do was sleep.

"Bill Walton is on the phone," Dinah said.

"No," Bird answered. "I'm done."

Just after midnight, the doorbell rang at Bird's Brookline home. Walton stood sheepishly on his doorstep.

"I know you're tired," said his friend, "and I know you're in bed. But I'm going to sit out here and listen to the Grateful Dead, and I'll be here when you wake up."

Bird shrugged, patted his friend on the shoulder, then headed back to his bedroom. Walton sat in his friend's kitchen all night, nursing a glass of Wild Turkey and reveling in the moment.

"I sat there and enjoyed how wonderful it was to be on a team with Larry Bird," Walton said. "I was an old broken-down player who could appreciate what had just happened. Larry, Kevin, and Robert were still young enough to think it would last forever.

"I knew that wasn't so."

When Bird awoke the next morning and got up to take a shower, he wasn't sure if he dreamed Bill Walton's visit. He poked his head into his kitchen and saw the big redhead sitting there, just as he had left him.

"Hey," Bird said. "Did you fall asleep?"

"Larry," Walton answered, "we are world champions. How do you expect me to sleep?"

Just as they had done the previous fall, Bird and Magic filmed another Converse ad in September, this time in conjunction with Isiah Thomas, McHale, Mark Aguirre, and Bernard King. The commercial, in which each player rapped a few lines that were both horribly corny and terrifically funny, opened with Magic holding his yellow-and-purple Converse shoe and rapping, "The Converse weapon, that's the shoe. Lets Magic do what he was born to do." From there Isiah, then McHale, then Aguirre, then Bernard King described what the shoe did for them. King's rap of "What can the Weapon do for the King? Why, I can do just about anything," was followed by a bubbly Bird who declared, "You already know what they did for me."

The collection of NBA players asked in unison, "What?"

"I walked away with the MVP!" said Bird, cradling his trophy and beaming like a Hollywood star.

No wonder Bird was so happy. At the time, he was a reigning NBA champion who was recognized as the best player in the league and had the hardware to prove it.

Within a year, the smile, the trophy, and the championship would be gone. His endorsement partner Magic Johnson would pilfer all three of them.

8

★ ★ ★

JUNE 9, 1987

Boston, Massachusetts

LARRY BIRD WAS OPEN, and there was nothing Magic Johnson could do about it.

The ball had swung around from one Celtics threat to the next, from Dennis Johnson to Danny Ainge and then, in the deep left corner, to Bird, the basketball player Magic feared most.

How could Bird be left alone like that, even for a second? Later, watching film, Magic would see that, a moment before, James Worthy had yanked Bird's number 33 jersey to prevent him from wriggling free. Had the referee spotted him it would have been a foul, but Worthy surmised correctly that the officials were concentrating on the top of the key, where D.J. was holding the ball. When D.J. passed it to Ainge on the left elbow, Worthy did what he was supposed to do: he rotated to put a hand in the face of Boston's young shooter. Ainge saw him coming and dumped the ball to Bird in the corner.

Lakers big man Mychal Thompson, a newcomer to this rivalry, was a sliver late in reacting. He knew instantly that his hesitation had cost him, so he charged to the baseline, his arms outstretched, in an urgent attempt to disrupt the sniper from hitting his mark. As Thompson lunged toward Bird, he looked for some indication that the forward was off-balance, or rushed, or distracted.

"There was none of that," Thompson said. "He was cold, lifeless. Like a shark."

Bird's shot was perfect — a dead-on three-pointer that instantaneously deflated the city of Los Angeles, as well as the proud franchise that bears its name. The Celtics, down 2–1 in the 1987 NBA Finals to the Lakers, had just gone ahead by two points with 12 seconds left, and it was all too familiar. As Magic jogged to the sidelines, trying to ignore the uproarious reaction of the Boston Garden fans, his temper flared.

"How could you leave him alone?" Magic berated his teammates in the huddle. "Everyone in the building knew he was taking that shot. Did any of you actually doubt he could hit it?"

No one responded. Magic surveyed their expressions and understood he needed to move on — quickly. "If we dwelled on the sting of Bird making that shot," he said, "we were going to lose."

Johnson thumped his hands together and changed his tone. "C'mon, fellas," he said, "plenty of time."

Coach Pat Riley drew them close in the huddle. The Lakers championship in 1985 had exorcised the doubt from 1984, and the coach detected a resolve in Magic that hadn't been present three seasons earlier. There was no hint of panic from him in the huddle. The young buck had grown up.

"Run 'fist,'" Riley told Magic as the Lakers returned to the parquet.

LA's patented "fist" play called for three Laker players to clear out while Johnson brought the ball up the left side of the floor with Kareem Abdul-Jabbar establishing position in the post. Once Magic made the entry pass into Kareem, the big man had the entire left side of the court to maneuver. Abdul-Jabbar gathered in the pass, wheeled to the middle, and was fouled.

Kareem had already missed three free throws in the game. Magic was relieved when his first throw dropped through, but the second one rolled off, and Kevin McHale and Robert Parish converged at the exact same moment in pursuit of the rebound. If they held on, Boston would have the ball, the lead, and very likely a tie series.

McHale appeared to have possession, but he collided with Parish and then received a bump from behind from Thompson, his friend and former college teammate. The incidental contact from the Laker forward was just enough to jar the ball free and send it bouncing harmlessly out of bounds.

So now the Lakers had the ball, down by one with seven ticks on the clock. For a decade, the only logical choice in the waning seconds of a game was Abdul-Jabbar. Riley could go to his big man again, as he had done one possession earlier, or he could diagram some screens for his own sniper, Byron Scott. There was Worthy, who was quick and elusive and could draw a foul. And then there was Magic, who had been waiting his entire career for a scenario like this: a chance to strike down Bird and Boston by finishing the job himself instead of dishing it off to someone else down the stretch.

Michael Cooper inbounded the ball under the basket. Magic, situated on the left side of the floor, came to meet the pass and McHale flashed out to meet him. The snapshot was framed: Magic, the 6-foot-9 point guard and 1987 MVP, against McHale, a first-ballot Hall of Famer and defensive force who had been hobbling through the series with a broken foot. Although McHale was a power forward, he made a living guarding smaller players, relying on his innate timing, his long, long arms, and his deceptive quickness for a man in a 6-foot-10-inch frame.

As McHale assumed his defensive stance, Magic instinctively thought "pass." He glanced over at Kareem, at Worthy, at Scott. They were all covered.

Magic leaned in, leaned out, and stutter-stepped past McHale, dribbling toward the middle. Parish moved over to help, but Magic was a step ahead of both.

Bird, sagging off Michael Cooper on the opposite side of the key, saw Johnson head toward the heart of the key. "Good," Bird said to himself. "He's going to the middle. We've got lots of help there."

With Boston's Big Three of McHale, Parish, and Bird flocking toward him, Magic left his feet.

"I still wasn't sure at that point if I was going to shoot it," Magic said.

Kurt Rambis, watching from the bench, thought Magic was contemplating flipping the ball over his head to Kareem. It was an option that Rambis prayed Magic wouldn't choose, because he was certain the ball would be deflected.

Magic swooped the ball into the air, extending up, up, up with a hook shot as the three Boston players extended along with him. Rambis was transfixed by the ball's high, arching trajectory. "It seemed to hang up there forever," he said.

The choice of weapon was no fluke. Magic had spent the previous summer at Michigan State working on his post moves with Jud Heathcote, honing the hook shot so he would be comfortable launching it with either hand.

Bird was surprised that Magic chose to keep the ball and equally stunned at how effortlessly he executed a shot that takes years to master. As he watched his rival expertly flip his wrist, Bird experienced the overwhelming and sinking feeling of helplessness.

Magic Johnson was open, and there was nothing Larry Bird could do about it.

Magic's "junior junior" hook dropped through like a plump raindrop into a bucket of water. On the sideline, Pat Riley raised his fist triumphantly.

"I had been waiting on that moment," Magic said. "I was calm, ready. I had been taking the last shot all year, so it was second nature to me.

"If I had taken it in '85, I probably would have missed. I would have been too excited. It wasn't until '87 that I really understood and appreciated what Larry had been doing all along by taking all those big shots."

Five seconds had elapsed during Magic's drive to the hoop, leaving two seconds for Bird to pull off a miracle for his team.

Boston's final play was simple. D.J. threw it in the corner to Bird in nearly the identical spot where he had drilled the three-pointer seconds earlier. As Bird launched the final shot, he experienced a momentary surge of excitement.

"Oh, God, it's in," Magic thought as he followed the flight of the ball. "He's going to do it to us again."

The jump shot was straight, perfectly on line with the basket. As he released it, Bird fell backward, nearly into the lap of the Lakers bench.

"It had perfect rotation," Bird said. "I was sure I had it."

Bird was only half-right. The ball was perfectly on line, but it hit iron and bounced out. The Lakers won and, with a 3–1 advantage in games, were in complete control of the series. As Bird left the court, he looked over at Riley, who was hugging Magic Johnson as if he hadn't seen him in a month. Bird briefly made eye contact with the Lakers coach, but said nothing.

"Riley knew he was lucky," Bird said. "I guarantee you he thought that shot was dropping."

"I thought it was in," Riley confessed. "We got lucky. But the game ended as it should. It truly was Magic's time."

Mychal Thompson, the number-one pick in the 1978 draft (five spots ahead of Larry Bird), spent seven years in Portland and a half-season with San Antonio gawking at the Lakers and Celtics. He was captivated by the rivalry of Bird and Magic and envious, like hundreds of other NBA stars, that he wasn't able to play a role in their sizzling competition.

"We used to sit around saying, 'When are we ever going to be good enough to pass those guys?'" Thompson said. "We knew the answer. They had Magic. They had Bird. Never."

Following their premature exit from the playoffs in 1986, the Lakers contemplated shuffling their personnel. Their futile efforts against Houston's Twin Towers and their ongoing struggles to contain McHale made acquiring a big man with size their top priority. Just as the Celtics had done two years earlier when they tailor-made their alterations to offset Magic by acquiring Dennis Johnson, the Lakers franchise was tweaking its roster specifically with Boston in mind.

Owner Jerry Buss talked seriously with Dallas about swapping Worthy for rookie center Roy Tarpley and Johnson's friend Mark Aguirre. Strong objections from West and Magic prevented the deal from going through. Tarpley evolved into one of the NBA's great teases: he exhibited flashes of brilliance but didn't excel because he was unable to control his drug problems. Worthy, meanwhile, just kept making the All-Star team. Aguirre eventually landed in Detroit with his other ally, Isiah Thomas.

During one of Magic's junkets to Las Vegas with Buss, his owner asked him what they needed to vault them over the top. Johnson had not forgotten his college visit with Mychal Thompson nearly ten years earlier. He felt that Thompson's personality would mesh well with the team, and he hoped that Thompson, who played at Minnesota alongside McHale, might have insight on how to contain Boston's rapidly improving low-post connoisseur.

On February 13, 1987, Thompson was dealt to the Lakers for Frank Brickowski, Petur Gudmundsson, two draft choices, and cash. Bird noted the transaction with little trepidation. Thompson wasn't someone he feared, although he knew McHale dreaded guarding him, a phobia that stemmed from their days together at Minnesota when Thompson embarrassed the freshman McHale in practice.

The Spurs tried to inform Thompson that he'd been traded, but San Antonio had a game that night, and he had already taken the phone off the hook and settled in for his customary pregame nap. In an era when text messages and cell phones were not yet part of everyday life, Thompson was unreachable.

When his nap was over, he got up, placed the receiver back on its cradle, and drove to the arena. As he jumped onto the table to get his ankles taped, the only two people in the locker room were his soon-to-be-ex-teammate Darnell Valentine and trainer John Anderson.

"Hey, I can't tape you, you've been traded," Anderson said.

"C'mon, no joking around today," Thompson said. "I want to do some extra shooting."

"Are you listening to me? You are no longer a Spur," Anderson persisted. "You've been traded to the Lakers."

Thompson looked at him for a moment, then at Valentine. Neither was laughing. He leaped up and hugged them both.

"I felt like I won the lottery," Thompson said.

Two days later, he was in the Lakers locker room preparing for a nationally televised afternoon game against the Celtics. As he dressed with Kareem to his left and Magic to his right, he leaned over to forward A. C. Green and cracked, "I feel like I'm with Mick Jagger and Keith Richards."

Green responded with a polite but restrained smile. Thompson noted that there was no idle chatter, no horsing around. The locker room was quiet, businesslike.

"You couldn't cut the tension with a chain saw," Thompson said.

The jovial big man, who had hammed it up with Magic many times before, was surprised to see that even Johnson was grim-faced. Thompson asked Byron Scott, "So why is everyone so serious around here?"

"Because we hate the Celtics," Scott replied.

Thompson's first taste of Boston-LA was every bit as electrifying as he had imagined. The Lakers won 106–103, and his initiation into the trench war included a stiff arm to his Adam's apple from Parish and a humiliating series of post-up acrobatics from his old friend McHale on the block. Yet Thompson acquitted himself well overall, and Johnson was optimistic they'd found a neutralizing weapon underneath.

It was one of the many new moves the Lakers made in 1986–87. Just as Bird felt cheated in '83 when his team didn't make it to the Finals, Magic was still rankled by his team's underwhelming '86 postseason performance. A month into a long summer of frustrated retrospection, Riley invited him to lunch.

"We've got to change things, Earvin," Riley said. "This has to be your team now."

Magic was mildly confused. He felt as though it had been his team for the last four or five years.

"You can't just be the guy that sets everyone else up anymore. I need you to score," Riley clarified.

"Have you talked to Kareem about this?" Magic asked.

"I talked to Kareem already," Riley answered. "He understands. Now you have to understand. When you come back, you have to have a different mindset."

Magic, who honestly believed he could put up the same numbers as Larry Bird, had spent years deferring to Abdul-Jabbar on the offensive end. Through the first seven seasons of his career, he averaged 12 shots a game. Now Riley was talking about him taking 15 to 20 a night. It would require more pick-and-rolls as well as setting Johnson up in the post so he could exploit the smaller guards.

Johnson went back to Lansing and asked his college coach, Heathcote, to walk him through the nuances of the post-up game. For hours, Heathcote fed his former Michigan State star passes on the block, monitoring his footwork on the drop step and the angle of his shoulder when he turned to take the hook.

Magic's summer league workout partners showed up expecting the usual no-look lobs above the rim, the half-court bounce passes up the middle, and the drive-and-kick feeds to the perimeter. Instead, Magic was driving and finishing. He was posting up forwards, guards, anyone he could pin down on the block. He was pulling up for jump shots on the break instead of dishing off to the trailer. When he arrived at training camp, he lingered after practice, studying Abdul-Jabbar's sweeping hook.

"What makes it work?" Magic asked. "Is it the position of the ball? The release? The footwork?"

Kareem demonstrated the proper way to turn the body, how to keep the sweeping motion far enough from the opponent so it could not be blocked. He replicated the flick of the wrist, which enabled the ball to arc properly.

Magic was genuinely concerned about how Abdul-Jabbar would

handle the subtle change in the team's pecking order. He had gone to great pains throughout his career to show the proper reverence to a player he had idolized since he was a child.

Yet Kareem continued to be an enigma. While at times he could be outgoing, even playful, those moments were offset by the more frequent occasions when he was difficult, standoffish. On those days, Johnson wrestled with whether he should call out the captain for his temperamental nature. If any other player had caused that kind of friction on the team, Magic would have admonished him. But Abdul-Jabbar was different. Keeping him happy required a delicate balance of respect and distance. It was indisputable that the team was more successful when their center was engaged and focused.

As far as his teammate could figure, there were two Abdul-Jabbars: the genuine, elegant, articulate man who brought Magic to tears at his retirement ceremony with his heartfelt remarks, and the bitter, stubborn man who snubbed Riley at his Hall of Fame induction.

"Thank God Kareem was my teammate, because I used to cringe at the way he treated people," Magic said. "There was a way to say no if you didn't want to sign an autograph. You could say, 'I'm busy right now,' or, 'Sorry, not today.' But Kareem didn't do it in a very kind way. Sometimes he'd have people in tears. It's hurt him now that he's done playing."

More than a decade after both men retired, Kareem approached Magic to learn more about Johnson's business acumen. Abdul-Jabbar had struggled to find his niche since he stopped playing, and he was looking to Magic, who had made millions off the court, for advice.

"I want to be like you," the center said.

Magic shook his head.

"No, you don't," Johnson answered. "To be like me, you've got to shake hands, hug people, attend luncheons. You've got to be nice to people all the time. You've got to make small talk. You've got to be *on*."

"Well, maybe I can do it another way," Abdul-Jabbar said.

"There is no other way," Magic explained. "You have to be cordial. You can't treat your teammates without any courtesy, or humiliate reporters, or blow off fans."

Magic shared a story with Abdul-Jabbar that happened in his second season in the pros and resonated with him for a decade. The Lakers were finishing up a pregame shoot-around when a man and his young son timidly approached Abdul-Jabbar and asked, "Kareem, can we please get a picture?"

"No," Abdul-Jabbar snapped, without breaking stride.

Magic, standing nearby, could see the young boy was crushed. Johnson was not yet an All-Star, an MVP, or a household name, although he was well on his way to accomplishing all of that. He walked over to the father and said, "How about a picture with me?"

As the grateful father lined up the shot, Magic joked, "Maybe I'll be in the Hall of Fame someday too."

Twenty-two years later, Johnson sat in a boardroom representing Magic Johnson Enterprises with hopes of generating some new business. After he made his pitch, an older gentleman approached him.

"We met before, a long, long time ago," the gentleman said. "You posed for a picture with my son. Kareem blew us off, but you were very nice."

The son was a grown man, a successful attorney in Los Angeles. His father was the CEO of the company Magic was soliciting.

"My son is 29 years old now," the man said, "and he still has that picture on his wall."

As Magic walked out of the meeting with a new multimillion-dollar client in his portfolio, he thought to himself, "See, Kareem? It could have been you."

Although his introspective personality was a mystery to Magic and the Lakers, Abdul-Jabbar handled his diminished role with dignity in 1986–87. He passed the mantle to Magic without complaint, remained a key member of the team's nucleus, and on any given day could submit a vintage Abdul-Jabbar night, sweeping hook and all.

"When he was on top of his game, no one could touch him," Magic said.

Riley was banking on Abdul-Jabbar and Magic to seamlessly carry his team onward together. The addition of Thompson provided LA with the added depth and younger legs in the front court. Scott and Worthy were reliable scorers, Cooper was still able to thwart Bird more effectively than anyone else in the league, and Green and Rambis understood and accepted their roles. The 1986–87 season proved to be a Career Best Effort across the board. Every single player improved at least 1 percent (and some as much as 20 percent) in his designated category.

Magic thrived in his new role as playmaker and scorer. He led the team in minutes, field goals attempted, scoring, assists, and steals. Riley reduced Abdul-Jabbar's playing time and held him out of practice more frequently. Nobody minded; the strategy had its distinct advantages.

"The scrimmages were better when Kareem wasn't playing," Magic said. "We'd run up and down and up and down with no big man to slow us down."

"Get your rest, Cap," Magic told Abdul-Jabbar after the spirited sessions ended. "Just be ready for the fourth quarter."

Los Angeles posted victories in 12 of its first 14 games. They won all but one of their games in March. In February, they streaked out to a 29–0 lead against the Sacramento Kings and prevented them from scoring a single field goal in the first quarter. When the shell-shocked Kings finally converted on a pair of free throws, Riley called time.

The Lakers gathered around him, anticipating some compliments for holding an NBA team that featured scorers Reggie Theus, Eddie Johnson, and Otis Thorpe without a point for so long.

"Goddammit!" Riley roared. "Why did you foul him and put him at the line?!"

The most meaningful Lakers regular season win was a 117–110 victory over the Celtics in December. Boston was in the midst of a 48-game winning streak at home when the Lakers, touting themselves as "Celtic busters," went in and manhandled their East Coast enemies. Magic reveled in silencing the hostile Boston crowd with his no-look feeds and his new offensive arsenal. Bird winced when he watched his rival confidently bank in a jumper from the left side of the floor with the shot clock ticking down.

"He was so much more offensive-minded," Bird said. "He controlled tempo, got them running. Before, he'd always pass off to the wings. Now, all of a sudden, you weren't sure if he might take it in himself."

The Lakers developed a lockdown mentality on the road that had been missing in past seasons. It became a constant topic of conversation on the plane flights. Magic was the instigator, reminding his team, "It's the 12 of us against all these people who hate us. Let's shut them all up."

The Celtics were strangely silent during that December loss to the Lakers. Although they were still among the elite in the East, the luck of the Irish, which had presided over the storied franchise for decades, had been decimated in one memorable night.

Boston held the number-two pick in the 1986 draft and selected Maryland forward Len Bias, a versatile forward who was, by all accounts, a sure bet to be an NBA star. Auerbach envisioned Bias as his bridge from one dynasty to the next. The plan was for him to learn alongside three future Hall of Fame players, then assume his place in the pantheon of Celtics greats.

Instead, after a night of partying to celebrate his new life as a Celtic, Bias collapsed and died of cocaine intoxication.

It was a devastating tragedy and a sobering lesson for the Celtics on how to conduct their predraft business. Auerbach had always relied on word of mouth from his considerable college sources for his background checks. Maryland coach Lefty Driesell, one of Auerbach's trusted contacts, had vouched for Bias's character. In the wake of Bias's death, Driesell was forced to resign and Maryland embarked on a thorough investigation of its student-athletes. In turn, the NBA and the Celtics began refining their research of draft picks.

Teams began hiring private investigators to determine the char-

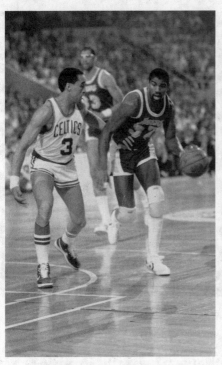

Dennis Johnson bodies Magic as he heads for the hoop.

Dick Raphael / NBAE / Getty Images

Michael Cooper allows Larry no space in the 1985 Finals.

Dick Raphael / NBAE / Getty Images

Larry shares tales of French Lick and West Baden with Magic between takes of a 1985 Converse commercial. © *John Goodman Studio 1985*

Bill Walton, who claimed Larry "saved my life" by welcoming him to the Celtics in 1986, offers a hand after another Boston victory.

Scott Cunningham/NBAE/Getty Images

The Big Three: Robert Parish, Larry Bird, and Kevin McHale, widely recognized as the greatest front line in NBA history.

Nathan S. Butler/NBAE/Getty Images

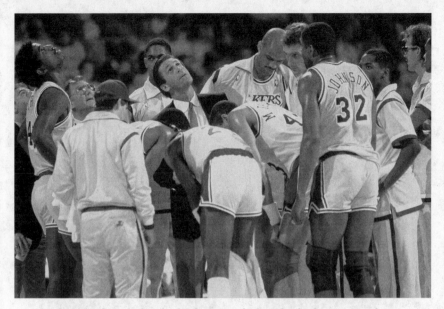

Lakers coach Pat Riley checks the game clock in the final moments of Game 4 of the 1987 Finals. *Richard Mackson/Sports Illustrated/Getty Images*

Magic unleashes his new "junior junior" hook, which later clinches Game 4 of the 1987 Finals.
Andrew D. Bernstein/ NBAE/Getty Images

Magic views the finishing touches of a Lakers victory alongside (right to left) his mentor, Kareem Abdul-Jabbar, and fellow Musketeers Byron Scott and Michael Cooper. *Scott Cunningham/NBAE/Getty Images*

Magic and Larry trade barbs in a pregame meeting of team captains.
Andrew D. Bernstein/NBAE/Getty Images

Toward the end of his career, Bird keeps his back loose during a game by lying on the parquet. *Nathan S. Butler/NBAE/Getty Images*

Magic, wearing his "optimistic" tie, announces to the world he is HIV-positive.
Stephen Dunn/Getty Images

Magic with his wife, Cookie, who steadfastly stood by him during his HIV crisis.
Andrew D. Bernstein/NBAE/ Getty Images

Magic can't hold back his tears during Kareem Abdul-Jabbar's emotional speech at Magic's retirement ceremony in 1991.

Mark J. Terrill/AP

NBA Commissioner David Stern sits next to a somber Larry as the Lakers hoist Magic's number 32 to the rafters.

Andrew D. Bernstein/NBAE/Getty Images

Larry Bird, David Stern, and Magic Johnson, the three men who were instrumental in saving the NBA.

Andrew D. Bernstein/NBAE/ Getty Images

Larry, Michael Jordan, and Magic show off their Dream Team uniforms in this outtake from a *Newsweek* cover shoot.

Neil Leifer/NBAE/Getty Images

Magic congratulates Larry at his retirement ceremony at Boston Garden in 1992. *Dick Raphael/NBAE/Getty Images*

Magic's efforts on behalf of AIDS and HIV patients continues through the work of the Magic Johnson Foundation.
Andy Hayt/NBAE/Getty Images

Coach Bird discusses the next course of action for his Indiana Pacers team with shooting guard Reggie Miller. *Marc Serota/NBAE/Getty Images*

Magic and Larry convene at center court to commemorate the 30th anniversary of the Michigan State–Indiana State game.
Andy Lyons/Sports Illustrated/Getty Images

acter of the athletes they were considering. Yet even that was an inexact science. Boston had used a service to investigate Bias and even subjected him to a predraft drug test. He passed with no trouble.

Bias's shocking death was the first of many bad omens. Bill Walton broke his pinky in a pickup basketball game, and then was pedaling on a stationary bike when he experienced a sharp pain in his right foot, which until that moment had been the healthy one. He was shelved until March, and even then was only an intermittent contributor the rest of the season.

Scott Wedman was the next to fall, with a heel injury that all but ended his Celtics career. Overnight the vaunted "Green Team" was reduced to a bunch of big names in expensive street clothes.

Kevin McHale, during a game in Phoenix on March 11, was jockeying for a rebound when he tromped on Larry Nance's foot. Although McHale was unaware of it at the time, he had suffered a stress fracture. He exacerbated the injury by continuing to play on it, and on March 27, when the Celts played Chicago, John Hefferon, the Bulls' team physician, looked at the x-rays and told McHale he had broken the navicular bone in his right foot. By the time the Celtics played the Pistons in the Eastern Conference Finals, McHale was aware that he was risking permanent damage by continuing to play. Even team doctor Thomas Silva conceded that he wasn't sure if McHale should be competing. Bird was not nearly as ambiguous in his opinion.

"Kevin, go home," Bird said.

"I'll be all right, Birdie," McHale answered. "You know you wouldn't go home either."

McHale was right. Bird's back was also a major worry. He needed to receive an hour of painful mobilization therapy from Dan Dyrek daily; otherwise, he couldn't loosen his back enough to play.

The Pistons were not interested in Boston's injury woes. Hungry to displace the Celtics as the best in the East, they adopted the moniker "Bad Boys" to accent their bruising style of play. Detroit's success was predicated on intimidation and defense, and their willingness to physically punish opponents caused them to be universally despised. The primary villains were Bill Laimbeer, a high-post offensive threat with a reputation for delivering blows after the whistle, and the rugged Rick Mahorn. Legendary Celtics radio announcer Johnny Most dubbed this duo "McFilthy and McNasty."

The ringleader of the Bad Boys was Isiah Thomas, the immensely clever point guard with an angelic face and an assassin's heart. Detroit also had crafty Joe Dumars in the backcourt and the combustible Dennis Rodman off the bench, as well as two veteran scorers in Adrian Dantley and Vinnie Johnson, nicknamed "the Microwave" by Danny Ainge because he heated up so quickly when he came into the game. The Pistons were a formidable opponent who proved to be one of the few teams that could match Boston's mental toughness.

The Pistons dropped Games 1 and 2 at Boston Garden, and when the NBA shifted its attention to Auburn Hills, Michigan, the series turned ugly.

In Game 3, Bird was fighting for a loose ball when he was roughly hauled down by Laimbeer. Bird was so incensed that he swung at the Pistons agitator as they both lay sprawled on the floor. When they were finally untangled, Bird fired the ball at Laimbeer's head. He was ejected, and the Celtics lost, 122–104.

"I wanted to fight him," Bird said. "Laimbeer tried to hurt people, and I wanted him to hurt."

As they lined up for introductions before Game 4, Bird refused to shake Laimbeer's hand. Robert Parish, who rarely expressed emotion on the floor, smiled broadly and clapped with approval. The Pistons then went out and evened the series 2–2.

In Game 5, back at the Garden, Laimbeer elbowed Parish in the midsection and the shoulder, and the Celtics big man lost his temper. The next time down the floor, Parish pummeled Laimbeer with a series of punches under the basket that sent the Pistons big man tumbling to the floor. No foul was called, nor was Parish ejected. Detroit general manager Jack McCloskey screamed at referee Jess Kersey, who stood less than a foot away from the Parish attack, to make a call. When he didn't, McCloskey did — to the league office demanding an explanation.

In the final seconds of Game 5, Isiah Thomas drilled a jumper to push his team in front. The Celtics placed the ball — and the outcome of the game — in Bird's hands. The franchise forward, guarded by Mahorn on the left side of the court, dribbled strong to the hole, but Rodman shifted over from the weak side and blocked his shot.

In the ensuing scrum for the loose ball, possession was awarded to the Pistons. Pistons big man John Salley and Rodman raised their arms aloft in unison. All Detroit had to do was run out the final five seconds of the clock and they would take a 3–2 series lead going back to Detroit. The two young forwards turned to run down the floor, still yipping with delight. Thomas grabbed the ball and hurried to inbound from the sideline near his own basket before the Celtics defense was set. He never saw his coach, Chuck Daly, signaling madly for a time-out, which would have given Detroit the ball at half-court.

Thomas considered throwing it to Rodman at midcourt, but Rodman was a poor free throw shooter and the Celtics would surely try to foul. Isiah had just five seconds to inbound the ball, and already three of them had ticked away.

Thomas settled on floating a pass to Laimbeer, who was waiting along the end line less than ten feet away. By the time Thomas saw Bird bolt from the foul line (where he was guarding Adrian Dantley) down to the basket to intercept the ball, it was too late.

"I had been counting down the seconds in my head," Bird said. "I knew he was running out of time."

For a moment Bird considered shooting the ball, but his momentum was going away from the basket, and it would have been an awkward, off-balance attempt. Out of the corner of his eye, he saw a streak of white heading for the hoop. It was Dennis Johnson. Bird relayed the ball, and D.J. knocked in the lay-up, sending the partisan Garden crowd into overdrive. Thomas and Laimbeer stood motionless for a moment, hands on their hips, then walked over to Daly knowing they had just literally thrown away their chance at a trip to the Finals.

Former coach and NBA star Doug Collins, who was broadcasting the game, expressed disbelief at Detroit's blunder. "To not call time-out in that situation is just cardinal sin," Collins told the viewers. "A veteran team should know better."

The Bird steal was the turning point of the series. Although the Pistons recovered to win Game 6 while Parish served the first one-game suspension in postseason history for his mugging of Laimbeer, Game 7 was back at the Garden, and Bird wasn't about to let the Bad Boys ruin his date with Magic and the Lakers. The Pistons encountered some colossally bad luck when Vinnie Johnson and Dantley collided and knocked heads, leaving a woozy Microwave unplugged for the rest of the day while Dantley was carted off to Massachusetts General Hospital in an ambulance. Boston finished off Detroit 117–114 in a win that left Bird pumping his fist with excitement.

All of the Lakers gathered at a team brunch to watch Boston eliminate the Pistons. Most of them were rooting for the Celtics, including Magic. And when Bird banked in an improbable lefty 15-foot bank shot, Magic turned to Cooper and said, "Here we go, Coop. We got 'em again."

In the aftermath of Detroit's incredibly crushing series defeat, Rodman spouted off about Bird being overrated. Thomas followed up with his observation that if Bird were black, "he'd be just another good guy." When apprised of Isiah's comments, Bird retorted, "It's a free country. He can say whatever he wants."

Bird maintained that stance throughout the controversy that followed, even as those around him hypothesized that he was deeply offended. When Thomas called to apologize, Bird's only request was that Isiah talk with Georgia Bird, who didn't understand why her favorite player had taken on her son.

"I really didn't care about it," Bird said. "I didn't know Isiah as a person. I liked to compete against him. Truthfully, what he said didn't mean a thing to me. I know what it's like to get beat in a big game. You get pissed off and you say things. No big deal."

Yet the fallout from Thomas's poor judgment was major news. The subject of race was still a sensitive topic, and the veteran had overstepped the boundaries. His comments about Bird quickly made headlines across the world.

Magic received a phone call from Lakers public relations director John Black the day after the Celtics-Pistons game. "Your boy Isiah has done it," Black said. "What do you want me to tell people?"

"Leave me out of it," Magic answered.

Johnson was angry with Thomas. It was an irresponsible comment, and the timing was atrocious, since the Celtics were moving on to play the Lakers.

But what frustrated Magic the most was that he had spent hours on the phone with Thomas consoling him over his loss to Boston, much in the way Isiah had done for him in 1984. The Bird steal had come to symbolize the Celtics' mental toughness and the Pistons' shortcomings, and Thomas was struggling to understand that. His Lakers confidant did the best he could to help him through it.

"Normally Isiah is a fighter," said Johnson. "Not after that play. He knew he had taken a major hit on that one. He was still fighting for his own stature in the league, and beating the Celtics was the only way he was going to get his.

"He took that loss hard. It was worse too because Isiah and Larry didn't like each other, and neither did the teams. It was a long phone conversation. By the time we got done talking, it was light out."

When Riley learned of Thomas's comments, he too went directly to Magic. It was a distraction that neither he nor his point guard needed to be addressing as they prepared for Boston.

"Earvin," Riley said, "we can't afford to spend time on this. What the hell was Isiah thinking?"

Johnson did not call his friend to find out. The call he placed instead was to Bird.

"Isiah does not speak for me," Magic said.

"It doesn't mean anything to me," Bird insisted. "Really, I could care less."

The conversation meandered briefly toward their impending Finals matchup before the two rivals signed off. The significance of the phone call was not lost on former Celtic Rick Carlisle, who had grown close to Bird and knew how intense the rivalry had once been.

"Their relationship had clearly changed," Carlisle said. "They were both at a juncture in their careers where they knew time was getting short, and they needed to live their basketball lives to the fullest.

"And whether they liked it or not, they were doing that together."

The 1987 Finals was the most coveted ticket in town in two cities — Boston and LA. Both Magic and Bird were inundated with requests for tickets to the games on their home turf. Magic's agent Lon Rosen came up with a brilliant solution: the superstars would swap tickets. Magic provided Larry with extra seats in Los Angeles, and Larry shared his quota of Boston tickets with Magic. The two players never discussed it, nor did they share their arrangement with their teammates.

"But if that doesn't tell you how far we'd come, I don't know what would," Magic said. "Because three years earlier, neither of us would have considered it."

With Detroit finally in its rearview mirror, Boston literally limped into the Finals. The space in McHale's foot was widening, and the forward was in excruciating pain. Bird's back was also in terrible shape. Robert Parish was severely hampered by a sprained ankle, and while Walton was on the team roster, he had missed most of the season and even the most optimistic Celtics fan knew better than to count on him.

The Lakers routed Boston 126–113 in Game 1 behind Magic's 29 points, 13 assists, 8 rebounds, and 0 turnovers, then rode a barrage of Cooper three-pointers to victory in Game 2. With Parish hobbling in Game 3, the Celtics' chances appeared bleak, but reserve center Greg Kite played the most memorable game of his career, bodying Kareem, rebounding the ball, setting bruising screens, and even blocking one of Magic's shots. He was the Player of the Game without scoring a single point.

Game 4 became a must-win situation for the faltering Boston team. They were at home, down 2–1, and needed a spark. Instead, they were felled by Magic's majestic "junior junior" hook. Like McHale's takedown of Rambis in 1984 and Kareem's revival in 1985, it was the signature moment of the series.

The Lakers went on to beat the Celtics in six games, and this time there were no bitter words, no angry barbs. Bird saluted Magic as "the best I've seen." A gracious Johnson maintained, "There's only one Larry Bird."

After eight years of envy, bitterness, anger, and despair, the two stars were finally able to step back and evaluate their rivalry with a hint of appreciation.

"I just knew no one else pushed me like he did," Bird said. "And I knew, the way my body was feeling, it wasn't going to last forever."

The 1987 playoffs represented the end of an era for the Boston Celtics. Walton's career was all but over. He spent the following summer in mourning, locking himself in his Cambridge home and listening to his Grateful Dead records over and over again. Bird went to visit a couple of times, but after a while he stopped. It was too depressing.

"The fun-loving guy I knew was gone," Larry said. "Bill was in such a deep funk, nobody could help him."

McHale underwent surgery to repair the gaping space in his foot and was told by the surgeon that he might suffer long-term effects from his decision to postpone the operation. He played six more seasons, but was never the same player.

Over the next four years, Bird underwent operations on both heels to remove bone spurs, then had major back surgery and played in constant pain for the remainder of his career. He approached each upcoming season as a new day, a new opportunity to coax his team back to the Finals against Magic and the Lakers, yet their West Coast foils appeared to be inching farther and farther away from their grasp.

Riley was still dripping with champagne in the Lakers locker room when he guaranteed a repeat of the 1987 championship. It was no off-the-cuff remark. He had been rehearsing what he'd say for days. The result was just as he desired: a locker room full of shocked players. No one else had to put the pressure on the Lakers. Their coach had taken care of that for them.

A few days later, after the parade and the rally where Riley repeated his guarantee in front of thousands of frothing Lakers fans, he sat down with Magic to explain his reasoning.

"Earv, this group will go down as one of the great teams in NBA history," Riley said. "But you want to go down as one of the greatest teams that ever played? The one way to do that is repeat."

One year later, the Lakers stood poised to do exactly that, but their opponent in the 1988 Finals would not be the Boston Celtics. The Pistons finally expunged their own Garden demons by clinching their first trip to the Finals on Boston's own floor. As the clock ticked down, the Celtics crowd implored Detroit, "Beat LA! Beat LA!"

So now it was Magic and the Lakers and Isiah and the Pistons, and it was an emotionally wrenching proposition. Isiah had been Magic's closest friend in the league. He had survived a childhood beset with poverty, violence, and tragedy in Chicago, and Johnson admired the odds he had overcome. He appreciated Thomas's fighting spirit and identified with his competitive nature, even though he often winced at some of the rash decisions Isiah made in the heat of competition, such as his comments regarding Bird in the 1987 playoffs. Magic had spoken to him about considering the ramifications of his actions instead of impulsively reacting to the situation at hand.

"It was one of the major differences between us," Magic said.

The summer after Thomas, who had just finished his sophomore year at Indiana, declared he would turn professional, Magic invited him to Lansing. Magic helped Isiah prepare for the pro game, just as Norm Nixon and Julius Erving had done for him.

Their off-season workouts became a tradition, along with annual visits with Aguirre to an amusement park in suburban Detroit. They flew to Hawaii together twice a summer: the first time to vacation with their girlfriends (later wives) and the second time to train. In between, they met in Chicago, Lansing, or Atlanta to push each other with new workout routines.

Aguirre, Thomas, and Johnson woke up each morning and ran four to five miles. They chugged up hills, lifted weights, ran through cardio drills, then went to the gym and did three-man weaves, full-court, and 1-on-1 competitions, also full-court.

After they were done, they sat in the gym and traded stories, bragging about their accomplishments and dreaming aloud of winning it all.

When Magic built his mansion in Bel Air, he nicknamed his guest quarters "the Isiah Room." If the Lakers were on the road and the Pistons were coming to town to play the Clippers, Johnson would leave Isiah the keys to his house or have his car waiting for him at the team hotel.

"He was like my brother," Johnson said.

But now the brothers stood poised to win a championship, and one of them was going to come up empty.

Isiah and Magic shared a pregame kiss before Game 1 as a sign of their respect and affection for each other. Bird, watching from his home in Brookline, Massachusetts, turned away, disgusted.

"I wanted to throw up," he said. "It was all show. I knew how bad they both wanted to win."

Pat Riley wasn't too happy about the public display either. He wanted the proper focus from his star, and he was concerned he wasn't going to get it. Michael Cooper, Magic's oldest friend on the Lakers, expressed similar doubts. Those questions lingered as Detroit stole a Game 1 win behind Adrian Dantley's 34 points. Before each game, Magic and Isiah reenacted their kiss, but at a price. Teammates in both locker rooms began wondering where their leaders' loyalties lay.

Those questions were answered in Game 4. The Pistons had emulated their enemies, the Celtics, by employing a physical style against the Lakers. But the difference, as Magic saw it, was that Boston hit you once on every play and Detroit hit you twice. Mahorn would deliver the hard foul, then Laimbeer would deliver another blow after the whistle had already blown.

"It was a line you shouldn't cross, and the Pistons crossed it all the time," Magic said.

Johnson was getting leveled every time he drove to the hoop, and he was growing tired of it. In the fourth quarter of Game 4, with

Detroit enjoying a sizable lead, Magic was tomahawked by two Pistons at the same time. It was time to make somebody pay.

Magic chose Isiah. As Thomas drove to the basket, Magic delivered his friend what he called a Laimbeer special — an elbow to the kidney. Thomas popped up, threw the ball at Magic, and went for his throat. The two friends raised their fists, ready to come to blows, before they were hastily separated. After the game, Magic told reporters he hadn't singled out Thomas and was planning on fouling the next Detroit player who drove to the basket.

"But that wasn't true," Magic admitted later. "I did target Isiah. Pat Riley had questioned me in front of the guys whether I'd take him out. I needed to show them I was willing to do it."

Before Game 5, Isiah and Magic again exchanged a pregame kiss, but suddenly the ritual was an uncomfortable formality. Both stars were still seething over their scuffle, and neither had picked up the phone to clarify what had happened.

Thomas responded with one of the gutsiest performances of his career in Game 6. He suffered a badly sprained ankle during the game but still returned to pump in 25 third-quarter points to keep his team afloat in the series. After the game, he left on crutches.

Isiah was hobbling badly in Game 7, and Magic exploited his lack of mobility. The Lakers became the first team since the 1968 and 1969 Celtics to win back-to-back championships. In the final seconds of the Finals, with LA up three points and Thomas hoping to sink a miracle three-pointer to prolong the action, he and Magic accidentally collided at midcourt. There was no call, no foul, no shot.

Johnson and Thomas did not speak after the game. There were no trips to Hawaii that summer, no shopping sprees in New York, no workouts in Lansing, no marathon phone calls. Thomas's son was born during the playoffs, and Magic never even went over to see him.

"I saw things differently," Magic said. "Our relationship was changing."

Almost immediately after the title was secure, Riley was gunning for a three-peat, even securing a patent on the phrase. He was obsessed with the Lakers legacy he was creating, and his approach with his players became even more controlling. Riley had become a national celebrity and was handsomely paid for it. He had more endorsements than most of his players, with Magic as the notable exception. His relationships with Cooper, Scott, and Worthy deteriorated. Johnson remained a Riley loyalist, but often he was a party of one.

Although LA advanced to the championship against the Pistons again in 1989 with a perfect 11–0 postseason record to that point, Riley made a tactical error. He took his team to Santa Barbara for a mini–training camp before the Finals and put his guys through two-a-day practices. Byron Scott tore his hamstring prior to Game 1, and Magic pulled up lame with a hamstring injury in Game 2. The Pistons swept the Lakers, ruining Kareem Abdul-Jabbar's final season.

Kareem retired in 1989, and the Lakers tried to make do with Thompson, Orlando Woolridge, and a young Serbian rookie named Vlade Divac in the middle. As Riley's demands increased, his players' patience wore thin. The Lakers still won 63 games in 1989–90, but in the second round of the playoffs against the Phoenix Suns, the tension between the coach and his players bubbled to the surface. The Lakers had difficulty containing point guard Kevin Johnson and were allowing journeyman Mark West to shred them inside. After a Game 4 loss that left the Lakers trailing in the series 3–1, Riley exploded in the team dressing room.

"Usually his outbursts were orchestrated," Magic said. "This time it wasn't."

As Riley disparaged his club for not getting back on defense, not following the game plan, and repeatedly allowing Kevin Johnson in the lane, he looked and saw a sea of blank faces. His players weren't listening. They had tuned him out.

Riley turned and slugged the mirror in frustration, shattering the glass and gashing his hand. As the blood began flowing down the sleeve of his custom-tailored white shirt, Riley walked out and closed the door. No one said a word. The Lakers silently dressed and exited to the bus, where they sat and waited. After 20 minutes, their coach took his customary place in the front seat with his hand heavily wrapped in gauze.

"It was never discussed," Magic said. "We couldn't discuss it. That would require Pat admitting he had a weakness, and he wasn't going to let us see that."

Two days later, the Suns ended the Lakers' season. Riley poked around aimlessly in his office behind his Brentwood home, the same room where he used to pore over Boston game film and excitedly call Magic at three in the morning when he discovered a new nugget on how to stop the Celtics.

Johnson was still his leader, still his trusted friend, but even Magic, he sensed, had grown weary of his coaching style. Once he realized that, Riley knew his days were numbered.

Owner Jerry Buss called his coach in and told him he thought it was best if he relieved Riley of his duties. It was an emotional meeting, with Buss thanking Riley profusely for his dedication to the Lakers and providing him with a handsome financial settlement. Buss agreed that Riley's exit would be worded as a "mutual parting of the ways."

Magic heard his doorbell ring and was surprised to see his coach standing in the foyer.

"Buck, I'm leaving," Riley said. "The guys aren't responding. It's time for me to go."

Tears formed around Riley's eyes. For the next hour, he sat on Magic's deck and wept.

They talked about the season that had just ended so badly and the ones that ended so much differently. They laughed at Riley's thinly veiled motivational techniques and lamented the passing of the days when their lives revolved around Larry Bird and the Boston Celtics.

Magic knew Riley was making the proper decision. He had lost the players, and even his treasured relationship with Jerry West had suffered. When his coach talked about a future without the Lakers, Magic wondered aloud if there was such a thing.

On the day Pat Riley's resignation was announced, Larry Bird felt a tinge of sadness he couldn't quite explain. Even though he had never played for Riley, Bird believed he was the best tactician he'd ever seen. Riley's innovative responses to Boston's offensive sets had earned Bird's grudging admiration, although he never — ever — admitted it publicly.

"So he's gone," Bird thought. "That's good for us."

Riley's departure turned out to be immaterial to Bird and the Celtics. Although neither Larry Bird nor Magic Johnson would have ever believed it at the time, they had already played in the final championship of their careers.

9

★ ★ ★

NOVEMBER 7, 1991

Los Angeles, California

YOU'VE GOT TO CALL Larry," Magic Johnson told his agent, Lon Rosen.

"Right away," Rosen assured him.

"Make sure you reach him before the announcement," Magic persisted. "I don't want him to find out about this on the news."

For 11 days Johnson had been harboring a harrowing secret: he had been diagnosed with HIV, the virus that causes AIDS. The condition was detected during a routine blood test, and Magic spent the next week meeting with specialists, undergoing additional examinations, and mulling his options. His wife Cookie was pregnant with the couple's first child, and although initial tests indicated she was not HIV-positive, it would be months before the baby could be pronounced risk-free with certainty.

How could he do this to her? He loved her and had planned to spend the rest of his life with her since his freshman year of college when he spotted her dancing at a nightclub in East Lansing, Michigan. But Magic couldn't commit. He had been swept up in the Hollywood scene, intoxicated by the beautiful, desirable women who propositioned him in the parking lot before games, in the hotel lobby after road games, in the stands *during* games. He broke off his engagement with Cookie twice, hurt her deeply, but then, finally, provided her with the wedding of her dreams. And now, some eight weeks after the day he pledged to love her forever, he had placed their happiness — their lives — in jeopardy.

Although Johnson had not contracted AIDS, only the virus that causes it, he knew so little about his condition that in conversations with Rosen he mistakenly kept referring to his illness as the fatal disease that was just beginning to creep into the public consciousness. An AIDS diagnosis would be an explosive story once the public became aware of it, and Magic wanted to keep it quiet until he knew all the facts. He needed to give his wife time to process what was happening. Cookie was frightened and upset and fretted about how she and her husband would be received once the news hit.

No secrets are safe for long, particularly in Los Angeles. Magic planned to hold a press conference on Friday, November 8, but the morning before, a reporter from KFWB, an all-news station in Los Angeles, called Rosen and told him they had learned Johnson had AIDS and planned to retire.

It was time to go public. Magic had already shared his condition with a small cadre of people — his parents, Cookie's parents, owner Jerry Buss, general manager Jerry West, assistant GM Mitch Kupchak, and commissioner David Stern — but none of LA's players had been apprised of what was ailing their star.

Magic compiled a short list of people who needed to be notified immediately: his former coach Pat Riley, now with the New York Knicks; his confidant Isiah Thomas; talk-show host and close friend Arsenio Hall; and former teammates Michael Cooper, Kareem Abdul-Jabbar, and Kurt Rambis.

It was also critical, Magic stressed, for Jordan and Bird to be contacted as soon as possible. Those two would be asked to comment more than any other current NBA player on his startling personal crisis.

As he ticked off the names, Magic paused to consider how each of them would react. They would be stunned, he was certain. Would they also be disappointed? Disgusted? Would it change the level of respect he enjoyed with each of them?

"You don't have a lot of time to think about it, because everything is happening so fast," Magic said. "But at some point I was wondering, 'What will Larry think? What will Michael think?'"

The unpleasant task of informing them fell to Rosen. He called Celtics public relations director Jeff Twiss and asked him to contact Larry with an urgent message. Twiss dialed Bird's number at his Brookline, Massachusetts, home shortly after one o'clock in the afternoon East Coast time with no expectation that Bird would pick up.

He didn't. After the Celtics were throttled the night before by Jordan and the Chicago Bulls, Bird had come home from practice that morning cranky, tired, and hurting. His Airness had scored 44 on Boston, and while Bird (30 points, 9 assists) had acquitted himself admirably, his chronically injured back had flared up, preventing him from sleeping most of the night. In fact, many nights the only way Bird could alleviate the searing pain was to sleep on the floor. When Dinah answered the phone call from Twiss, Bird was napping.

Dinah poked her head in to wake him.

"You need to call Lon Rosen," she said. "It sounds important."

Bird pulled himself up and dialed the number.

"Hey, Lon, what's going on?" Bird asked.

"Larry, I'm just going to tell you, because we don't have a lot of time," Rosen said. "Magic has the HIV virus. He's going to announce his retirement this afternoon. He wanted you to know before the news hit."

Bird grabbed on to the wall to steady himself. He wasn't sure what he was expecting — an endorsement opportunity perhaps? — but this revelation literally took his breath away.

"I felt like someone had sucked the air out of my lungs," Bird said. "I had this terrible empty feeling, like how I felt when my dad took his own life."

Rosen waited on the other line for a response. He was already growing accustomed to the chilling effect his phone calls were having on some of the biggest stars in the game. Moments earlier, he had elicited a similar, shocked reaction from Jordan.

"What can I do? What does he need?" Bird asked Rosen, struggling to control his voice.

"He's doing okay," Rosen answered. "You'll hear from him in a couple of days."

"I need to talk to him now," Bird said. "Can I call him?"

Magic was at his Beverly Hills home attempting to pick out a tasteful suit and an "upbeat tie" for his press conference when Bird reached him.

"Magic, I'm so sorry," Bird said.

"No, it's going to be all right," Magic said. "I have to take some medication and do some different stuff, but I'm going to fight this thing."

The two superstars talked briefly. If Johnson was reeling from his diagnosis, he adeptly concealed it.

"So," Magic said, "how are the Celtics looking?"

Bird was momentarily speechless.

"Ah, hell," he replied. "We'll probably kick your ass."

When Bird hung up the phone, he turned to Dinah and reported, "He was trying to cheer *me* up."

For the next three hours, Bird lay on the bed in his room, ruminating on his complex relationship with his lifelong rival — and, in recent years, his friend. Their journey had elicited a range of emotions: jealousy over Magic's NCAA championship in '79, euphoria over beating him head-to-head in '84, determination in '85 after the Lakers stole back the title, and grudging respect in '87 when it became clear that Magic had truly reached his peak.

Bird had devoted his entire career to establishing the upper hand over Earvin Johnson and the Los Angeles Lakers, and suddenly none of it mattered.

"My God," Bird said to Dinah, "Magic's gonna die."

The official word was that Magic Johnson caught the flu. In reality, the life of the Lakers star began unraveling shortly after he took a blood test for a team life insurance policy in early October 1991. The team was about to leave for Paris to play in the McDonald's Open when Rosen was notified by the Lakers that there was a problem with Magic's results. The insurance company needed Johnson to sign a document to release his medical file to the team and his physician, Dr. Michael Mellman.

When Rosen called the insurance company to inquire why Johnson's results had been flagged, they were tightlipped.

"Is it safe for him to play?" Rosen asked.

"I can't discuss Mr. Johnson's results with you," the insurance man answered.

The response left Rosen skittish. The previous March a college star named Hank Gathers had collapsed and died while playing for Loyola Marymount. A subsequent autopsy found that Gathers had suffered from a heart condition called hypertrophic cardiomyopathy. What if the insurance company had detected a similar problem during Magic's tests?

"I need to know if it's safe for him to play," Rosen persisted. "If he drops dead like Hank Gathers, we'll sue."

"I'm sorry, sir," the insurance agent replied. "Mr. Johnson's results are confidential. We need that release."

As soon as he hung up the phone, Rosen contacted Magic's personal physician, Mellman, who was as perplexed as Rosen about the results.

"It could be anything," Mellman told him, "but every physical I've given him has shown that he's fine. He looks healthy to me. Let's wait and see."

Johnson flew to Paris unconcerned about what he dismissed as a minor clerical detail. On October 18, the Lakers trounced CSP Limoges 132–101, then beat Spain's Joventut Badalona 116–114 the next day. Rosen faxed a signed release to the insurance company from Paris, but they did not accept it as an official document.

"We need this done in person," the official explained.

Magic arrived back in Los Angeles on October 21 feeling jet-lagged and fatigued. The Lakers were scheduled to play an exhibition game against the Utah Jazz in Salt Lake City four days later, but Johnson was dragging and discussed skipping the trip with assistant GM Kupchak. His former teammate urged him to play. Although the Jazz game had sold out, there were still tickets remaining for the next game in Vancouver, and they'd have no chance of a full house without Magic there.

"Besides, there are thousands of Utah fans that bought tickets to the game just to see you," Kupchak reminded him.

"All right, I'll go," Magic said. "But limit my minutes, okay? I'm beat."

Before he left for Salt Lake, a representative from the insurance company drove to his home and witnessed him signing the release form. Instead of overnighting the document via Federal Express, the representative inexplicably sent it via regular mail.

On the afternoon of October 25, shortly after he checked into the team hotel in Salt Lake City, Johnson received a phone call from Mellman, who had finally been mailed the results of his blood test.

"Earvin, you need to come back to Los Angeles immediately," Mellman said.

"I just landed in Utah," Johnson protested.

"This can't wait," Mellman said.

Rosen hastily arranged for Johnson to catch a Delta Airlines flight back to LA that landed at 5:30 P.M. He picked Magic up at the airport and drove him directly to Mellman's office. By then, Rosen feared the worst: cancer, a serious heart condition, a fatal disease.

Johnson was more curious than worried. A heart murmur maybe? Some kind of knee trouble?

"I'm a positive guy by nature," Magic said. "I wasn't thinking, 'Oh, no, something is really wrong.' I felt so good, I couldn't imagine I was sick."

But when Mellman finally opened the door and waved him into his office without any of his usual cheerfulness, Johnson quickly realized the news was dire.

The HIV-positive diagnosis was equally shocking and surprising.

Magic did not initially react; he sat transfixed for a moment, as if he were intently watching a dramatic movie in which the plot was about to be revealed.

"Honestly, I think I was numb," he said.

Within seconds, he had a flood of questions: How did I get it? When did I get it? What does it mean? Am I going to die? What about my career? What about Cookie? The last question left him breathless. Only then did the scope of the somber diagnosis finally register with him.

"Oh, no," Magic said. "What about Cookie? She's pregnant."

Mellman recommended an additional blood test to make sure the results were accurate and advised him to have Cookie tested immediately. From there, Magic needed to meet with HIV specialists to chart a course of treatment. All of this would take time. Hence, the "flu" alibi was hatched.

"How am I going to tell her?" Magic asked Rosen as they left Mellman's office.

The two men stopped at an Italian restaurant in Santa Monica to have dinner and map out the immediate future. Magic wondered aloud if he would have to retire. He agonized over what he would say to Cookie, who was at home, still unaware that anything was amiss. As the waiter took their order, he handed Johnson a note from the adjacent table. They were planning an AIDS fundraiser and were hoping Magic would be willing to speak at their event. Johnson spent the rest of dinner absent-mindedly turning over their business card in his hands.

On his way home from the restaurant, Magic called his wife to tell her he'd been sent home from Utah.

"What's wrong?" she asked.

"I'll be home in a few minutes, and we'll talk all about it," he said calmly.

Cookie hung up the phone, her hand shaking.

"In my mind I was thinking, 'He's going to tell me he has AIDS,'" she said, "because that was my worst possible fear."

The moment Earvin "Magic" Johnson stepped into his house he knew his wife had already figured out his news was devastating.

"She knew me too well," he said.

He told her what Dr. Mellman had said and then fell into her arms. Cookie experienced a range of emotions: shock, fear, anger, disappointment, concern.

"At that time, any discussion of AIDS meant you were going to die," Cookie said. "I thought my heart was going to jump out of my chest. For a minute, I felt like I was going to pass out."

She sat down and held her husband, and then did what she always did when she was frightened or in trouble: she prayed.

"I wouldn't blame you if you left," said Magic through his tears.

"Are you crazy?" Cookie answered. "I am staying. God will get us through this."

Her faith did not completely overrule the terror of what lay in front of them. She fretted about her unborn child, about what the future held for her husband. The next morning Cookie went to visit her minister, the Reverend Rick Hunter, and he told her, "We will pray, and ask for a miracle."

Mellman drove to the Johnsons' home and took blood from Cookie and Magic. He retested the Lakers star's blood under the assumed name "Frank Kelly" in order to protect his privacy.

As the days droned on, Johnson's absence from the Lakers became more and more difficult to explain. Vitti, the trainer, who traveled with the team on the road and was a witness to Magic's cavalier lifestyle, guessed immediately what Johnson was facing. He was sworn to secrecy, which was the easy part. The more difficult task for the emotional Vitti was to prevent himself from breaking down every time he saw his friend.

The so-called flu that Magic was battling made no sense to a keen group of veteran reporters or a seasoned group of Lakers players. A week after Magic was summoned home from Salt Lake, Lakers coach Mike Dunleavy, who lived around the corner from Rosen, dropped by the agent's house unannounced.

"Lon," he said, "I need to know what the hell is going on."

"I can't tell you yet," Rosen answered, "but it's not good."

"I already know that," Dunleavy said. "Every time I ask Vitti about it he starts crying."

On Wednesday, November 6, Magic met with Dr. David Ho, an expert on HIV and AIDS who had been researching the disease since 1981. The second blood test confirmed the diagnosis. Ho recommended that Johnson stop playing basketball.

The doctor's reasons were sound. It was too early to determine how much Johnson's immune system had been compromised. There was no way of telling how Magic would react to AZT (zidovudine), the medication he planned to prescribe. At the time, AZT, which had demonstrated the ability to help prevent HIV from spreading, was the only FDA-approved drug available. Normally that painstaking approval process takes anywhere from seven to ten years, but the FDA pushed AZT through in twenty months under pressure from the AIDS community, which stood by helplessly while thousands of people suffered an agonizing death without treatment.

AZT was not a perfect antidote. Its side effects included nausea, vomiting, diarrhea, anemia, and, in some cases, evidence of severe muscle atrophy. In subsequent years, other, less toxic drugs would prove to be a far better course of treatment. But in 1991 it was AZT or nothing.

Dr. Ho explained to Magic that he needed to alter his diet, get plenty of rest, and limit his physical activity. Although there was no hard evidence that playing basketball would compromise his health, there was also no blueprint to chart how a full, rigorous NBA season would affect an HIV-positive patient. Magic, as far as Ho knew, was the first.

Although he was aware that his career was in jeopardy from the moment Mellman handed him the manila envelope with the results of his blood test, Magic couldn't completely grasp why he shouldn't play. He had plenty of energy and no discernible symptoms. The disease was baffling to him. If it was so deadly, why did he feel so alive?

While he awaited the results of his new round of tests, he dabbled at the side baskets in practice, shooting lightly while the Lakers went through their regular daily routine. At least twice, he contemplated jumping into the scrimmages before he retreated to the sidelines again.

It was unlike Johnson to miss so much time. He put a premium on the team's workout sessions, attacking them with the same enthusiasm that he would a playoff game against the Celtics. Byron Scott couldn't understand what was taking Magic so long. His friend didn't look ill, although he did show up one day with a small wrap on his arm, an indication that someone had drawn blood. When Scott noticed the bandage, he couldn't resist a jab at his expense.

"Hey, Buck, is your arm too sore to shoot?" Scott said jovially. "Since when are you too sick to play?"

"I've got to wait until the doctors clear me," Magic curtly replied.

The exchange left Scott suspicious and Magic uneasy. Johnson was uncomfortable with deceiving his friends. He wanted to tell Scott that he was sick, and frightened, but he remained silent.

By the morning of November 7, that no longer was possible. Dunleavy, his face ashen, interrupted practice and told his players to listen carefully to instructions from Vitti. Choking back sobs, Vitti told them to walk directly to their cars and drive straight to the Forum. They were not to speak with anyone. Those who didn't comply would be fined $20,000.

"Hurry," Vitti said.

It was too late. The story had leaked. Several media outlets breathlessly — and erroneously — reported that Magic Johnson had AIDS. As he drove to the Forum, Worthy turned on the radio and heard that horrifying, albeit inaccurate, information.

"I almost went off the road," said Worthy. "I was in such a daze, I don't even remember how I got there."

Magic mistakenly tuned into the urgent news of his demise on his car radio. Although he had been living with the diagnosis for nearly two weeks, it was jarring to hear it broadcast publicly. His private life was about to be dissected and analyzed and scrutinized. When the man who had captivated the NBA with his infectious smile walked into the Lakers dressing room — his sanctuary — all he could muster was a feeble wave.

"Hey, fellas," he said, his voice cracking.

As he stood before his teammates, who were overcome with emotion, Magic broke down. The Lakers were his family, his livelihood, the center of his world. And quite abruptly, that world had collapsed. He explained the diagnosis and the course of treatment. He told them how truly sorry he was for letting them down. And then he grieved with them, abandoning his original intent of maintaining a stoic resolve.

Johnson walked around the locker room hugging each Laker individually. More than one of them stiffened as he approached. He whispered something private in each of their ears, and when he came to Scott, his most trusted friend on the team, he squeezed him extra tightly and whispered, "Don't worry, B, I'll be all right. I'm going to beat this."

"I know, Earv," Scott responded. "If anyone can beat it, it's you."

"I said that, but I didn't believe it," Scott admitted. "From what little I knew about the disease, Magic had been given a death sentence."

One hour later, dressed impeccably in a dark blue suit, crisp white shirt, and an "optimistic" multicolored tie with bright hues, Magic walked up to the same podium where he had accepted his MVP trophy a year and a half earlier. Flanked by Commissioner Stern, Dr. Mellman, Lon Rosen, Jerry West, Jerry Buss, Kareem, Rambis, and Cookie, the NBA's ambassador swallowed hard and told himself, "Remember. Hold it together."

Moments before, Rosen had quickly reviewed what Magic should say. "I'm just going to tell them," Johnson said. "I'm going to tell them I have AIDS."

"But, Earvin," Rosen said, "you don't have AIDS. You have the virus that causes AIDS. Make sure you make that clear. There's a big difference between the two."

Though the press conference was overflowing with reporters, friends, teammates, and Lakers officials, an eerie silence permeated the room. It had the feeling, Buss noted later, of a funeral procession.

"Good afternoon," Johnson said. "Because of the HIV virus that I have obtained, I will have to retire from the Lakers today. I just want to make clear, first of all, that I do not have the AIDS disease. I know a lot of you want to know that. I have the HIV virus. My wife is fine. She's negative, so no problem with her.

"I plan on living for a long time, bugging you guys like I always have. So you'll see me around."

Johnson outlined his plans to be an HIV spokesman. He preached the need to practice safe sex. He was somber but composed. West, his eyes bloodshot from a morning of grieving, marveled at Johnson's ability to contain his emotions.

"Sometimes we think only gay people can get [AIDS], or 'It's not going to happen to me,'" Magic told the rapt audience. "Here I am, saying it can happen to everybody. Even me — Magic Johnson."

The point guard who had come to define the Lakers — and the NBA — stood facing his audience. West's shoulders heaved. Buss teetered forward, his knees buckling. The only reason the Lakers owner didn't collapse was that an alert Abdul-Jabbar grabbed Buss and pulled him upright before he toppled over.

Back in Lansing, Michigan, Christine Johnson summoned her children to the Middle Street home where young Earvin was raised. She asked them to join hands and bow their heads, then told them their brother had been diagnosed with HIV. The Johnson family knelt down in their cramped family room and cried and prayed together. Christine informed her family that she had hired grief counselors to talk with each of them. She warned them that the world of Magic Johnson was about to change. There would be supporters, but there would also be detractors and a hungry horde of media people trying to advance the story.

"We are a family. We will stick together," she advised her children.

"If any of these people say anything, I'm going to crack them upside their heads," said Magic's big brother Larry, his voice quaking.

237

Most of Magic's friends learned of his condition from his live press conference broadcast on CNN. All of them remember exactly where they were the moment they discovered Magic was HIV-positive.

Mychal Thompson was playing professional basketball in Caserta, Italy, and working on his post moves when former Seton Hall star Anthony Avent grabbed Thompson by the sleeve and misinformed him that Johnson had AIDS and would likely be dead within a year.

"Even my Italian teammates understood the magnitude of that news," Thompson said. "We were devastated."

Former Michigan State star Greg Kelser was in a hotel room in Denver preparing for a broadcast between the Nuggets and the Minnesota Timberwolves for Prime Sports Network when his wife called him and told him to turn on the television. "I was stunned," Kelser said. "It was my first broadcast, and I had been preparing for days, but when we went on the air, all I could talk about was Magic."

When Pat Riley was informed that Johnson had tested HIV-positive, he immediately felt ill. Riley was a pragmatic, solutions-oriented person, but as he sat in his office with his stomach churning, he couldn't think of a single way to fix this.

"I'm not coaching tonight," he told Rosen through his tears.

Rosen explained that Magic wanted — *needed* — the people he loved to carry on as usual. "If you don't," Rosen explained, "he'll think he's dying."

Riley agreed to coach that evening, but moments before the Knicks and Magic tipped off another otherwise meaningless regular season game, Riley asked the 19,763 fans in attendance to join him in a moment of silence. Then, through choked pauses, he read the Lord's Prayer.

As word of Magic's condition spread, Bird's phone began ringing incessantly. After an hour, he finally thought to take it off the hook. The world wanted to hear from Magic's most ardent competitor, but number 33 was in no mood to share his feelings.

"I didn't want to talk to anyone," Bird said.

Twenty-four hours later, on November 8, the Celtics hosted the Atlanta Hawks at Boston Garden. Bird engaged in his usual pre-game routine — stretches to loosen his back, laps in the corridors of the stands, jump shots from eight different spots on the floor — but he slogged through the motions without his trademark intensity.

"For the first time in my life," Bird said, "I didn't feel like playing."

The Hawks notched a rare 100–95 win at the Garden. Bird scored 17 points with 9 rebounds and 6 assists in 40 minutes of playing time, but he turned the ball over 4 times and was clearly laboring.

"Everything that went on that night was foggy," Bird said. "I played, but I didn't play. Everybody wanted to talk to me about it. The only guy I wanted to talk to was Magic, and I had to wait. I figured he had an awful lot on his plate."

Johnson was inundated with letters, phone calls, telegrams, and flowers. Some wished him well; others chided him for the choices he'd made that put his wife and unborn baby in jeopardy. For every fruit basket and inspirational message there were insults and blackmail attempts.

Magic lived in a gated community, so reporters and gawking fans were temporarily kept at bay, yet the tabloids remained undeterred. Johnson changed his unlisted phone number, but within 48 hours the *National Enquirer* was already dialing the new number. Reporters rifled through the trash in Rosen's yard, searching for clues to his client's personal life.

Magic and Cookie flew to Maui with some friends to a private home overlooking the ocean. They were having dinner, with the French doors open, when they heard a rustling noise outside. Their friend Michael Stennis went out to investigate: a photographer sprang from behind the shrub and sprinted off — but not before he snapped one final shot.

"It seemed like every bush we walked by had a lens sticking out of it," Magic said. "Cookie was upset about it. But I wouldn't let it stop us. I told her, 'Let's live our lives.'"

Johnson's approach to his illness was proactive. He couldn't change the diagnosis, so he set about changing the way HIV-positive patients were viewed. The day after his announcement Magic went on *The Arsenio Hall Show* and received a prolonged standing ovation when he walked onto the set. When he assured the live audience that he wasn't a homosexual, they burst into applause again. Gay activists across the country cringed. Johnson's diagnosis had given them hope that the public might finally recognize the AIDS epidemic that was sweeping the world. Magic had enough star power to make a difference, but not if he planned on presenting himself as an isolated case. When Johnson received a barrage of feedback from the AIDS community after his appearance with Arsenio, he pledged to embrace the plight of homosexuals with AIDS rather than separate himself from them.

"The gay community misunderstood what happened there," Magic said. "I wasn't putting down gays. I was asked a question, and I answered it. I told them, 'Don't be upset with me. I'm trying to help gays — and everyone else with HIV — by promoting research, getting tested, and finding a cure.'"

His message that heterosexuals were at risk for HIV infection was carefully monitored in one segment of the population: the NBA, where many athletes besides Johnson feared that their sexual encounters had left them at risk.

"Right after we found out about Magic, a bunch of us ran out and got tested too," Worthy said. "It was one of the most traumatic things I've ever been through."

Almost immediately there were whispers and innuendo about Magic's sexuality. Rumors persisted that he had engaged in a relationship with a man, or in a three-way encounter with a man and a woman. Magic felt confident that his friends would dismiss these falsehoods for him, but then was distraught to learn from Rosen and other NBA friends that Isiah Thomas had called asking curious questions. According to Rosen, Thomas told him, "I keep hearing Magic is gay."

"C'mon, Isiah, you know Earvin better than anyone," Rosen responded.

"I know, but I don't know what he's doing when he's out there in LA."

"Isiah kept questioning people about it," Magic said. "I couldn't believe that. Everyone else — Byron, Arsenio, Michael, Larry — they were all supporting me. And the one guy I thought I could count on had all these doubts. It was like he kicked me in the stomach."

"Of all the things that happened, I think that hurt Earvin the most," Cookie said. "But we had no choice but to move on from people like that. Whenever something like that happened, I reminded him, 'They just don't get it.'"

Johnson needed some guidance to navigate his way through this monumental personal crisis. Lon Rosen contacted Elizabeth Glaser, an AIDS activist who contracted the virus from a tainted blood transfusion following the birth of her daughter Ariel, and she was happy to provide it.

Glaser, whose husband, Paul Michael Glaser, was the star of the popular television series *Starsky and Hutch*, unknowingly passed the disease on to her daughter and son Jake. After Ariel died at the age of seven, Glaser helped found the Pediatric AIDS Foundation and became a tireless advocate for the rights of infected patients.

"I didn't know anyone with AIDS," Magic said. "She helped me wrap my mind around it. She was very sick when I met her. She told me, 'You are going to be here a long time. It's too late for me, but not for you.'"

While Glaser conceded it would not be an easy road, she implored Magic and Cookie to assume a leadership role in educating the country about HIV and AIDS.

"You don't have time to wallow in this," Glaser told them. "You have to fight."

It wasn't just about raising money. It was about raising awareness. Most people (including Magic at the outset) didn't distinguish AIDS from HIV. It was important for the public to understand that neither disease could be transmitted by sharing a cup, or hugging someone who was infected, or coming in contact with their sweat.

The last point was of critical importance to NBA players, who were still reeling from the downfall of one of their most notable stars.

"We were starved for information," said Rambis. "How did it happen? Is it contagious? Nobody knew the answers. What about sweat? What if we bump heads? Guys were scared. Really scared."

When Johnson returned from Hawaii, he showed up at the Forum out of habit. Although he was no longer on the roster, he dressed in his practice gear to get some shooting in and do some drills before practice. When some of his teammates wandered in early, he expected an enthusiastic greeting. Instead, Magic was met with polite small talk before the players hurriedly moved to another basket. When he tried to coax a couple of them into a game of 1-on-1, there were no takers.

"It took me a while to realize they didn't want my sweat on their body," Magic said.

Only Byron Scott embraced him when he walked in. Only Scott engaged in a meaningful conversation with him and lingered, asking, "Are you feeling okay? Are you taking care of yourself?"

"I wanted to shout at those other guys, 'Hey, I'm one of the boys, remember?'" Magic said. "I won't lie to you. It crushed me for a minute."

Magic, the rare superstar who actually liked to walk freely among his fans, noted subtle changes in the way he was treated. Suddenly, people weren't clamoring for autographs. Fans backed away when he passed by. Friends kept him at arm's length. Even his signature high-fives were an issue. People didn't want to touch him because they were terrified they'd get infected. For the first time in his life, nobody wanted a piece of the Magic Man.

"I'm a warm guy," Magic said. "I'm a hugger. I'm a person who wants to greet people, and when someone pulled away, it was difficult. I kept telling myself, 'You have to respect what they're feeling, because they don't know.' And for a while I could do that. But when my teammates shied away from me — and to be honest, most of them did — that got me a little down."

Elizabeth Glaser warned him that he would experience bouts of isolation. Her daughter was excluded from play dates and birthday parties because of her condition. Johnson nodded sympathetically when she shared those anecdotes, but he naively thought it would be different for him. He was Magic Johnson. He had difficulty believing people would avert their stare when he walked into a room or cross the road so they wouldn't get too close — until it happened.

"I know those kinds of things hurt him to the core," Scott said.

Lakers forward A. C. Green, a deeply Christian man, had always preached abstinence and warned his teammates that promiscuity was a sin. After Magic contracted HIV, Green told him he would pray for him. Green never chided Magic with "I told you so," but the Lakers star knew how he felt. Following Magic's diagnosis, A.C. was distant, aloof. Although he did not publicly condemn Johnson's choices, Green did urge him to include abstinence as part of his educational platform on HIV and AIDS.

"Even as I sit here, I don't have a problem with A.C.," Magic said. "He has a right to his opinions and his beliefs. He has lived his life a certain way, and I couldn't be mad at him when he said, 'See? This is what I'm talking about. You can't run around with all these women. Look what happened to Magic.'

"At least I knew where I stood with A.C. He never went behind my back. The so-called friends that did that to me were the ones that hurt me the most."

In the first months after his diagnosis, Earvin wondered what his teammates were thinking. James Worthy, who won three championships with Magic, was always a quiet man. He became even more withdrawn after Johnson's diagnosis. Initially Magic was devastated by his teammate's silence, but over time he came to understand that many people, Worthy among them, didn't know what to say — so they said nothing.

"James is a caring guy," Magic said. "But he kept his emotions in check. I'm sure he was sitting there thinking, 'What does this all mean?' It was tough for him to see me. I scared him."

Although most of Johnson's public appearances elicited tremendous support, it didn't fool him into believing the world was ready to embrace an HIV-positive icon. Each time a stranger — or a friend — backed away, it was another reminder of the stigma he carried. When he went to a comedy show, entertainer Damon Wayans performed a five-minute skit ridiculing Magic, HIV, and his lifestyle without knowing Johnson was in the audience.

The slights strengthened Johnson's resolve to shatter some of the stereotypes regarding infected people. Although most of his friends were queasy about discussing his illness and the AIDS epidemic in detail, Magic kept talking about it.

"When I was diagnosed with HIV, there was no such thing as an open conversation about AIDS," Magic said. "People didn't want to discuss things like that. So my mission was, 'Okay, let me see if I can change a few perceptions,' because I could see the look on people's faces when they met me. They're wondering, 'Can I shake his hand? I know I don't want to hug him.' Those people made me feel like I had a disease, and I was trying to get past that."

A week after his appearance on Arsenio Hall's show, Magic received an invitation from President George H. W. Bush to join his National Commission on AIDS. Johnson was genuinely flattered and eager to get involved, but first he needed to do his homework. Glaser and another activist, Derek Hodl, pointed out the serious flaws in the Bush administration's approach to AIDS. They armed Magic with statistics to back up the assertion that the president wasn't doing enough. Johnson presented those facts and figures to Bush when he met with him at the White House. The president accepted the data, then presented Magic with a pair of cuff links and gave him a tour of the White House horseshoe pit. Johnson left hopeful that Bush and the commission would become a major player in the fight against AIDS and HIV.

The support did not materialize. While Magic forged ahead with an educational television program on HIV aimed at teenagers and young adults and wrote a book for the same target group, the president failed to adequately fund research or treatment for the disease. It soon became evident to Johnson that the commission was an impotent organization hamstrung by a president who simply had not made AIDS or HIV a priority.

"It was the worst thing I've ever been a part of," Magic said. "They were so hung up on their 'regulations,' we couldn't get anything accomplished."

The final indignity came in the fall of 1992 when Johnson toured a new hospice in Boston. The gleaming facility featured state-of-the-art equipment and twenty new beds for AIDS patients, but only two of those beds were filled.

"There were hundreds of people trying to get in there," Magic explained, "but the only way they could was to have the proper 'certification.' And they couldn't get the certification because of all this political red tape that Bush had created. I said to one of the committee members, 'Are you joking? These people are dying and they need these beds, and they're sitting here empty because you guys say they need some piece of paper?'

"I quit the next day."

On September 25, Johnson drafted a letter to President Bush and formally resigned from the commission, citing the president's lack of support in the fight against AIDS.

"I cannot in good conscience continue to serve on a commission whose important work is so utterly ignored by your administration," Magic wrote.

Johnson's resignation triggered headlines across the country. Bird smiled when he read Magic's comments in the morning paper.

"I was glad he quit," Bird said. "Sometimes people just want to use your name. It happens all the time with people like Magic and me. I knew how seriously he took his fight against AIDS. I figured he'd get a whole lot more done doing it his way."

The Magic Johnson Foundation was created in 1991 with the aim of raising awareness of AIDS and HIV by providing education, treatment, and research. One of the first donations he received was a sizable check from actor and devout Lakers fan Jack Nicholson. He was also genuinely touched to receive a personal check for $50,000 from Charlotte Hornets and Washington Bullets guard

Rex Chapman, who was not particularly close to Magic but who explained in his brief note that he felt "compelled to help with a wonderful cause."

The foundation would aid 135,000,000 people through community grants, education on HIV, scholarships, the opening of HIV/AIDS clinics, the provision of mobile testing units to underserved communities in Los Angeles, and a partnership program with Abbott Laboratories, called "I STAND With Magic," aimed at decreasing the alarming number of new HIV/AIDS infections in African-American communities.

The inroads the foundation made would be both rewarding and gratifying, but the foundation did not fill the void created by Magic's retirement.

Even though he would not play for the Lakers during the 1991–92 season, Johnson's name still appeared on the All-Star ballot, which had been printed months before his announcement that he was HIV-positive. As the votes began to be tallied, it was clear that the fans had every intention of voting Magic in as a starter for the Western Conference.

First, Johnson was touched. Then he was tempted. Then he was determined to play.

"I'll call Stern," Rosen said.

The commissioner had done his homework since Magic's diagnosis. He consulted specialists. He read every piece of literature he could find on the subject of HIV, including an English publication that purported to have found an incident of an English soccer player having become HIV-positive through skin-to-skin contact.

"We were being told that couldn't happen," Stern said. "It had to be an open sore to open sore, and even then it was unlikely. But that was the kind of information that was circulating at the time."

Stern supported Magic's return for the All-Star Game, although he initially balked at the notion that Johnson, who had not played a minute of the 1991–92 regular season, should be a starter.

"If he doesn't start, he's not coming," Rosen said.

The commissioner had been prepared to name Golden State

guard Tim Hardaway instead, but Hardaway graciously stepped aside to allow Magic to have center stage.

As news spread of Stern's decision to allow an HIV-positive athlete to compete among some of the world's most gifted athletes, his phone began ringing in earnest. Some of the calls were supportive, but an overwhelming number of them were skeptical, even outraged. Some NBA owners, concerned about their investment, weighed in with their protests.

"Aren't you getting a little too ahead of the curve on this?" asked one owner. "Why don't we do some polling?"

"No," Stern answered. "That doesn't work for me. I think we can affect the polls."

"Do you know what you are doing?" asked another powerful NBA owner. "Because this is some helluva risk you are taking."

Stern and Magic shared a common goal: they wanted to change the way the world looked at HIV. Yet Stern did not welcome Magic back to the fold without some trepidation. He knew that if his decision backfired, it could lead to serious consequences — for him, his league, and Magic Johnson. Although the backlash over Johnson's inclusion in the All-Star Game was heated and, at times, contentious, Stern successfully concealed most of that dissension from his discerning fan base.

"We were not aggressive in public," Stern said. "We didn't say anything. We were under fire from many of our own people, but the public didn't need to know that."

Magic was the first player to arrive at the 1992 All-Star Game in Orlando, Florida, and he brought along Glaser to speak to players and their wives about HIV. She debunked many of the myths about how the disease is transmitted and explained in detail the battle she and others were waging to stem the tide of AIDS. By the time she was done, many members of the audience were crying.

One particularly distraught woman approached Glaser after the program and confessed that her son was scheduled to present the MVP of the All-Star Game with a trophy.

"I'm so ashamed," she said in between sobs. "I told my son that he was, under no circumstances, to touch Magic Johnson if he won that award."

The wife of a prominent NBA star also walked up to Glaser after her moving presentation and told her, "I'm praying for you and your family. But I'm sorry, I still don't want my husband out there playing basketball with Magic Johnson."

On the surface, Magic's All-Star return was a heartwarming story with a fairy-tale ending. He scored 25 points and dished out 9 assists in a 153–113 win for the West and walked off with the MVP trophy. Yet there were underlying issues throughout the weekend that suggested a more complicated story line.

Philadelphia forward Charles Barkley, whom Magic counted among his NBA friends and who had petitioned to have his number changed to 32 in Johnson's honor once he was diagnosed, had no issue with Johnson's HIV status, but declared that it was unfair for a retired superstar to take away a spot from a younger player who might have been making his All-Star debut. The intimation: Johnson was being selfish.

Magic attempted to address that issue in a press conference two days before the game. "I have to be out there for myself," he conceded, "but for others too. Whether they have a disease or they are handicapped, they have to keep on living. That's what I'm doing — I'm living."

When he walked into the West locker room on All-Star Sunday, it was loaded with familiar faces: Clyde Drexler, Chris Mullin, Karl Malone, David Robinson, Hakeem Olajuwon, Otis Thorpe, Jeff Hornacek, Dikembe Mutombo, Dan Majerle, Hardaway, and Worthy. Yet something had changed. He was a visitor, not a regular. And, he feared, he was also a bit of a curiosity. After a decade of playing the role of the most dynamic personality in the room, suddenly Magic was the hesitant one.

The salutations when he entered the room were cordial, but awkward. Nobody jumped up to embrace him, and only a couple of players offered a handshake. He was a guest at his own party.

"Everybody was a little hands-off," Magic conceded. "You could sense it."

"The tension was unmistakable," David Robinson recalled. "It was a scary time. Players had gone behind Magic's back to get him out of the All-Star Game. They were afraid. They didn't know."

Robinson, sensing Magic's discomfort, made a point to walk up to him and offer his hand.

"I'm glad you're here," said the Admiral.

"I'm glad I'm here too," Johnson answered.

Before the game started, the two teams lined up opposite one another at center court. Isiah Thomas broke ranks with the East and crossed over to give Magic a hug. Soon most of the East squad followed suit, yet the player who truly eased the tension was Pistons forward Dennis Rodman, who vowed before the game to be aggressive with Johnson on the court.

Since Magic hadn't played all season, the expectation was that he would be treated delicately. Yet Johnson wanted no part of being a charity case. He worked out religiously in the weeks leading up to the game, telling Lon Rosen, "If they think I'm showing up just to make a couple of passes, they're wrong."

Rodman eliminated the awkwardness on his very first trip down the floor, when he elbowed Magic in the back, then bodied up on him and bumped him in the post.

"C'mon now," Rodman said to Magic. "Show me what you got."

Magic wheeled and rolled in a hook shot.

"How did that look?" Johnson said, after the shot dropped through.

"Let's go," Rodman said. "Is that all you have?"

Johnson ran and passed and sweated and tumbled into people just like everyone else. After a few minutes, the players seemed to relax.

"I made a nice pass, and guys were saying, 'Oh, I remember him. He's still Magic,'" Johnson said. "It calmed everyone down. After that, it was just about basketball.

"That game helped change the perception of HIV all over the world. People watching it said, 'It's okay. He can do this.'"

As the game clock ran down, Isiah pushed the ball up the floor with Magic guarding him. Thomas urged Magic to come closer. He dribbled the ball in and out of his legs, behind his back, stutter-stepping back and forth in a staccato rhythm, challenging his old friend. Magic, in turn, motioned with his hand.

"C'mon, bring it," Magic said.

Thomas whipped the ball through his legs one more time. As the shot clock dwindled down to its final seconds, Thomas hoisted a long jumper over Magic's outstretched arms. It never reached the rim.

The capacity crowd hooted appreciatively, anticipating a theatrical finish. So now it was Michael Jordan with the ball and Magic matching up opposite him. Jordan faked left, burst right to the basket, then pulled up for a shot over Magic. It too was short.

Finally, it was Magic's turn for Showtime. He made a V cut, then a backdoor cut, and popped out to the three-point circle, all with Isiah in pursuit. Teammate Clyde Drexler lofted him the ball and Johnson launched a three-point bomb.

"I didn't have to look," Magic said. "I knew it was good."

Magic was mobbed by his teammates, just like the old days. Mullin came over for a double high-five, Drexler slapped him on the back, and East big man Kevin Willis approached Magic without hesitation and wrapped himself around him. As they left the court, Isiah leaned over and pecked Magic on the cheek.

Christine Johnson and Earvin Johnson Sr., watching from the stands, finally exhaled. Like Cookie, they had been unsure how their son's illness would be received. The pregame murmurs from the crowd were mixed. For every fan who appeared delighted to witness Magic's return there was another casting doubt on his decision to play in Orlando.

Johnson's dramatic three-pointer in the final seconds was a perfect ending — except that now the game, and his career, was over. As Magic drove to the airport with Rosen, he told his agent what an arena filled to capacity with basketball fans in Florida already knew: he didn't want to stop.

* * *

While Magic pondered whether he should resume his career, Bird was back in Boston debating whether he should end his own re-markable run. He too had been voted in as an All-Star starter but was unable to make the trip to Florida. His back was so horribly damaged that he spent much of his downtime in a fiberglass body brace that extended from his chest down to his hips. Bird hated the brace so much that when doctors told him he no longer needed it, he took it out behind his home in Indiana and blasted it to pieces with a shotgun.

By 1992, his back injuries were the cumulative result of years of diving into the stands, trading elbows with seven-footers, and re-peatedly hurling his body onto the parquet after loose balls. The L-4 vertebra on Bird's back was compressed and twisted on the L-5 vertebra, and a nerve was trapped in between the two. The condi-tion left Bird with unstable bones pushed into the nerves, and a piercing, burning pain shooting down his leg. Physical therapist Dan Dyrek, who spent most of the year attempting to manipulate Bird's spine to relieve some of the pressure of bone on nerve, begged him to retire.

"I had genuine concerns about what it would mean for the rest of his life," Dyrek said.

Bird had already undergone back surgery in the summer of 1991 to shave down a problematic disc and widen the canal where the nerves led to the spinal cord. The afternoon after the procedure, he walked six miles with minimal discomfort. He was elated — and, he thought, cured.

Two months later, while executing a routine cut in practice, he experienced the telltale shooting pain in his leg. He missed 37 games in 1991–92, his final season, but even more frustrating, he was unable to participate in the team practices.

"I've always said practice is what makes you great," he said. "I needed that repetition. Without it, I didn't feel like the same player."

The rigors of the team's travel schedule were counterproductive to his recovery, particularly since the team flew commercially, so

Bird did not accompany the Celtics on their annual February swing to the West Coast.

But against his doctor's advice, he jetted to Los Angeles for the February 16, 1992, game against the Lakers. Magic's number 32 was being retired at halftime, and he had asked Bird to be part of the ceremony. It was only seven days since Johnson had brought down the house in Orlando with his dramatic All-Star performance, and legendary Lakers announcer Chick Hearn proclaimed, "Let's make this an afternoon the world will never forget."

Magic wore a chocolate brown suit and the expression of an emotionally torn man. He could not bring himself to smile when Hearn introduced him or when Hearn highlighted his legacy with the Lakers. The first glint of a grin came when Hearn welcomed Bird to step up to the podium. As Boston's franchise forward made his way to the microphone, the Forum regulars greeted him with a warm reception that lasted several minutes. Bird tried twice to begin reading his prepared script, but the applause did not subside before he finally chastised the crowd, "Hey, I'm not the one retiring here."

"When are you going to?" shouted a good-natured heckler.

"Pretty soon," Bird replied wistfully.

He presented Magic with a piece of the Boston Garden parquet, recited the accolades prepared for him, then departed from the script as he finished, saying, "Magic's not done yet. We're going to Barcelona to bring home the gold."

Although Bird had agreed to be part of Magic's ceremony, he truthfully would have preferred to skip it. He felt uncomfortable, misplaced.

"The whole time I was thinking, 'What the hell am I doing here, hanging with all these Lakers, when my own team is standing right over there?'" he admitted.

As Bird listened to Kareem thank Magic for teaching him how to enjoy the game, he began reflecting on his own teammates, who were standing court-side, in uniform, watching the tribute. Bird glanced over at McHale, Parish, and D.J. He wondered what it would be like to say goodbye to them. He knew he'd be doing it soon — sooner than anyone realized.

As Johnson embraced Abdul-Jabbar, sobbing as he pulled the Hall of Fame center closer, Bird felt a lump catch in his throat.

"I was sitting there wondering how long it would be before he was gone," Bird said.

When Magic finally took the microphone, he thanked his family and his teammates. Then he turned to his lifelong rival and embraced him.

"It's sort of too bad Larry and I couldn't go on forever," Magic told the crowd. "I enjoyed so many of those battles, whether we won or lost, because you got a chance to play at your highest level when you played the Celtics and Larry.

"I want to thank Larry Bird personally for bringing out the best of Magic Johnson because, without you, I could have never risen to the top."

Johnson ended his own retirement ceremony by telling the fans he hoped they wouldn't be too mad if he decided to come back and do it all over again. The crowd cheered; Jerry West blanched.

Later that winter, Johnson and Rosen went on a business trip to New York. The Knicks were playing that night, and Magic called ahead to Riley to see if he could work out at Madison Square Garden in between the two teams' shoot-arounds.

Riley met his former point guard at the gym and put him through a rigorous workout. For more than an hour, Riley ran Magic through wind sprints, dribbling drills, and shooting repetitions. Riley normally adhered to a strict pregame routine that included watching film and reviewing his notes of the opponent, but for one afternoon he abandoned all of it. On this day, his only focus was on rebounding for a friend. Just before tip-off of the game between the Knicks and the Lakers, the Madison Square Garden scoreboard ran a video highlight of the career of Earvin Johnson to the tune of "Do You Believe in Magic?"

"It was," said Magic, "the nicest thing anyone did for me during that time."

When Magic returned to Los Angeles and resumed his workouts, he discovered that he had company during off-hours at the Forum. Miami Heat center Rony Seikaly, who was rehabilitating an injury, could often be found shooting down at the far end of the court. One afternoon he called down, "Want to play?"

Johnson looked around. He had no personal relationship with Seikaly and wasn't sure if the center was talking to him.

"Magic," Seikaly said. "C'mon, let's get some work in."

It was a small gesture, yet one that Magic grew to cherish during a tumultuous time in his life. It gave him hope that someday he would regain his place in the NBA. It was a baby step toward resuming his life as he had known it.

10

★ ★ ★

AUGUST 7, 1992

Barcelona, Spain

I T BEGAN AS a friendly game of pool.

Magic Johnson awaited his turn while Michael Jordan, a premium Cuban stogie dangling from his mouth, lined up his shot in the game room of the Ambassador Hotel in Barcelona, Spain, a cordoned-off area on the second floor designated as a sanctuary for the members of the U.S. Olympic basketball team.

It was a welcome and needed hideaway. This traveling troupe of basketball legends, whom coach Chuck Daly likened to a band of rock stars, caused a near-stampede simply by arriving. Spectators grappled with one another for a glimpse of Michael and Magic and Larry as they exited the team bus and checked into the hotel. As fans clamored to photograph this historic sports moment, the unruly crowd surged forward. Bird, skittish in large gatherings since he was a child, held his breath. The mob made him anxious.

An arm's length away, Magic surveyed the maze of faces and also held his breath. He found their energy to be exciting, exhilarating.

"Isn't this amazing?" he said to Bird.

"Are you kidding me? I want to get the hell out of here," Bird answered.

The "Dream Team" needed buffers, for their privacy and their safety. During their 16 days in Barcelona, the Ambassador's game room served as an exclusive club where the players could shoot pool, play cards, enjoy a beer, and invent occasions to compete with one another.

By day the room was littered with books, toys, movies, and video games, a haven for the players' families. Earvin Johnson III, barely eight weeks old, sat wide-eyed in his bouncy seat, intently following the movements of the older children. Conner Bird, a toddler who kept his mother and father awake half the nights during the Olympic Games, loved to jump on the leather couches and throw balls from the pool table down the hotel's elegant marble steps.

On the night of August 7, little Conner and baby E.J. were already asleep. Their daddies were wide awake, embroiled in an emotional debate over a simple question posed by Bird: which NBA team was the greatest of all time?

"Obviously one of our Laker teams," answered Magic, leaning on his pool stick. "We won five championships. More than all of you."

"No, it's the great Celtics teams with my man Bill Russell," said center Patrick Ewing, who played for the New York Knicks but was raised in Cambridge, Massachusetts. "He won 11 rings."

"You're forgetting the '86 Celtics, with the best front line in the history of basketball, including this guy right here," added NBC commentator Ahmad Rashad, pointing to Bird.

"That Celtics front line was brutal," agreed Charles Barkley.

Jordan, refusing to allow the chatter to disrupt his concentration, knocked his ball into the corner pocket and puffed on his cigar. He was 29 years old and had just won his second straight championship and his sixth consecutive scoring title. His counterparts in the room were decorated NBA veterans, yet their body of work was nearly complete. The maestro of the Bulls was only just beginning to add new strokes to his championship canvas.

"You haven't even seen the best NBA team of all time yet," Jordan announced. "I'm just getting started. I'm going to win more championships than all of you guys. Tell you what. Let's have this conversation after I'm done playing."

"You aren't winning five championships," Magic protested.

"Michael, I'm going to steal at least one of them from you," Barkley shot back.

The flurry of protests continued, with five of the greatest players in NBA history sparring over their own place in basketball history. Magic was indignant at the suggestion that the best team could be *anyone* other than his 1987 Lakers, the team he had determined was the finest of his title years.

"Put me with Kareem, James Worthy, Coop, and Byron Scott, and we'd dominate your Bulls team," Magic claimed.

Barkley was about to chime in again, but Bird, taking a slug of his beer, shot his hand up.

"Quiet," Bird said. "Charles, you ain't won nothing. You're out of this discussion. Ahmad, same thing. You're gone. Patrick, you don't have any championships either, so you need to shut up and sit down right here and learn some things."

Barkley, subdued by the unfortunate reality of his basketball résumé, wandered off. Ewing, who had once considered Bird a bitter adversary but would develop an unusual kinship with him during their Olympic experience, dutifully sat on the bench next to his new friend. Rashad lingered also, fascinated by the banter between these elite basketball stars, each of whom at some juncture of his career could have argued that he was the best player in the game.

Jordan insisted that his Chicago teams belonged in the conversation about the all-time greats; Bird reminded Jordan that he used to torture Scottie Pippen regularly before his back betrayed him.

"I feel sorry for you," Magic told Jordan. "You will never have what Larry and I had. We went two weeks without sleep knowing, if we made one mistake, the other guy was going to take it and use it to beat us. Who do you measure yourself against?"

The conversation lurched on with no resolution until the topic switched to the inevitable follow-up: who was the best 1-on-1 player of all time?

"Gentlemen," said Jordan, "give it up. You've got no chance on this one. Larry, you don't have the speed to stay with me. Magic, I can guard you, but you could never guard me. Neither one of you guys can play defense the way I can. And neither one of you can score like me."

"I don't know about that," Magic retorted. "I could have scored more if I wanted to. It would have been a good one."

Jordan's face darkened. He had been uncommonly conciliatory in Barcelona, stepping aside as Bird and Magic shared the title of captain and revered elder statesman. Jordan deferred to Magic, allowed him to become the face of the Dream Team, even though Jordan was the reigning back-to-back league MVP. He did so because he understood that Magic's career was at an end and this was his final basketball indulgence.

"I didn't want to burst his bubble," Jordan said.

But now Jordan expected Magic to acknowledge the obvious: that Michael Jordan was the best player in the world. He turned to Magic, plucked the cigar out of his mouth, and approached his fellow future Hall of Famer with his voice rising.

"You better give it up," Jordan told Magic. "I'll come into your gym and drop 60 on you. I've already done it to the Celtics. Ask your friend Larry. You and Bird were great players. You did some amazing things. But it's over. This is my game now."

"Michael, don't you forget," Magic said. "Larry and I turned this league around. We *are* the NBA."

"Well, I've taken it to a new level," Jordan replied. "And it's not your league anymore."

"You're not there yet," Magic insisted.

Bird watched silently as the debate between Magic and Michael escalated. He detected a swagger in Jordan that he hadn't seen before. Bird recognized that strain of confidence, bordering on arrogance. It was exactly how he had felt when he was on top of the basketball world.

"There were plenty of years when I knew in my heart I was the best guy in the room," Bird said. "That night I knew in my heart it wasn't me anymore. And it wasn't Magic either."

Rashad, a friend to both Michael and Magic, tried to soften the increasingly heated rhetoric. He was unsuccessful. Jordan wanted concessions from Johnson that Magic stubbornly refused to provide, and His Airness remained relentless in pursuing them.

"I just think it's too bad we couldn't all have been young together," Magic said. "We could have all been the face of the NBA at the same time."

"Your time has passed," Jordan said. "C'mon, old man, give it up."

"I'm not sure about that," Magic persisted.

"Magic," Bird finally interjected, "stop. We had our moment. There was a period when nobody was better than you and me. But not anymore. Michael is the best now.

"Let's pass the torch and be on our way."

Magic Johnson wouldn't stop pestering Larry Bird. Magic desperately wanted to play in the 1992 Olympic Games with him, but Bird's back was so badly damaged that he could barely run up and down the court for the Boston Celtics.

"I was in so much pain, I didn't even want to play basketball anymore," Bird said.

Although he had not told anyone except his wife and Dan Dyrek, Bird had already determined that the 1991–92 season would be his last. It had become a daily chore for him to lace up his sneakers without doubling over. He was 35 years old, and he was done.

But Magic wasn't taking no for an answer.

"Larry, we've got to do this," Magic implored him. "I've been waiting my whole career to play with you one more time."

Dave Gavitt, the CEO of the Celtics and president of USA Basketball, also wanted Bird in the fold. Four years earlier, in Seoul, South Korea, the U.S. team, made up completely of college players, suffered a stunning loss to the Soviet Union in the Olympic Games and trudged home with a bronze medal instead of the customary—and expected—gold. Even before the embarrassing defeat, there had been discussions about opening up Olympic competition to NBA players. In 1989 the International Basketball Federation voted to allow professionals to play.

Members of USA Basketball were split over the decision. Some were vehemently opposed to inviting NBA stars to compete internationally, and others worried that, since the pros would not receive financial compensation, they might be less committed. There was also the thorny issue of asking the stars to tack two months of training onto an already taxing NBA season.

Gavitt reasoned that the professionals would embrace the idea only if the team was turned into a phenomenon, a coveted, once-in-a-lifetime showcase with enough cachet to capture the curiosity of the world. The goal was to assemble the greatest basketball team in history, and to do that Gavitt needed three people: Magic, Larry, and Michael.

It had been nine months since Magic retired in the wake of his devastating HIV diagnosis, but he continued to feel physically strong and played basketball nearly every day. He enthusiastically endorsed the idea of playing for his country in Barcelona.

Jordan, who won a gold medal in Los Angeles in 1984 as an undergraduate at North Carolina, was intrigued with Gavitt's vision but remained noncommittal.

Bird, whose back continued to deteriorate, couldn't have been any more adamant.

"I'm not playing," he told Gavitt. "I'm too old. Give my spot to one of the younger guys."

Gavitt remained undeterred. He asked Bird if he followed the Olympics as a child and if he had ever dreamed of representing his country. Bird conceded that he had. The United States needed to reclaim the gold, Gavitt explained, and to do so they needed the finest available players. He had Magic. He was close to convincing Jordan.

"And if we have you, we'll make history," Gavitt said.

Bird was unmoved. Gavitt backed off, but in the interim he made it known that he wanted Bird on the roster. Boston's franchise forward was inundated with phone calls urging him to reconsider.

"Larry," Magic said during one of their conversations, "you can't let this opportunity go by. All I want to do is throw you one pass and have you hit a shot. Do that, and then you don't have to play anymore."

Had he been healthy, Bird would have already signed on with the Dream Team, but his mobility was limited and his game had suffered. He was no longer the same player who was widely recognized as one of the greatest clutch performers of all time.

"I don't want to be a charity case," Bird told Gavitt.

"Larry," Gavitt said, "the Olympics are played under international rules. That includes zone defenses. You'll destroy them with your outside shooting."

Bird considered Gavitt's argument, the first valid reason that swayed him. He could still shoot. And he did always wonder what it would be like to have a gold medal around his neck.

"All right," Bird said. "I'm in."

Within days, Jordan and Barkley also joined the fold, and interest in the team swelled. Suddenly a spot on the Dream Team had become the most prestigious invitation in all of sports.

A committee made up of USA Basketball, NBA, and college officials fleshed out the remaining roster. Jordan's Chicago teammate Scottie Pippen was added, along with Utah's prolific duo of forward Karl Malone and point guard John Stockton. Ewing and Spurs big man David Robinson were invited to anchor the middle. Chris Mullin, a three-point shooter, was asked to help exploit the zone defenses. The final two spots were later filled by Portland guard Clyde Drexler and the lone college representative, Duke star Christian Laettner, who beat out a young, powerful center from Louisiana State University, Shaquille O'Neal, bypassed in favor of Laettner because the Duke star had logged more time with USA Basketball.

Predictably, the selection process was not without controversy. The list of snubbed NBA stars could have captured a gold medal of its own: Atlanta star Dominique Wilkins, Magic's Laker counterpart James Worthy, Indiana's clutch shooter Reggie Miller, and Detroit stars Joe Dumars and Dennis Rodman.

Yet the most glaring omission was Isiah Thomas, the point guard of the Pistons' back-to-back championships in 1988 and 1989.

Thomas was an eleven-time All-Star and three-time first-team All-NBA selection, and his coach, Chuck Daly, had been tabbed to coach the Dream Team.

Bird was startled that Thomas didn't make the cut. He shouldn't have been. Jordan had made it clear that he wanted no part of playing alongside Thomas in the backcourt. Michael had not forgotten the All-Star freeze-out in 1985 or the 1991 Eastern Conference Finals, when the Bulls supplanted the Pistons in the East and Isiah, Bill Laimbeer, and Mark Aguirre walked off the court with four seconds left on the game clock rather than congratulate the Bulls. It was a blatant sign of disrespect that was roundly condemned throughout the league.

Magic, still wounded by Thomas's reaction to his HIV diagnosis, did not hear from him during the Dream Team selection process. Pistons public relations director Matt Dobek called Magic on Isiah's behalf, but Magic refused to advocate for him.

"Our relationship was really strained at that point," Magic explained. "We didn't speak for years, and Isiah knew why. He questioned me when I got my HIV diagnosis. How can a so-called friend question your sexuality like that? I know why he did it, because we used to kiss before games, and now if people were wondering about me, that meant they were wondering about *him* too.

"I was so upset by that. When I started working for NBC, [*New York Post* reporter] Peter Vecsey tried to get us together. He was telling me, 'Isiah is hurting, you guys need to talk.' But I wasn't interested. I told him, 'Forget it.'

"Isiah killed his own chances when it came to the Olympics. Nobody on that team wanted to play with him.

"Isiah's problem was he always felt he had to fight for everything. Even when he finally got among the elite, he couldn't stop fighting.

"The comments about Larry being overrated [in the 1987 Conference Finals] were out of pure frustration. He was jealous. He felt Larry was getting too much attention and he wasn't getting his.

"He always wanted to be in that conversation when people talked about the great players. Michael, Larry, and I were always in that discussion. He could have been if he had handled things differently.

But because of the petty decisions he's made, no one gives him his due.

"I'm sad for Isiah. He has alienated so many people in his life, and he still doesn't get it. He doesn't understand why he wasn't chosen for that Olympic team, and that's really too bad. You should be aware when you have ticked off more than half of the NBA.

"If you went strictly on terms of ability, then Isiah should have been chosen for the Dream Team. But Michael didn't want to play with him. Scottie wanted no part of him. Bird wasn't pushing for him. Karl Malone didn't want him. Who was saying, 'We need this guy'? Nobody.

"Michael got singled out as the guy that kept Isiah off, but that really isn't fair. It was everybody. We all understood the camaraderie wouldn't be the same.

"What happened with Isiah has been the biggest personal disappointment of my life. Nothing else is even close. Here's a guy I trained with, I vacationed with, who I counseled, and he counseled me. And he threw it all away out of jealousy.

"When I see him now, we're cordial. That's about it. When the Knicks were looking for someone to run their team, [Madison Square Garden Sports president] Steve Mills, who is a good friend of mine, called me asking what I thought. I told him, 'Hey, you should talk to Isiah.'

"I can separate the personal from the professional. In spite of what happened between us, I still respect his knowledge of the game.

"But even with the Knicks situation, he had to be stubborn. When things went bad there, he kept fighting and fighting instead of saying, 'Okay, I better give up something here.' If he was willing to compromise, he might have saved himself a lot of trouble. But he couldn't. He doesn't know how.

"I don't wish anything bad on him. We will never be the same, and I will never trust him again, but I hope he finds peace with himself.

"In the meantime, I've moved on."

* * *

Once the Dream Team roster was finalized, the players hunkered down in La Jolla, California, at the Sheraton Grande Torre Pines Resort and went about the process of evolving from rivals into united teammates. The transition, Bird and Magic noted, was remarkably smooth, with the prospect of a gold medal outweighing any lingering disagreements from the NBA season.

It quickly became apparent to Daly that, if there was going to be a problem with the squad, it was their tendency to pass the ball *too much*. The players, often in competition to outdo each other on the court, delighted in making the difficult play.

Daly's private wish was to go through the entire Olympic process without ever having to call a time-out. Known as a player's coach for his ability to juggle egos and personalities, Daly was pleased at how self-motivated his players were in practice. Ewing would dominate play in the middle with jump hooks and turnarounds, then Robinson would counter with rainbow jumpers and fast-break jams. Barkley would post up Malone, declare his supremacy, then steel himself for Malone's response, which often involved a forearm in the back and a brute physical move around the basket. At stake were bragging rights to being the best power forward in the world that day. Yet all those battles paled in comparison to the verbal (and physical) skirmishes involving Magic and Michael.

In their mano-a-mano battles, the stakes were high: basketball legacies and superstar bragging rights.

"C'mon, Magic, keep up," Jordan would tease Johnson after blowing past him in the open court.

"Michael, you've got to see the whole floor," Magic would chastise him, after firing one of his pinpoint no-look passes into the hands of a startled teammate.

On June 23, USA Basketball assembled eight of its top college players to scrimmage against Daly's studs: Michigan forward Chris Webber, Memphis State guard Anfernee "Penny" Hardaway, Duke star Grant Hill, North Carolina center Eric Montross, Kentucky forward Jamal Mashburn, Tennessee sniper Allan Houston, Wake Forest scorer Rodney Rogers, and Duke point guard Bobby Hurley.

Daly instructed coach George Raveling to encourage his college team to push tempo and shoot three-pointers. The kids buried 10 treys and outscored the Dream Team 62–54 in a 20-minute scrimmage.

"They beat the hell out of us," Bird said. "I was pretty ticked off. Allan Houston murdered us with the threes, and Bobby Hurley was absolutely killing us with his quickness. Nobody wanted to guard him because nobody could stay with him.

"Those kids embarrassed us. And they did us a favor. Our attitude changed after that. No fooling around."

The next day the Dream Team demanded a full-game rematch and beat the kids by 50. All eight of the college All-Stars graduated to the NBA and enjoyed lengthy careers, save Hurley, who was injured in a serious car accident and was never the same player.

The Dream Team migrated from La Jolla to Portland for the Tournament of the Americas, where four of the ten teams advanced from the zone qualifier to the Olympic Games. Months earlier, Rosen had fielded a call from USA Basketball asking him what number Magic wanted.

"How high do the numbers go?" Rosen asked.

"To 15," the official answered.

"Earvin will take 15," Rosen said.

That way, Magic's agent figured, his client would be introduced last.

The Americans pummeled Cuba 136–57 in the first game, with Bird and Magic re-creating the on-court chemistry they had demonstrated 14 years earlier at the World Invitational Tournament.

Magic repeatedly pushed tempo, penetrated the lane, then kicked it back out to Bird on the perimeter. Each time Larry buried the shot on a feed from Magic, the fans celebrated as if the gold medal had just been won. Seconds before halftime, Johnson drove all the way to the hoop, with Bird trailing on the wing. Magic was about to lay in the ball when he turned and fired a no-look bullet to Bird, who stopped and drained the three as the buzzer sounded.

It was precisely the play Magic had envisioned when he coaxed Bird onto the roster.

"I'll remember that basket for the rest of my life," Magic said.

"To this day," Bird said, "I have no idea how he saw me."

Bird was buoyed to have played without pain and to find that, even with all his downtime, his shooting stroke was intact. He went to his designated cubicle for his postgame interviews and regaled the press with pithy one-liners. But when Bird shifted slightly in his seat halfway through the session, he felt that familiar jolt of pain traveling down his leg. The pain was so sudden and so severe that Bird, nauseous from the burning sensation, began sweating profusely. He abruptly ended his interview, hobbled back to the hotel, and laid himself out on the floor.

That is where his brother Mark discovered him when he burst into Bird's room exclaiming, "That was awesome! Let's go celebrate!"

"I'm done," Bird said quietly. "It's over for me."

"What do you mean?" his brother asked.

"I mean, this is it," Bird said. "I can't keep going on like this."

Mark Bird hurried out to find the Dream Team (and Boston Celtics) trainer Ed Lacerte. Lacerte tried to alleviate the burning sensation of the compressed nerves by manipulating Bird's muscles, but his back was rock-hard, like an impenetrable brick wall.

"I'm sorry, Larry," Lacerte said. "I'm not sure what else I can do."

Bird had played his first and last game in the Tournament of the Americas — and quite possibly the final game of his career. He was relegated to the sidelines for the remainder of the pre-Olympic competition.

He had company. Patrick Ewing had cut and dislocated his finger on the rim during the team workouts in La Jolla and missed the win over Cuba. He was held out of practice for a few days, and in the interest of preserving his conditioning, he jumped on an exercise bike on the sidelines while the team went through their drills. Bird did the same. It made for an awkward scene: two tall, proud men who had been heated adversaries for years sitting side by side, pedaling furiously, going nowhere and having nothing to say about it.

Although he wasn't playing, Bird still offered some caustic commentary from his perch on the bike. When Barkley muscled Malone in the post, Bird kidded Utah's chiseled forward, "Charles owns you, Karl. Get used to it. You're a backup on this team."

Ewing eventually joined the verbal fray. When David Robinson jammed home an alley-oop pass, Ewing shouted, "Enjoy it now, David. When I get back out there, you'll be eating that." Bird chuckled. The two men got to talking.

They recounted their playing days against one another, when Bird would lure Ewing out to the wing and inform him, "You're no center. You're a glorified power forward. And there's no way you can stop me out here."

Bird usually punctuated his point with a jumper. Then it would be Ewing's turn to jog back and inform Boston's forward, "I'm going to take you into the post and kick your ass."

At the time, the acrimony was real. Years later, pedaling side by side, their past bravado seemed contrived. When Magic glanced over and caught Ewing and Bird guffawing over the misadventures of Clyde Drexler, who had been pickpocketed by Jordan on back-to-back possessions, he shook his head.

"I wasn't expecting that," Magic said. "Two of the quietest guys, and suddenly they were best friends."

Bird bestowed the nickname "Harry" on Ewing. Most of the guys thought it was after the big but lovable character in the movie *Harry and the Hendersons*, but Bird was harkening back to his junior season of college, when he played alongside Harry Morgan at Indiana State.

"Just call us Harry and Larry," he announced.

Lacerte printed up T-shirts that read THE HARRY AND LARRY SHOW . . . TO BE CONTINUED IN BARCELONA — a takeoff on a Reebok Olympic advertising campaign that featured American decathletes Dan (Johnson) and Dave (O'Brien).

It was an unlikely friendship. Ewing grew up in Boston resenting the way the public fawned over Larry Legend. He saw Bird as another overhyped white guy and used to scoff with his friends, "Oh, please. He's not that good. He can't run, and he can't jump."

But Ewing changed his mind when he arrived in the NBA and bore witness to Bird's considerable skills.

"I take it back," Ewing told his Cambridge friends. "This guy is incredible. He can shoot, rebound, pass . . . he's the greatest competitor I've ever seen."

In the 1990 playoffs, Ewing traded elbows and insults with Bird as the Celtics took a 2–0 lead in the best-of-five first-round series. Everyone in Boston was certain the Knicks were done, but Ewing anchored a New York comeback that culminated in a Game 5 win over the Celtics on the Garden parquet. It was a shocking development that forced Bird to examine Ewing in a new light. He had always recognized the big man's skills, but now he grudgingly acknowledged Ewing's mental resolve, the quality Bird always felt separated the great players from the good ones.

Ewing was able to return to action after a few days of the Tournament of the Americas, but John Stockton fractured his right fibula midway through the Dream Team's win over Canada, and Clyde Drexler was forced to sit out the victory over Argentina with a bruised right knee.

Stockton was clearly going to be sidelined for a few weeks, which initiated a discussion of whether to add another player. Isiah's name came up in a conference call, but again he was rejected by his peers.

Even without a full complement of players, the Dream Team lived up to its weighty name. Magic, Barkley, and Jordan dominated, and their opponents literally applauded them for it, sometimes in the middle of the game. When they played Argentina, Magic guarded a player on the block who refused to make a move to the basket.

"What are you doing?" Magic asked him.

"I'm waiting," the player replied.

Johnson, clearly flummoxed, finally knocked the ball out of his hands — but only after a player on the Argentina bench had successfully snapped a Polaroid of Magic guarding his friend.

As he ran back down the court, Magic noticed the player was weeping.

"Mr. Johnson, I cannot believe it's you," he said. "I used to watch you late at night. This is the thrill of my life."

When the United States played Puerto Rico, Bird remained flat on his stomach on the court in his warm-ups, too injured to play. One of the game officials ran past the U.S. bench and begged Bird to check in, if only for a second, so he could tell his family he had refereed a game in which the great Bird competed.

The referee left disappointed. He wasn't the only one. Brazilian star Oscar Schmidt, whose silky smooth shooting stroke was the pride of his nation, idolized Bird as a child and had anxiously awaited the opportunity to test his skills against his hero. He had to settle for an autographed copy of Bird's autobiography *Drive*.

"Sorry, Oscar," Bird told him before the U.S. game against Brazil. "I'd love to drop 50 on you, but I can't move right now." The United States cruised to another lopsided win, after which the Brazilian coach touted the Americans as "a team from another planet."

The U.S. team proved to be an undefeated juggernaut in the Tournament of the Americas, overpowering clubs by an average of 51.5 points. Magic led the team in assists and minutes played and was chosen to carry the U.S. flag in the closing ceremonies.

When Bird stopped to consider Magic's prognosis during a quiet moment, it left him pensive, even melancholy. Magic Johnson would be dead soon. Based on the scant information the Dream Team had about an HIV diagnosis, his teammates were certain of that. And yet this exuberant man, who thrived in Barcelona as the unofficial U.S. basketball ambassador, seemed more vibrant than all of them.

By contrast, Bird's physical struggles had become increasingly transparent. He was forced to wear his fiberglass body brace around the clock. It had become part of him, like buttoning up his shirt each day, but it felt like a piece of concrete around his waist and was so tight that his breathing was labored when he sat down. He wore it to bed but could only lie on his back or his stomach because, when he tried to sleep on his side, the fiberglass dug into his skin, leaving welts and cuts.

When the team broke camp 15 days before reconvening in Monte Carlo, Bird went back to Boston and showed up at Massachusetts

General Hospital unannounced. He found Dan Dyrek, his physical therapist, and begged him to accompany him to Barcelona.

"I don't think I can make it without your help," Bird said.

Dyrek opened his daybook. He was teaching a graduate school course and had a full calendar of commitments. But he wasn't about to be the person who prevented Larry Bird from realizing his Olympic dream. Dyrek hopped aboard the Dream Team caravan and before long was treating many of Bird's teammates as well, including Ewing and his chronically sore knees.

By that point, "Harry" and Larry were inseparable. When the team flew to Monte Carlo for their final pre-Olympic training, Ewing sat poolside with Larry, Dinah, and their friend Quinn Buckner, wearing dark glasses and trying not to stare at the topless women. He ordered a round of draft beer for Bird and his friends, unfazed by the $8 price tag.

Bird was incredulous each time his new friend ordered another round.

"Do you know how much those beers cost?" Bird asked Ewing.

"Nah, I don't drink," Ewing replied.

"They are $8 each!" Bird exclaimed. "I would never pay that for a beer!"

In his rookie season, the first time Bird went to New York with the Celtics, he and Rick Robey popped into a bar to have a brew. When he saw the prices on the tavern's menu, Larry abruptly stood up and walked out. Years later, while dining with his teammates in a trendy New York eatery, the players began collecting money for the bill. Told they were going to give the waiter a 20 percent tip, Bird said, "What for? All he did was deliver the food."

He stood up, grabbed the tip money, and strode unannounced into the kitchen. He handed the astonished cook a fistful of bills, then walked out.

While Larry rang up the bar tab in Monte Carlo, Magic hung with Jordan at the casino and tried to bring him luck at the blackjack table. When the clock struck midnight, Johnson, Jordan, Barkley, and Pippen flocked to Jimmy Z's, an exclusive Monte Carlo night-club with a retractable roof and a maze of dance floors.

For the first time since his HIV diagnosis, Magic felt like one of the boys again. The Dream Team was all about inclusion, right down to their 12th man, Laettner, with whom Bird regularly sat on the bus so he would not feel isolated from his more celebrated team-mates.

While the team was still in Portland, a representative from *Newsweek* magazine had approached Magic about appearing on their cover with Michael Jordan. Johnson had agreed, but with one stip-ulation — he wanted Bird included in the shot too.

"No Larry, no cover," Magic said.

On July 6, 1992, Magic, Michael, and Larry had graced the front of *Newsweek* with the heading "Team Dream" trumpeting their up-coming journey.

When the team arrived in Monte Carlo on Sunday, July 19, Bird had still not been cleared for contact, but the following morning he scrimmaged for five minutes. Stockton, also on the mend, split his time between the swimming pool and the stationary bike. That eve-ning the Dream Team attended a reception hosted by Prince Rain-ier and Prince Albert, and Magic, resplendent in a black-and-white tuxedo, declared that the Rainiers were the only royalty who super-seded Jordan.

Magic led the United States to a 111–71 win over the French Na-tional Team, the last tune-up before Barcelona. Johnson went to the casino, won big, and blew kisses to the crowd on his way out the door.

"He absolutely captivated those people," Daly said.

On Wednesday, July 22, the West (Magic, Drexler, Robinson, Malone, and Barkley) lined up opposite the East (Bird, Jordan, Pip-pen, Ewing, Mullin, and Laettner) for an in-practice scrimmage. Magic, feeling particularly spry, sparked his team to an early 14–2 advantage with a dazzling display of artistic passes; after driving to the hole, he sneered good-naturedly, "Hey, M.J., you better get with it."

Jordan's fists clenched. He called for the ball, drove to the basket, elevated, then dunked it through.

"That good enough for you?" he said.

Pippen immediately perked up when he saw Jordan's suddenly glowering visage.

"Y'all have done it now," Pippen said, grinning.

Jordan swarmed the West team with traps and full-court pressure. He jumped the passing lanes, knocked down one-handed slams, pushed Magic off the block, and hit fadeaways, barking at the West's suddenly impotent squad as he continued his scoring rampage. Within minutes, the score was tied. Johnson, rankled by the calls (or no calls) of the coaching staff, complained, "It's like I'm in Chicago Stadium! They moved it to Monte Carlo!"

"Welcome to the nineties," Jordan retorted.

"You want to be like Mike?" Pippen baited Magic. "Try drinking some Gatorade!"

When the "regulation" scrimmage ended in a tie, both Jordan and Johnson instructed their respective teams to remain on the floor.

"We're going again," Jordan said.

"No," Daly interjected. "We don't need any more injuries."

For the first and only time, the players ignored Daly's pleas. Five more minutes of high-octane basketball followed, with Ewing and Robinson grinding in the post, Barkley and Malone wrestling for the boards, Bird angling for the perimeter dagger, and Magic controlling tempo. Yet it was Jordan who had the last word, with a melodious display of basketball trickery that Gavitt would later maintain was the most amazing five minutes of basketball he'd ever seen.

As Jordan and Bird skipped off the floor victorious, gloating shamelessly about their turnaround, Magic left the court demanding a new officiating crew.

"Magic was cursing at the refs, his teammates, and his coaches," Jordan recalled. "He couldn't stand that we beat them.

"It was the most fun I've ever had playing basketball."

Two days after that epic scrimmage, the Dream Team arrived

in Barcelona and practiced lightly before Magic gathered them in a semicircle and reminded them of their duty, both as Americans and as representatives of the NBA. He stressed the need to focus despite all the alluring distractions and encouraged the young players on the squad to come to him with any questions or concerns.

"I don't know what was more impressive — his wealth of knowledge or his willingness to share it," Stockton noted.

Bird was cautiously optimistic about his prospects in Barcelona. Earlier during the Celtics season, his team doctors had prescribed oral steroid pills to alleviate the inflammation in his back and the burning pain down his leg. Although he took them only intermittently, once he committed to playing in the Olympics he stopped taking them altogether. Even though he was taking them for proper medicinal purposes, steroids were one of the many banned substances in the Games, and Bird was concerned that any remnants of his treatment in his system would automatically disqualify him.

The Olympic drug-testing techniques were surprisingly archaic. Moments after each game, officials approached the trainer, Lacerte, and had him randomly draw three numbers from a box. Bird's number 7 came up both the first and the second time. He submitted his sample with some uneasiness; for a moment, the worst-case scenario of being sent home fleetingly crossed his mind. He ended up passing both tests without incident, but admitted, "That was the most stressful part of the Olympics."

The actual basketball games turned out to be a mere formality. It was a foregone conclusion that the Dream Team would advance to the medal round, and they rarely practiced once they got to Barcelona. Jordan routinely played 36 holes of golf a day, sometimes finishing up 10 minutes before the team bus pulled out of the hotel.

Because they were the most high-profile athletes in the Games, the Dream Team was housed at the Ambassador during their entire stay. The hotel was roped off and patrolled by gun-toting security guards around the clock, and entrance to the building required a special ID issued by USA Basketball. The United States was roundly criticized for providing elite accommodations for their elite athletes, particularly since the Ambassador had amenities that were not available to other competing basketball teams in the Olympic Village, such as air conditioning and oversized beds to fit the seven-foot frames of Ewing and Robinson.

Daly was unmoved by the complaints. He was aware of death threats that had already been made against some of his players and worried about his multimillionaire "amateurs" clubbing in Barcelona at night. The players joked about the unmarked cars that always flanked their team bus, but there were reasons the extra security was in place.

The night before their first game, the Dream Team held a private dinner in a downtown restaurant, with Barkley as their toastmaster. His job: to keep the guys loose and happy.

"Hey, Larry," Barkley said. "You used to be a great player, but now you're sitting on the bench waving a towel like M. L. Carr!"

"Laettner! You are forbidden to talk!" Barkley roared. "Finish college, then maybe we'll listen to you."

"And Drexler," Barkley said. "Your college team [Houston] was the dumbest in the history of basketball. How can a team that had you and [Hakeem] Olajuwon on the same team lose to N.C. State in the championship?!"

The night before the opening ceremonies, Magic Johnson lay awake, too excited to sleep. His crested blue blazer, white straw hat, and star-spangled red, white, and blue tie, the designated outfit for all the male American athletes who would be marching, was laid out carefully in anticipation.

Down the hall, Larry Bird also lay awake, unable to sleep because of a flurry of back spasms. He wanted desperately to march with his team, but as the night wore on and his discomfort increased, he knew his chances were diminishing with each hour.

The following morning, when told he would be standing around a minimum of two hours before the procession began, Bird put his straw hat and blue blazer back in the hotel closet and watched the ceremonies from his customary prone position on the floor.

Hardly anyone expected the Dream Team to lose, including their competition. It was not uncommon for opposing players to ask

Bird, Magic, and Jordan to pose for pregame photographs, and often, after being shellacked by 30 points or more, the other team would politely request postgame autographs. Before each game, teams exchanged flags or pins from their native country. There was often a mild scrum among the opposition as they tried to line up opposite Jordan, Bird, or Magic.

"You could tell they got a little disappointed if they got stuck with one of the rest of us," Stockton said.

The Dream Team beat Angola 116–48 in its opening game and put the game away with a resounding 46–1 spurt. Magic had 10 assists, and Bird chipped in with 9 points and 3 rebounds in 16 minutes of playing time. When he stepped onto the court for that first game, Bird's goal in Barcelona had been accomplished.

"I really don't care what happens after this," he told Magic.

The margin of victory for the Dream Team in Barcelona was an average of 45.8 points. Jordan occasionally toyed with opponents before applying suffocating full-court pressure that usually generated a turnover, fast-break lay-up, or both. Bird felt that Jordan's defensive pressure was the single biggest reason the United States dominated, and he wasn't surprised to see in 2008 that Olympic coach Mike Krzyzewski (an assistant on the Dream Team) employed the same tactics using Kobe Bryant.

Although Bird's friendship with Ewing generated the most attention in Barcelona, he also enjoyed the chance to connect with Michael Jordan. They had met for the first time in 1984, when Jordan was playing for the Olympic team and Bird was part of a group of NBA players scrimmaging them at the Hoosier Dome. Both clubs were warming up before the game when Jordan's ball rolled over half-court toward Bird.

"He came running after it with a big smile on his face," Bird said. "I threw it over his head. I don't know why I did that. He looked kind of ticked off. I guess I embarrassed him."

As Jordan prepared to play against Bird for the first time in his NBA rookie season, he sat in the Bulls locker room listening to veteran teammates Orlando Woolridge and Sid Green rev themselves up for the game. Woolridge's assignment was to check Bird, while Green would be guarding McHale.

"Larry Bird's not that good," Woolridge said. "He's slow. I can take him."

"Yeah, McHale's overrated too," Green added.

As Bird warmed up before the game, he approached Bulls coach Doug Collins.

"What's the record for an opposing player in this building?" Bird asked.

"Why, are you going for it?" Collins said.

"They messed up my tickets, so someone's got to pay," he said.

Forty-five minutes later, Bird and McHale had combined for 35 points and 28 rebounds in a routine Celtics victory.

"Larry absolutely destroyed us, but he never said a word," Jordan said. "He didn't have to."

One year later, Jordan hit a jump shot over Bird's outstretched hand and then, as he backpedaled on defense, told Larry, "Take that, All-Star."

"Come on, you little bitch, bring it back here," Bird said, then went down and drained a perimeter shot of his own.

"You know, you are the biggest prima donna I've ever seen," Jordan said.

"What the hell is a prima donna?" Bird asked.

In later years, Bird and Jordan collaborated on a number of McDonald's commercials and appeared together in the movie *Space Jam* alongside Bill Murray and Bugs Bunny. The groundwork for their friendship was laid in Barcelona, around a pool table, a conversation, and a couple of beers.

While Jordan and Magic ventured out to watch track and field, swimming, and women's basketball during their free time, Bird limited his activities because it was too difficult for him to sit in the stands. He also dreaded walking through the front entrance of the hotel, where hundreds of fans kept a vigil around the clock, patiently awaiting a Dream Team sighting.

One morning as Bird stood in the lobby, warily taking stock of the crowd, he asked the security guard, "Is there any other way out?"

The guard directed him to a side door that led to a vacant street. Bird jammed a baseball cap over his head, slipped out the exit, hopped on the subway, and went to the U.S. baseball game. He walked in with a small group of Americans who had ridden the subway with him and took turns buying beers at the concession stand. Bird happily talked balls and strikes, Major League Baseball, and even a little Dream Team gossip with his new friends. When the game ended, one hopeful fan said, "See you tomorrow, Larry?"

"You bet," he answered, and showed up the next day with his wife Dinah.

Bird appeared back in the hotel lobby the same time as Magic, who, flanked by four security guards with machine guns, was preparing to go to the boxing venue. For a moment, Bird considered telling Magic about his little side door, but then thought better of it.

"He was having fun doing it his way," Bird said.

Magic awoke each morning to a full docket of plans, whether it was a media interview, pushing baby E.J. in his carriage, an Oscar de la Hoya boxing match, or yet another act of charity.

One year earlier, Johnson and the Lakers had played in the McDonald's Open in Paris during the exhibition season, and the Make-a-Wish Foundation had asked Magic if he would meet with a seriously ill young European boy. Magic agreed, but the boy was so sick that the meeting had to be canceled. The boy was feeling stronger when the Dream Team arrived in Barcelona, but the Make-a-Wish Foundation hesitated to ask Magic to spare some time in the middle of the Olympic competition.

"I can always find time for kids," Magic answered. He took the boy to lunch, played video games with him for hours, and invited him to visit the locker room that housed the best players in the world. The boy died three months later, his own Olympic dream fulfilled.

The United States disposed of Puerto Rico 115–77 in the Olympic quarterfinals, then trounced Lithuania and its legendary center,

Arvydas Sabonis, 127–76, in the semifinals. As they were warming up for the gold medal game against Croatia, Bird began to consider how to commemorate the final game of his career. He decided to dunk in the lay-up line, but when he went to lift off, his limited mobility prevented him from getting high enough to slam it through.

"Hey, leave that stuff to me," said Jordan.

The next time down the court, Bird held his breath, extended himself as high as he could, then stuffed the ball through.

"Larry, what are you trying to do?" Magic said.

Daly had tried to conjure up some urgency before the United States played Croatia in the gold medal game. The Dream Team had already crushed the Europeans in an earlier round by 33 points, and the coach was guarding against overconfidence. When the United States trailed Croatia 25–23 early in the first half, his fears appeared somewhat justified. He was about to call his first time-out when Jordan and Johnson led them on a quick run.

The Dream Team led 52–46 at the half, but Bird still hadn't taken off his warm-ups. Assistant P. J. Carlesimo grabbed him and said, "Hey, Coach forgot about you in the first half. He's going to start you in the second half."

Bird laughed. He wasn't concerned with minutes. His goal — to step on the court in the Olympic Games representing his country — had already been reached. But he did find it amusing that Chuck Daly, who had spent much of his career in Detroit attempting to dethrone Bird and the Celtics, forgot him.

"As many times as I had broken that guy's heart, you'd think he'd remember," Bird said.

The fans wanted Bird in the game and would not stop chanting "Larr-eee, Larr-eee!" until he entered. The United States coasted to a 117–85 win, and as the buzzer sounded, Bird and Magic turned to one another and embraced. Amid cameras flashing and confetti flying, Ewing tapped them both on the shoulder.

"They had been battling each other for so long, it was nice to see them finally on the same side," he said.

As Bird stood on the medal stand with Ewing at his side and

Magic in front of him, he remembered his father, Joe Bird, a veteran of the Korean War who loved his country and stood straight and proud whenever the national anthem was played.

Magic's eyes were moist as he faced his country's flag. The Olympic Games had exceeded all of his hopes and expectations and given him one final chance to enjoy the precious gift of being part of a team that was as close to perfect as he had ever experienced.

"You had to thank Larry and Magic and Michael for making it work," Barkley said. "They were the ones who checked their egos at the door. Nobody big-timed anyone in Barcelona."

Barkley couldn't help but notice the contrast between the 1992 Olympians and the 1996 Olympic squad, which he also played on. Unlike the Dream Team, which managed to sidestep any incidents regarding minutes, the 1996 Olympians bickered over everything from who started to who wore which uniform numbers.

"It was one big ego fest," Barkley said. "Guys actually boycotted practice because they weren't happy with their playing time. It was ridiculous."

One afternoon when his '96 Olympic teammates were complaining about their minutes, Barkley finally snapped. "You should be ashamed of yourselves," he berated them. "Michael and Magic and Larry shared the ball. They shared the spotlight. And because of that, it was the experience of a lifetime. You guys are a bunch of selfish jerks."

After Barcelona, Jordan backed up his bravado from the game room of the Ambassador Hotel by winning six titles — one more than Magic, three more than Bird. He proved to be the most recognizable NBA star ever, but playing alongside Magic and Larry on the Dream Team remains one of the most cherished memories of his career.

"It was," Jordan said, "the best time I've ever had."

In the final hours before they jetted back home from Barcelona, Magic and Larry emptied their lockers and packed their bags.

"So this is it for you?" Magic asked his friend.

"Yeah, it probably is," Bird answered.

The two superstars, who spent their entire careers affixing their signatures to pictures, posters, papers, and sneakers for complete strangers, each pulled a ball from their gym bag and signed it for the other. Then they turned and walked away, leaving the game just as they had come to it — together.

★ ★ ★

11

AUGUST 18, 1992

Boston, Massachusetts

L ARRY BIRD STRODE into Dave Gavitt's office on a humid August morning. He had been home from Barcelona only nine days, and there was one unfinished piece of business that had been nagging him.

"Dave," Bird said, "I'm done. I'm retiring."

"Larry, are you sure?" Gavitt said. "I think you should take a few weeks to think it over a little longer."

Gavitt, who had watched Bird suffer in Barcelona, knew better than anyone that his star couldn't physically play anymore. Yet there was a reason why he wanted to put off Bird's announcement. If the franchise forward waited two more weeks, his contract for the following two seasons at $5 million each would kick in, and the Celtics would be obligated to pay him, even if he did retire. After everything number 33 had done for the Boston Celtics, Gavitt felt he deserved the money.

"I know what you are doing," Bird said. "I don't want the money. I didn't earn it, and I won't take it. Let's just get this over with."

281

Although there had been rumors of Bird's retirement for months, no one save Dinah and a few select Dream Team teammates could say for sure whether Bird was really done.

His final game at Boston Garden was on May 15, 1992, against the Cleveland Cavaliers. At the time, the Celtics were down 3–2 in the second round of the playoffs, and Bird steeled himself to face the fact that any game from that point on could be his last. His friend Reggie Lewis was turning into a star before his eyes, and it was Lewis's young legs (not to mention some critical free throws) that extended Bird's career. Lewis dropped 28 on the Cavs, while Bird had 16 points and 14 assists in his final game on his beloved home court.

He went to Cleveland firmly believing Boston could win Game 7, but as the Cavaliers put the finishing touches on their 122–104 victory, Bird glanced around the Richfield Coliseum and said to himself, "Well, I guess this is it."

It was a markedly subdued ending to a superlative career. Coach Chris Ford, aware that Larry was in constant pain, played his forward 33 minutes. Bird submitted 12 points (on 6-of-9 shooting) with 5 rebounds and 4 assists, but the box score was reflective of his lack of mobility. Larry didn't attempt a single free throw or three-point shot.

"I wasn't myself," Bird admitted. "If I was, maybe I would have felt worse about stopping. But I knew it was time. Hell, I should have retired after the first back surgery."

There were no grand pronouncements when the game ended. Although speculation swirled that Bird was considering retirement, no one in the locker room mentioned it — least of all Bird himself. He just quietly slipped the game ball into his gym bag and went home.

Larry would have preferred an equally low-key retirement celebration, but Gavitt had already hatched an idea to hold a tribute celebration at Boston Garden in Bird's honor and donate the proceeds to local charities.

"Let me do this for you," said Gavitt. "Let me do it for your fans. You deserve a proper sendoff."

"I don't know," Bird said. "Why would anyone want to come see me if I'm not playing ball?"

"You still don't get it, Birdie," Gavitt laughed. "You have no idea what you mean to these people."

Bird finally agreed to holding a Larry Bird Night, and the tickets sold out within an hour.

But first Bird had to make his retirement official. After he met with Gavitt, he called his attorney, Bob Woolf, who tried in vain to talk his client out of the hasty press conference.

"Larry, let's do this right," Woolf said. "Give me some time. You want this announcement to get the proper attention it deserves."

"Nope, Bob," Bird said. "I'm done now. Today. I'll see you at the press conference."

The harried Celtics public relations staff got the word out as quickly as they could. The local media flocked to the Garden, and the national pundits, aware of what the press conference meant, solemnly delivered the news that Larry Bird's basketball career was about to officially end.

Magic Johnson had already arrived at work at his downtown offices when his phone started ringing.

"You better clear some time in my schedule," Magic informed his assistant. "I think I might be kind of busy today."

Larry Bird told the people of Boston that if you didn't play for the Celtics, then you didn't play professional basketball. He told them he cherished the fact that he had played in one place his entire career. He promised them he would never — ever — make a comeback.

And then it was over.

Dinah had decided to go back to Indiana once she knew her husband was about to make his retirement official. There were too many memories, and, she surmised, it would be too emotional. She was sitting in a chair at the hairdresser's when the announcement breathlessly came across the radio.

Though Bird experienced a wave of nostalgia after the press conference, what he felt mostly was a huge sense of relief. He was in so much pain that he was ecstatic not to have to play anymore.

"At that moment," he said, "it was one of the happiest days of my life."

Larry Bird Night raised more than $1 million for 33 charities, among them WGBH, the local PBS affiliate that televised all the kids' shows that Bird's young son Conner loved to watch with his daddy.

While numerous dignitaries, celebrities, and Hall of Famers were present, the highlight was the arrival of Magic Johnson, who came nattily dressed in a suit and tie.

The Lakers had previously shipped Magic's uniform to the Garden, and as Magic began to change, he realized he'd forgotten to bring a T-shirt to wear underneath. The team tossed him a Celtics jersey and he snapped up his gold-and-purple warm-ups to cover it.

As the two legends bantered onstage during the ceremony, Bird suddenly lunged toward Magic and ripped open the Lakers warmup jacket to reveal Celtics green. The Boston fans howled with delight.

Magic, matching Bird's gesture from his own retirement, presented him with a piece of the Forum floor signed by Kareem Abdul-Jabbar, Jerry West, Elgin Baylor, and, Magic chuckled, "all those other guys you don't care about."

He told the crowd that in all the years Bird had played in Boston, he had only ever told them one lie.

"Do you know what it was?" Magic asked Bird, who was genuinely perplexed by the line of questioning.

"You said there would be another Larry Bird," Magic continued. "And I'm telling you, you're wrong. There will never be another Larry Bird. You can take that to the bank."

A year and a half following his retirement, Bird underwent spinal fusion surgery, a major medical procedure that often leaves patients permanently unable to engage in most athletic activities. The surgery was successful, and Bird was able to play golf and an occasional tennis match through the years. It was made abundantly clear to him, however, that his basketball days were over.

Magic's prognosis was much murkier. He had been living with HIV for almost a year, and his T cell count (the white blood cells called lymphocytes that protect the body against infection) was holding steady. His energy level was high, and his health was good.

He kept busy during his time away from the game. He built up his business and still rubbed shoulders with celebrities and musicians.

By the early nineties, the Jackson Five had disbanded, but the youngest brother, Michael, had become a pop icon with his *Off the Wall* album. His handlers called Magic one night and invited him to dinner. When Johnson arrived, he was presented with an elegant plate of freshly prepared chicken garnished with parsley and a bed of rice.

Magic was about to dig in when he noticed that Michael Jackson had nothing in front of him. On cue, a servant came from the kitchen and placed a bucket of Kentucky Fried Chicken on Jackson's plate.

"Is that your dinner?" Magic asked.

"You bet it is. I love this stuff," Jackson answered.

"Well, then, pass some over," Magic said. "I love it too!"

Over their fast-food meal, Jackson asked Magic to appear in his new video "Remember the Time." Eddie Murphy had agreed to play the role of a pharaoh, and Magic would be cast as his servant.

The video was cutting-edge for those times, and more than nine minutes long. Magic wore a funky Egyptian midriff and headband and banged a gong. He loved every minute of it, even though his friends teased him mercilessly for his bizarre attire. The video premiered in March 1992 and drew rave reviews.

While Magic enjoyed the opportunity to try new endeavors, he wasn't kidding himself or anyone close to him. He wanted to play basketball again, and with his health stabilized, he couldn't come up with a reason why he shouldn't.

He called Commissioner David Stern at his New York office.

"David," Magic said, "I want to make a comeback."

Stern was not particularly surprised by the phone call. He'd seen Magic at various NBA functions and could sense his restlessness. He did not object to Johnson's return but was keenly aware of how difficult it would be to sell a permanent comeback as opposed to a one-time All-Star exhibition.

In the wake of Magic's diagnosis, the NBA had taken specific steps to protect its players. Every league trainer was required to wear plastic gloves when treating an athlete. If a player was cut on the court, he had to come out until the wound was covered with a bandage.

Warm memories of the All-Star Game and his appearance in Barcelona with the Olympic team had convinced Magic that he was no different than anybody else, in spite of his medical condition. Yet once word circulated that Magic was coming back for the long haul, the goodwill toward him began to vanish. One by one, a small number of his NBA peers began publicly questioning whether someone who was HIV-positive should be playing in the league. Utah forward Karl Malone, Magic's Dream Team teammate, told the *New York Times* on November 1, 1992, that players were nervous about playing against Magic, particularly if they had any open cuts on their bodies.

"Just because he came back doesn't mean nothing to me," Malone told the paper. "I'm no fan, no cheerleader. It may be good for basketball, but you have to look far beyond that. You have a lot of young men who have a long life ahead of them. The Dream Team was a concept everyone loved. But now we're back to reality."

In the same article, Suns president Jerry Colangelo, who had been so supportive of Magic remaining a part of the Olympic squad, also conceded that players were concerned about the potential exchange of blood through cuts, even though the Players Association had repeatedly reassured them that the chances of that happening were practically nil.

"Risk is risk," Colangelo told the *Times*. "I have a son-in-law who does surgery every day, and he wears gloves, goggles, masks, and lives in mortal fear."

Magic was blindsided by the comments. Malone had said nothing in Barcelona; why was it an issue now? Johnson was particularly stung that Malone and Colangelo did not share their reservations with him before going public.

Their comments reignited the debate on whether Magic belonged in the NBA. It was a major blow to Johnson, who mistakenly believed that his peers would warmly welcome him back.

"I was really ticked off at Malone," Byron Scott said. "He had just played with Earvin in the Olympics. He knew the deal. He knew we had the best team with Earvin, and if Earv didn't play, Utah would have a better shot of getting to the Finals.

"I couldn't believe Karl would stab him in the back like that. I've never forgiven him."

Colangelo said Malone's fears were shared by many of his peers at that time, whether they articulated them or not. It was, he conceded, the result of a lack of knowledge about AIDS and HIV.

"It's pretty easy to look back now," said Colangelo, "but at the time, players were frightened. When they heard 'HIV,' a lot of red flags went up.

"I wish we had been more informed. In retrospect, had we known what we know now, I wish nothing was said. But at that time, we were saying what a lot of other people were secretly thinking."

The pressure for Stern to ban Magic increased tenfold. The commissioner stood his ground and stressed in confidential meetings with his owners that if the NBA tried to ban Johnson, they would have a major lawsuit — and public relations disaster — on their hands. It would also force the league to implement mandatory HIV testing for all of its athletes, a concept the Players Association vehemently opposed.

"Are you completely sure that Magic is our only HIV-positive player?" Stern asked his owners. "Because I'm not."

His reasoning did little to quell the cries for Stern to turn Magic away. The commissioner stubbornly held his ground, telling owners, sponsors, players, and media the same thing: "We will not be railroaded."

Within a week of the controversial *Times* article, Johnson's fate was sealed. As he was driving to the basket in an exhibition game against the Cleveland Cavaliers in Chapel Hill, North Carolina, Magic was scratched on the right arm. Under the new guidelines established by the league, game action was halted and Johnson's "wound" was attended to by trainer Gary Vitti.

Once they realized it was Magic who was cut, the crowd emitted a collective gasp. As Magic walked toward Vitti, the arena grew deathly silent.

Vitti understood what he was required to do. He needed to put on his rubber gloves and attend to the cut. But for weeks Magic's teammates had been secretly streaming into Vitti's office asking for reassurances that it was okay to play alongside Johnson. The trainer explained again and again that there was virtually no risk involved.

"That's what I was telling them," Vitti said. "Now here comes a little scratch, and I'm going to put on those gloves? To me, it was sending the wrong message."

The gloves were in his pocket. Vitti reached for them, then looked at the Laker players, who were monitoring his every move. He pulled his hand out of his pockets without the gloves and placed a Band-Aid on Magic with his bare hands.

Cleveland coach Lenny Wilkens thought the crowd's response seemed awfully dramatic for a little scratch. He looked up to the stands and realized that the fans were fixated on his players, wondering what they'd do next.

"I think they were waiting to see if we'd run off the floor," Wilkens said.

The coach scanned the expressions on the faces of his players as he waved them to the sideline. He recognized fear when he saw it. Wilkens was a longtime NBA alumnus, a Hall of Fame player for 15 seasons, and a Hall of Fame coach for another 32. He had not forgotten what Magic Johnson had done to revitalize the league during one of its most dismal periods. Wilkens admired his skill and, in the wake of his diagnosis, his courage.

As the Cavaliers huddled together, it was apparent that some players were unfazed by Magic's "injury," while others were genuinely unglued.

"I don't know about this," said one of the Cavalier starters.

"I want to go home to my family without worrying about whether I'm going to pass on some infection. Let's stop this thing," said another.

"Guys, you have to calm down," Wilkens said. "You are not in danger. It's only a scratch. Now let's get back to work."

Danny Ferry was in the Cleveland huddle. He had already guarded Magic in the game and was ready to resume playing. Yet he understood why some of his teammates were hesitant.

"The NBA tried to educate us, but to be honest, it was an uphill battle," Ferry said. "They told us we were more likely to be run over by a car than contract HIV, but some of the guys in that huddle just couldn't wrap their minds around that."

As Wilkens coaxed his team back onto the floor, he glanced over at Magic Johnson. His face was steeped in disappointment. There would be no more high-fives that day, no joyous behind-the-back passes, no playful gestures to the crowd. The look of devastation on his face was unmistakable.

"His expression said, 'I can't do this anymore,'" Wilkens said.

The collective gasp of the Chapel Hill crowd haunted Magic for years. And when Cleveland veteran Mark Price publicly joined the fray as yet another NBA player who had reservations about Johnson playing, Magic knew what had to be done. He called Cookie and told her, "It's over."

"I'm not going to hurt the league Larry and I spent so much time building up," he said.

Over the weekend, Magic called Rosen and met him at Duke's, his favorite breakfast spot. He told him he was retiring and instructed Rosen to call a press conference.

For the first time in his career, Magic didn't bother to show up.

"He was so hurt by the criticism," Rosen said. "It devastated him. I'm not sure there was ever a lower point in his life."

The morning after the Charlotte exhibition, a photograph of trainer Gary Vitti ministering to Magic Johnson was on the front page of papers throughout the country. There, in plain sight, was proof that the trainer had not used his gloves. Within days he was reported to the Occupational Safety and Health Administration (OSHA) for not following protocol. The complaint came from a Rhode Island doctor.

"Who knows what motivated him?" Vitti said. "Maybe he was a guy the OSHA had been hassling. Maybe he was an overzealous Celtics fan. All I know is that I was investigated for the next year regarding everything I'd ever done with the Lakers."

Vitti was eventually cleared by the OSHA, but while his "impropriety" made the front page, his exoneration was a one-line news item buried in the back.

By then, Magic was retired from the NBA and had organized All-Star and barnstorming teams to play in exhibition games throughout Europe. He was received with great fanfare — and little mention of his medical condition — as he played against, and beat, the top players in the world. Over time, new cases of HIV cropped up daily, and so did new courses of treatment. Americans learned to live with HIV, just as Magic Johnson did.

On January 30, 1996, nearly five years after his first retirement, Magic Johnson embarked on one final comeback. Fears about HIV had subsided considerably, and prevention and treatment of the disease were part of the daily conversation in America. This time he felt certain that he could resume playing the game he loved without any further static regarding his condition.

In his return against Golden State, Magic assumed his new role on the Lakers as a power forward/sixth man and put up 19 points, 10 rebounds, and 8 assists. He was 27 pounds heavier, less mobile, and no longer an MVP candidate, but his court vision and his unabashed enthusiasm for the game were still unparalleled.

The Lakers were a different team in 1995–96. The roster no longer included Abdul-Jabbar, Worthy, Cooper, or Scott. Magic's new running mates were Elden Campbell, Vlade Divac, George Lynch, Eddie Jones, Cedric Ceballos, and Nick Van Exel, who became annoyed when Johnson's presence began to overshadow his own accomplishments. Van Exel and Ceballos objected to the inordinate amount of attention their elder statesman received. Magic was 36 years old, past his prime. He was, they felt, horning in on the peak years of their careers.

"They couldn't deal with me," Magic said. "They were worrying about publicity and their points more than winning. It was unfortunate. Even guys like Eddie Jones, who I really respected, got caught up in it. They were so busy fighting for their turf, they forgot why they were there — to win games."

Johnson talked to them about leadership and commitment and preparation, but his sermons fell on deaf ears. He was the Lakers' past, and they were only interested in the Lakers' future. The team posted a 17–5 record in the first weeks of Magic's comeback, but Ceballos, upset over his diminished minutes, failed to show up for the team's charter flight to Seattle and was AWOL for four days. He claimed to be attending to "personal issues" but was spotted water-skiing on Lake Havasu in Arizona. Magic was incredulous when he heard about his teammate's unauthorized sabbatical, and even more disgusted when Ceballos vocalized his frustration over Johnson stealing his minutes.

The Lakers won 53 games that season, but lost in the first round of the playoffs to the Houston Rockets. When the series ended, Magic stepped on the team plane, turned to assistant coach Larry Drew, and told him, "I'm done."

He announced his retirement and vowed this time to stick to it.

"I'm glad I came back," Magic said. "I wanted to end it on my terms, not on someone else's terms."

Johnson has come to accept that his legacy will always include the fact he is HIV-positive. It has become his mission and his responsibility. When tennis star Arthur Ashe contracted AIDS following a blood transfusion after heart surgery, he called and asked Magic for his help preparing his public announcement.

Since his 1991 diagnosis, Johnson has maintained a rigorous workout schedule and a carefully monitored diet. In 2003 doctors told him there was no detectable evidence of the virus in his system, prompting Cookie to declare in a published interview, "The Lord definitely healed Earvin." While Cookie noted that her husband's physicians credited the medicine for his robust health, she said, "We claim it in the name of Jesus."

Her comments triggered an outcry from HIV and AIDS activists and the medical community. The message, they stressed, should not be that Magic was cured, but that his virus was dormant. They were gravely concerned that Cookie's comments would impede the message of how to treat and manage HIV.

"People needed to look closely at what Cookie said," Magic said. "She said, 'I feel he is cured.' She feels in her heart this is so, and God played a role in that.

"I have my own faith, but I didn't stop taking my medication. That's what the AIDS community was worried about. Their fear was people would read that and say, 'Oh, Magic says he's cured, we can stop taking our medicine now too.'

"That wasn't our message. We went out and corrected that little thing. We said, 'Everyone is entitled to their faith. Please respect that.' People calmed down once we clarified things."

Johnson is acutely aware that people remain skeptical about his explanation for how he contracted the disease. At the time he was diagnosed, the majority of HIV cases were among homosexuals, and there are many who still believe he was involved with another man.

"I've been a straight shooter all along," Magic said. "I never denied I contracted the virus, and I didn't lie about the fact I had been with many women throughout my career, even though I knew it would be hurtful to Cookie, and to my reputation.

"It was the truth, and the truth needed to be told, especially with the disease starting to run rampant in our society. If I was engaging in gay sex, don't you think somebody would have come forward by now? I'm Magic Johnson. I was only at the top of my game when I got my diagnosis. If there was someone that had been with me, don't you think we would have heard about it, just like all those politicians who keep getting themselves in trouble?

"Believe me, the tabloids tried. The [*National*] *Enquirer* had a whole fleet of people on the story. They contacted all of my friends, my family members, and a good number of my acquaintances. But they couldn't find anything about a gay lifestyle because it wasn't there.

"Honestly? I don't care what people think at this point. I know the truth. That's all that matters.

"My whole mission is to educate people. That's how I felt then, and that's how I feel now. It hurts heterosexuals if they think this can't happen to them. Here's a statistic for you: 80 percent of all new cases of HIV are heterosexual. The homosexual community has worked hard to curb the problem. They practice safe sex. They use condoms.

"It's the Latino and black population that's being hit hard now. That's why I'm still out there speaking to schools and churches and companies, because there is too much false information circulating."

There are new advances in HIV research each day, so whenever Johnson speaks to schools, businesses, or church groups, he brings along two doctors to answer medical questions.

He is heartened by his foundation's success at educating people on HIV and AIDS, yet every once in a while another incident crops up to remind him how far our society still has to go in understanding the disease and its ramifications.

In October 2008, a conservative radio host of KTLK Radio in Minnesota named Langdon Perry suggested that Magic "faked AIDS."

"You think Magic faked AIDS for sympathy?" asked his cohost, Chris Baker.

"I'm convinced Magic faked AIDS," Perry answered.

"Me too," Baker chimed in.

Within hours, Magic and HIV were in the news. The misinformed claims of the hosts quickly appeared on blogs, websites, and chat rooms across the country. Outraged AIDS activists demanded that both Perry and Baker be fired.

Magic digested the news with a measure of sadness and resignation. The talk-show host's ignorance regarding his condition was mildly surprising, but his sentiments merely picked at an old, familiar wound.

"It hurt our cause more than it hurt me," Magic said. "So many people are doing such great work trying to educate young people, and then this idiot comes along.

"It was irresponsible. When you say something, your audience takes it at face value. The station should have taken some action, but they didn't, so I guess that shows you where their minds are.

"If nothing else, get your facts straight. I never had AIDS. I still don't. They couldn't even get that right."

When Magic first announced he was HIV-positive, AZT was the only drug on the market. Now there are more than 30 options for patients. Johnson takes the antiviral medication Trizivir as well as Kaletra, a protease inhibitor made up of lopinavir and ritonavir. He hopes to dispel the misconception that because of his celebrity status and his financial means he has been provided with treatment that is not available to the masses.

"It's just not the case," Magic said. "I take the same meds as everyone else. I do what my doctors tell me to do, even though I feel great. I haven't stopped taking my medication just because I feel good. That's a mistake, I think, some HIV-positive patients make. Don't stop doing what got you to this point.

"I've been blessed. I've had this since 1991, and nothing has happened. Other people aren't doing so well. When the virus spreads, it's not good.

"This is something I'll be fighting for the rest of my life. And it's not just me. My family is affected too.

"When I'm speaking, I tell people, 'I thought the hardest thing I'd ever do is play against Larry Bird and Michael Jordan.' They start laughing. Then I say, 'But the hardest thing I've ever had to do, by far, was tell my wife I had HIV.'

"I don't know how or why I've been blessed with Cookie, but I thank God every day she's still beside me.

"The reason I'm still alive is because she stayed. If she left, I wouldn't still be here. When you deal with something of this magnitude, you need your support system. You need someone to say, 'Hey, did you work out? Did you take your meds? Are you eating right?' Or, 'You've been working too hard and too long.' Or, 'Come here, give me a hug.'

"Cookie knows me. She knows what I need. I'm a knucklehead. I need someone to take care of me. She does that. And she's an unbelievable mother too."

As the years passed and Magic's condition remained stable, Bird all but forgot about his friend's illness. As their paths crossed at the occasional private signing or appearance for the league, the topic rarely came up. Magic immersed himself in the business world, investing in everything from coffee to movie theaters to strip malls. When he opened a new Starbucks, the first person he sent a gift card to was Larry Bird.

Ten days later, Magic opened a handwritten envelope addressed to him from Indianapolis.

"Thanks for the card," Bird wrote. "Get a job."

12

★ ★ ★

SEPTEMBER 27, 2002

Springfield, Massachusetts

L
ARRY BIRD BOUNDED into the room and lowered himself into a chair a mere five feet away from the man who motivated him like no other.

"Magic Johnson," he said, in his trademark midwestern drawl.

"Larry Bird," his longtime rival responded. "Hell, man. We're back together again."

It had been almost three years since the two had seen each other. The previous occasion had not been nearly as momentous — a Fox Sports special to commemorate the 20th anniversary of their Michigan State–Indiana State clash.

On a rainy day in September 2002, the two men who shared a legacy also shared a microphone to honor the induction of Earvin "Magic" Johnson into the Basketball Hall of Fame.

Magic's original wish was for the two superstars to go into the Hall together. Each of them retired in 1992 after their Dream Team gold rush in Barcelona, but a pair of brief comebacks derailed Johnson from following the same schedule as Bird. The Hall of Fame requires players to be retired a minimum of five years before they are eligible, so in 1998 Larry went in without his Lakers rival, whose final comeback ended with the completion of the 1995–96 season.

There was never any doubt that Magic would be a first-ballot inductee; the only suspense revolved around who he'd choose to present him.

According to Hall of Fame guidelines, Johnson was required to ask someone who was already enshrined, thereby eliminating the obvious choice of Pat Riley as a candidate.

There were other members of the Lakers family Magic could have selected — Jerry West, Kareem Abdul-Jabbar, Elgin Baylor — but all along he had someone else in mind.

"I wanted Larry," Johnson said. "When I think back on my career, he's the first person who pops into my head."

He called the former Celtic and asked him to pull out his calendar.

"Larry," Magic said, "how does September look for you?"

"Why?" Bird said. "You taking me fishing?"

"I was hoping you'd present me in the Hall of Fame," Magic said.

Bird caught his breath. Magic's invitation surprised him. It was an unexpected pleasure — and an unorthodox decision to tap the very man who had tormented him for a significant portion of his professional life to present him for basketball's highest honor.

"Really?" Bird said. "Well, I'd be honored."

After he hung up the phone, Larry considered what Magic had told him. No matter where Johnson went or how many speeches he made, the first question from the audience was always the same: have you seen Larry lately? Bird experienced the same phenomenon in his travels. Without fail, someone was bound to ask him, "How is Magic feeling? Have you talked to him?"

"We're connected," Magic told Larry. "We have been for a long time, for better or for worse. And we don't see enough of each other anyway. Let's have some fun in Springfield."

Three months later, when the two convened at the Hall of Fame for a joint press conference, Bird entertained the rapt audience with the story of the day he came back from the World Invitational Tournament and breathlessly extolled Magic's basketball virtues to his brother.

"Aw, he can't be that good," Mark Bird said at the time.

After Johnson and his Spartans upended Bird's undefeated Indiana State in the NCAA championship, Mark Bird amended his comments.

"You're right," Mark told Larry. "Magic *is* better than you."

The audience roared as Bird recounted the story. Magic playfully grabbed Larry's arm, then told him, "You pushed me. You made me a better player. I shot 800 jump shots every day in the summer because I knew you were somewhere, shooting just as many."

For the next half-hour, in front of more than 100 media members, the two stars traded compliments and barbs, heartbreaks and heroics. Afterward, Magic would say, it felt as if no one else was in the room.

"Just two old friends, catching up on everything," he said.

That evening Bird stood on a podium at the Springfield Civic Center and addressed a capacity crowd teeming with Massachusetts natives and Celtics fans.

"I'd like to call out to all of you New Englanders," Bird said. "It's time to lay down your weapons. The battle is finally over. It's time to move on."

Magic fought back tears as he addressed the crowd, including Cookie and their three children, Andre, E.J., and Elisa. When he had been diagnosed with HIV, he spent countless lonely nights lying awake and dreading the moment his health would begin to deteriorate. His T cell count was so low that the doctors told him he'd live three years at the most. During those dark moments, it occurred to him that he might not live long enough to attend his own Hall of Fame induction.

"Eleven years ago," he said, wiping his eyes, "I didn't know if I'd be here to accept this honor. It's truly a blessing.

"I can't tell you what a great moment this is for me and my family. Long after I'm gone, my picture will still be up there."

"Right next to mine," said Bird.

* * *

For months after Magic Johnson retired, he had recurring dreams of playing basketball, of playing against Bird. Sometimes Magic couldn't make his body move in his dream. The game was so slow, and he'd reach for the ball, but he couldn't quite get his hands around it . . . and then he would wake up.

In Bird's dream, he would be gliding up the court, floating as if he were on a cloud, but then he'd look down to shoot, and the ball was gone. Suddenly, he was in a gym he didn't recognize, with players he'd never seen. And no matter how many times he tried, he couldn't figure out how that ball was snatched from his hands.

"Retirement" was a challenge for both men. They were presented with numerous opportunities related to basketball, but they all paled in comparison to the rush of competing against the best athletes in the world.

In March 1994, owner Jerry Buss approached Magic to ask a favor. The Lakers had stumbled out to a 21–47 start, and Buss planned to fire coach Randy Pfund.

"Could you take over as head coach until the end of the season?" Buss asked.

The team played a different brand of Laker basketball. Kareem and Michael Cooper were long gone, and Byron Scott was too. James Worthy was in his final season with the Lakers and averaging a career-low 10.2 points a game.

Magic had never coached before, yet he couldn't fathom saying no to Buss, the man who had nurtured him through his rookie season, rewarded him with the most lucrative contract in NBA history, advised him regularly on his business ventures, and tirelessly scoured the medical community to make sure Johnson was given the best possible care after his HIV diagnosis.

Johnson's disease had not affected him adversely. He painstakingly monitored his diet, his exercise, and his medication and felt healthy enough to do almost anything — even coach the Lakers.

"There's only 16 games left," Magic said, when discussing it with Cookie. "How bad could it be?"

Bird learned of Magic's new vocation on ESPN's *SportsCenter*. In all the years he had been around Johnson, he'd never heard him discuss a desire to sit on the bench. Although it would be three more years before Bird's own foray into coaching, he already knew it was a daunting undertaking that required careful research and preparation.

"You can't just say, 'Oh, I think I'll coach now,'" Bird said. "It's crazy to ask someone to do that. But that's exactly what the Lakers did with Magic."

His first day on the job, Johnson drove to practice an hour and a half early to work with the point guards. When he arrived, he was surprised to discover that no one was in the gym. Magic sat and waited. Most of the Lakers rolled in five minutes before they were due or even, in some cases, after practice was under way.

"This isn't going to work," Magic said to longtime assistant coach Bill Bertka, who had been with Johnson through the Lakers' glory years. "We used to come an hour and a half before. We used to stay an hour afterward. Don't these guys realize they need to do that to get better?"

"Earvin," Bertka replied, "it's a different time."

Johnson notched the first victory of his coaching tenure on March 27 against the Milwaukee Bucks and his old Lakers coach Mike Dunleavy. The night before the game, Magic received a one-hour pep talk from Pat Riley, who also offered some coaching tips. George Lynch, a swing player from North Carolina who Magic felt could become a force if he developed a perimeter game to complement his slashing style, scored 30 points in the win.

Yet Lynch proved to be as inconsistent as the Lakers team. Two nights after looking like an All-Star, Lynch managed just 4 points against the lowly expansion Minnesota Timberwolves, and the Lakers barely eked out a 91–89 win.

"George," Magic said to him, "you are not a good outside shooter, but in games you regularly take that shot. Why don't you come early before the next practice and we'll spend some time on shooting?"

"Sure," Lynch shrugged.

The next day Magic arrived an hour and a half ahead of time. Again, he was alone in the gym. When Lynch showed up with just three minutes to spare, Johnson waved him over.

"If you take a shot tomorrow and don't hit it, I'm yanking you out of the game," he said.

Magic turned his attention to guard Nick Van Exel, who Johnson believed would thrive in an up-tempo system. When the Lakers played Seattle on March 31, point guard Gary Payton (nicknamed "the Glove" because of his superior defense) hawked Van Exel from end line to end line. Payton disrupted his concentration and made it difficult for him to get into his offensive sets. Van Exel kept glancing over to Johnson on the sidelines for instructions.

"Don't look at me!" Magic shouted. "You call the play. You've got to get into the flow of the game."

After the 95–92 loss, Johnson offered to spend some time with Van Exel on how to see the floor and establish tempo.

"Come early before practice tomorrow and we'll do some drills," Magic said.

"I can't," Van Exel replied. "I've got an appointment."

"Another time then," Magic said.

Johnson eventually abandoned his waiting game. Van Exel never came early, and neither did Lynch. Only Rambis, Johnson's former teammate who had returned as a seldom-used bench player with the Lakers, engaged in any extra court work in advance of the scheduled practice.

On April 6, Johnson's old friend Worthy reached back into his All-Star archives and gave Magic 31 vintage points off the bench, and the Lakers came back from a 12-point deficit to edge Sacramento in overtime. Although Magic couldn't have known it, that victory, his fifth in six games, would be his last.

"Fellas, we've got to get back to fundamentals," Magic told his team after the narrow win. "You've got to pass the ball."

He explained to them that Showtime was successful because of the unselfish nature of the team. He lectured them on the value of a player like Michael Cooper, whose career average was 8.9 points a game but whose defensive commitment was a critical part of the team's success.

"You think the Celtics didn't fear Michael Cooper?" he said. "Larry Bird said he was the toughest guy he ever faced, that Coop belongs in the Hall of Fame. It's not all about getting your shots. There's so much more to the game than that."

Their reaction was muted, save a yawn from Elden Campbell. It wasn't as though Cooper was an unknown name from the past. He was an assistant coach, working with the Lakers every day. On the way out to the floor, one of the players murmured, "Who gives a shit about Showtime?"

The 1993–94 Los Angeles Lakers lost their final ten consecutive games. In a span of two and a half weeks, Magic's career coaching mark went from 5–1 to 5–11.

Before the team's last practice of the year, Magic grabbed Rambis, Worthy, and assistant coaches Larry Drew and Cooper and told them to start stretching. He laced up his sneakers and called in his team.

"I'm going to prove a point today," Magic said. "I'm going to prove to you that you don't know how to play this game. I'm going to take all these old guys, and we're going to give you a whooping."

The "old guys" won the first game 15–11. They won the second 15–8. By the third game, the young Lakers were so busy cussing at one another that Magic stopped keeping score.

In his final game as coach, Magic started Rambis, Worthy, 38-year-old center James Edwards, Van Exel, and journeyman guard Tony Smith.

"These are the guys who are willing to play the right way," he said when explaining his line-up.

LA lost that game too, and for the first time in 18 seasons the Lakers did not make the playoffs. Coach Earvin Johnson stepped down the next day. Asked how he felt, Magic responded, "Relieved."

Bird's first job in his basketball afterlife proved to be equally unfulfilling. He went to work in the Celtics front office as a special assistant to Dave Gavitt, but the team was floundering and Gavitt was at odds with owner Paul Gaston, who had assumed control of the team from his father, Don Gaston, earning him the nickname "Thanks-Dad" from *Boston Globe* columnist Dan Shaughnessy.

The Lakers and Celtics were no longer the marquee NBA franchises. Jordan's Chicago Bulls dominated the nineties, with Houston opportunistically taking advantage of Jordan's brief and quixotic sabbatical to pursue professional baseball.

Boston was left shorthanded by the sudden demise of the Big Three. The Celtics bungled the 1993 draft by selecting Acie Earl, an awkward forward from Iowa. They won just 32 games and missed the playoffs for the first time in 14 years. Gavitt was fired, and Earl was eventually traded.

Bird stayed on after M. L. Carr was named vice president of basketball operations, but he operated largely as a figurehead. A disturbing pattern developed when it came to Bird's input on basketball decisions: Gaston and Carr would ask his opinion, listen carefully, then make decisions that were often at odds with what Larry recommended.

A month after Bird told them Sherman Douglas was their best player, the Celtics traded him to Milwaukee for Todd Day (who failed to grasp the team concept the Celtics stressed) and fading veteran Alton Lister. When the team contemplated signing 34-year-old Dominique Wilkins as a free agent, Bird, who suspected it was a public relations ploy to sell tickets rather than bolster the roster, warned them, "Don't do it. There's nothing worse than a superstar past his prime. 'Nique will need to be 'the man,' and it's going to ruin your chemistry."

Gaston nodded. M.L. did too. One week later, they announced with great fanfare the signing of Wilkins to a three-year, $11 million contract. 'Nique's brief tenure with Boston was a colossal disappointment. He bickered with coach Chris Ford, shot 42 percent from the floor, and eventually asked out of his deal so he could escape overseas. Wilkins's only contribution of any significance in a Celtics uniform was to score the final points in the legendary Boston Garden before it was torn down.

Bird officially terminated his relationship with the Celtics in 1997, but his connection to the only franchise he had ever played for had been damaged beyond repair long before that. The only reason

Larry didn't leave sooner was that, after undergoing fusion surgery on his back, his surgeon warned him the recovery would be slow and fraught with potential difficulty. Bird stayed on the Celtics payroll so he could continue to be treated by his Boston medical team.

Although Magic often publicly lamented Bird's fractured relationship with the Celtics, number 33 refused to dwell on the split.

"I'm pretty good at moving on," he said.

Upon his departure from the Celtics, Bird retreated to Naples, Florida, where he fished, played golf, splashed in his pool with his young children, Conner and Mariah, and spent many evenings watching the Miami Heat play. He became fixated on Pat Riley's ability to motivate his players, and as Bird took mental notes of Riley's strategies, for the first time he experienced the urge to try coaching himself.

In May 1997, Pacers president Donnie Walsh contacted Bird about Indiana's coaching vacancy, in part because he was Larry Legend from Indiana and would generate some buzz for the team. Yet Walsh also wanted some assurances that Bird had given some thought to his coaching style.

"So what would you do with this team?" Walsh asked Bird.

He was expecting a general answer. Instead, Bird took Walsh from his first practice all the way through the NBA Finals, something Walsh had never seen before and does not expect to see again. Bird's detailed response included specific examples of how he'd run practice, what time the plane would leave, what offense he'd use, how he'd deal with the media, and a breakdown of each player outlined by their strengths and weaknesses.

"Oh, and one more thing," Bird said. "I'm only coaching three years. No matter what happens. After three years, your players tune you out."

Some of his ideas were his own. Others he adopted from conversations with Portland assistant coach Rick Carlisle, who had given him a binder overflowing with coaching techniques before the interview.

After Bird landed the job, he lured Carlisle and fellow Portland assistant coach Dick Harter to Indianapolis. In their first meeting,

Bird told them, "I'm going to pump these guys up and give them so much confidence that by my third year here we'll make the Finals."

He gave Harter the responsibility of running the defense and put Carlisle in charge of the offense, including diagramming the plays in the huddle. It was a highly unusual move to give so much responsibility to an assistant, but Bird didn't care. He was learning. Carlisle was better than he was at drawing up the plays.

Bird's expectations were straightforward: be in shape, be respectful, be on time. He enforced all three. In his first year, the Pacers were taking a charter flight to Nashville, Tennessee, for an exhibition game against the Charlotte Hornets. At precisely 4:00 P.M., Bird signaled for the pilot to start the engine and take off. At 4:03, Dale Davis and Travis Best ran out onto the tarmac, bags in hand. The pilot cut the engine. Bird signaled for him to rev it up again. The door remained closed and the plane took off, leaving two of the team's key players standing on the runway in disbelief.

Bird was enthused about the team's nucleus: Reggie Miller, his scorer and his leader; center Rik Smits; veteran point guard Mark Jackson; and redoubtable forwards Dale Davis and Antonio Davis (no relation). His bench included Best and the versatile Jalen Rose, and when he acquired former Dream Team teammate Chris Mullin, Bird felt that he had the ammunition to make a run at Jordan and his Bulls.

Indiana catapulted from 39 to 58 wins, the biggest turnaround in franchise history. Bird was voted NBA Coach of the Year, and the team advanced to the Eastern Conference Finals, where they lost to the Bulls in seven games.

The Pacers limped home knowing they had been one play away from shocking Jordan's team. Midway through the fourth quarter of Game 7, Indiana was up by three points when a jump ball was called between Jordan and the seven-foot Smits.

As the players gathered around the circle, Bird noticed Scottie Pippen and Reggie Miller jockeying for position. He didn't like how Pippen was a shade in front of Miller.

"Reggie could get beat on that," he thought to himself.

Indiana's alignment was set up perfectly for Smits to tip behind his head — except that, as Bird realized in a moment of horror, his center never tipped that way.

The coach turned to his assistants to make sure he had a timeout. In that moment of hesitation, the ball was tossed. Bird hollered for time, but it was too late. Pippen stepped in front of Miller to intercept the tip, and the Bulls turned the possession into a Steve Kerr three-pointer. Indiana went on to lose the game and the series.

For the next three months, Bird brooded over his rookie mistake. He knew from his own playing days that chances at the Finals were fleeting, and it gnawed at him that he had cost his veterans a chance to get there.

The following season Smits battled foot troubles, and some of the older players began grumbling about their reduced roles. Again the Pacers made it to the Eastern Conference Finals, and again they were denied a trip to the Finals, this time by Patrick Ewing of "Harry and Larry" fame.

The Pacers juggled their personnel during the off-season, trading Antonio Davis for high school phenom Jonathan Bender and placing Jalen Rose in the starting lineup. He responded by leading the team in scoring. Bird perused the NBA rosters, searching for a scorer and rebounder who could put them over the top. He called the seaside town of Split, Croatia, and tracked down former Celtic Dino Radja, who had played two and a half seasons with Boston but left under vague circumstances.

"Dino, this is Larry Bird," he said. "I want to talk to you about coming back to the NBA and playing with the Pacers."

"How did you get this number?" Radja said.

"I don't remember who gave it to me — what difference does it make?" Bird said. "If this is a bad time, I can call you back. I'm trying to make you an offer to come back and play."

"Oh, okay . . . I see," Radja said.

"We have a chance to win a championship," Bird said. "We could use another front-court player. I thought you would fit in nicely with what we are trying to do."

"I'm sorry," Radja said. "How did you say you got this number?"

An exasperated Bird finally hung up. Years later, he ran into

Radja during a scouting trip in Croatia. "You know, Dino, you cost me a real good chance of winning a championship," he said.

"I know, Larry," Radja said. "I'm sorry. I was going through some tough times."

In November 1999, in Bird's third (and final) season as head coach, the team stood at 7–7 and had just been thrashed by Seattle on the road. With Portland up next, Indiana was looking at the prospect of its first losing month since Bird arrived.

Bird had said little about the poor showing against the Sonics the night before. But when he gathered his team together minutes before tip-off against the Blazers, he let them know he hadn't forgotten.

"Listen," Bird said, "I'm going to give you guys one more chance tonight, because what happened in Seattle was an embarrassment to the game of basketball. If you guys don't play, don't worry. I'll find someone who will."

Indiana went on to beat Portland and won 15 of its next 17 games. It was the springboard to a 56-win season, a 25-game winning streak at home, and the elusive trip to the Finals against league MVP Shaquille O'Neal, Kobe Bryant, and the Los Angeles Lakers.

The Lakers were heavily favored, and the Pacers couldn't match their depth or talent, even when Kobe went down with an injured ankle. After Indiana fell in six games, Smits retired, Jackson signed elsewhere, and Dale Davis was traded. Bird resigned, just as he said he would, despite entreaties from Walsh to remain.

He drove back down to Florida, looked around his beautiful home, and asked Dinah, "Now what am I going to do?"

Both Magic and Bird had visions of owning an NBA franchise. Johnson joined a bid to buy the Toronto Raptors headed by construction magnate Larry Tanenbaum and Labatt Breweries (a founding partner of the Toronto Blue Jays baseball team), but they lost out to a group that swayed the expansion committee by proposing a centrally located downtown site accessible by public transportation.

Bird and businessman Steve Belkin formed a group to buy a new franchise in Charlotte, but the expansion committee instead chose a group headed by billionaire Robert Johnson, the founder of Black Entertainment Television (BET), making him the first African American majority owner in the NBA.

Both Magic and Larry walked away from their ownership bids bitterly disappointed. While they still enjoyed unparalleled cachet in basketball circles, when it came to buying an NBA team they were simply two more businessmen trying to cash in on the success of the very league they helped grow into a flourishing multimillion-dollar empire. Magic had already been a minority owner of the Lakers for years, but he still wistfully wondered what it would be like to have his own team.

Although Bird had been retired from basketball for almost a decade, he was still in demand for private shows and appearances for Fortune 500 companies. The most lucrative requests were for Magic and Larry to appear in tandem. During these occasional rendezvous, both men noted that the laughter came more easily and the camaraderie more naturally now that there were no championships at stake.

And every time they made solo appearances, they fielded the same questions: What's Larry like? What's Magic like? Their lives had become intertwined, like vines from an old tree that had crossed paths so many times they were permanently entangled. The world remained fixated on their relationship.

"When I came into the league," Bird told an audience of financiers, "I wanted to make a million dollars. Magic wanted to make a hundred million dollars. And we both got what we wanted."

As a player, Magic cut his own licensing agreement with the NBA and left other players kicking themselves for not thinking of it first. When the Lakers were on the road, he'd hobnob with corporate executives in each city, becoming friendly with power brokers like Hollywood's Michael Ovitz and Starbucks CEO Howard Schultz.

Johnson's mission was to establish thriving businesses in underserved communities. Where others saw urban blight and decay,

Magic saw opportunity. He signed a partnership with Sony Entertainment and opened a 13-screen multiplex theater at the Baldwin Hills Crenshaw Plaza in Los Angeles. His inner-city theaters featured murals of African American heroes like Martin Luther King Jr. and Jackie Robinson. He insisted on multiple concession stands offering cultural snacks and stadium seating.

As Magic conceptualized the revitalization of city neighborhoods, it was apparent to him that the glaring omission in his vision was the lack of a meeting place. In 1998, through a partnership with Starbucks, he opened his first Urban Coffee Opportunities store in Los Angeles.

His formula proved to be a stunning success. Magic Johnson Enterprises grew to be worth more than $700 million, yet it was his unique way of assisting minorities while still turning a profit that made him the envy of his NBA peers. Players who used to flock to Johnson for basketball advice now approached him as their business guru.

"Forget all the basketball stuff," said Charles Barkley. "The economic opportunities he provided poor people in their own communities is the most remarkable thing he's ever done."

Johnson continued to educate the world about HIV and AIDS, writing children's books and appearing regularly on the talk-show circuit. When both diseases emerged as a major problem in China, he filmed public service announcements with national hero Yao Ming.

"My goal after I found out I was HIV-positive was not to let that define me," Johnson said. "It has been a long road, but I think people only see that as a small part of my life now."

In 2002 Bird finally relented and accepted an offer from Donnie Walsh to return to the Pacers in a front-office role as president of basketball operations.

On the surface, the Pacers had all the tools to contend for a title. They had Reggie Miller, one of the most lethal shooters of all time, and Jermaine O'Neal, a blue-chip center in the prime of his career. Forward Ron Artest, the most versatile player on the roster, was powerful, hit shots, could defend, and was notably unselfish on the floor. In 2003–2004, Artest averaged 18.3 points, 5.7 rebounds, and 3.7 assists and was named Defensive Player of the Year.

After Artest led Indiana to the Eastern Conference Finals in 2004, Bird and Walsh briefly discussed trading him while his value was at its peak. Ultimately, the Pacers stood pat, and for a while the decision paid dividends.

Artest, O'Neal, and the mercurial Stephen Jackson set the tone in practice with hard fouls and incessant trash-talking. Their emotions were their greatest asset and their biggest weakness. Reggie Miller, the consummate professional, tried to provide a calming influence, but there was only so much he could do.

"Some days he'd just look at me and shake his head," Bird said.

On the night of November 19, 2004, Bird sat in his living room watching his team put the finishing touches on a critical win over the Detroit Pistons in Auburn Hills, Michigan. There were only 45.9 seconds to go when Artest thumped Detroit big man Ben Wallace as he drove to the basket. It was a hard foul in a game that was already decided, and Wallace wheeled around and shoved Artest to articulate his displeasure. That ignited a mild skirmish between both benches, but officials separated the players and appeared to successfully quell any further tensions.

Yet Bird could not avert his eyes from two disturbing images on his high-definition screen: Wallace lingering on the court several minutes after order had seemingly been restored, and Artest reclining on top of the scorer's table with his hands behind his head.

"Ronny, get out of there," Bird shouted at the television set in his suburban Indianapolis home.

Artest lay serenely on his back, as if he were blissfully unaware of the turmoil he had helped generate.

"This is not good," Bird said to his son Conner, who sat beside him on the couch.

In twelve years, Larry's son had grown from a toddler tossing pool balls down the stairs in Barcelona to an active teenager who loved the NBA and his dad's team, the Pacers. Conner didn't completely grasp what was unfolding at the Palace of Auburn Hills that night, but he accurately read the level of concern on his father's face.

"Dad, what's wrong?" Conner asked.

Within seconds, everyone in America knew the answer. As both Birds looked on, a Pistons season ticket holder hurled a cup of beer at Artest's chest. The liquid splattered across his uniform, and Artest vaulted himself over the scorer's table, fracturing four vertebrae in the back of Pacers radio play-by-play man Mark Boyle as he flailed and clawed his way into the stands.

Stephen Jackson immediately bolted after him, and for a split-second Bird was hopeful that "Jack" would pull Artest away. Instead, Jackson joined Artest in the seats, throwing punches and escalating the confrontation into a full-scale brawl between NBA players and their paying public.

Jack's actions surprised Bird. He knew how important it was to Jackson to establish himself as a centerpiece of the Pacers. In 2003, the year before he actually joined the team, he was a free agent and told both Bird and Donnie Walsh that he would play for them at a reduced rate.

"I think you guys have a great team," Jackson said at the time. "I'd play for nothing just to be here."

"You don't hear that too often," Bird said after the meeting.

"You're not kidding," Walsh answered. "I wish we had the money for him."

Indiana didn't have the cap room to sign Jackson for 2003–2004, so Jackson signed a one-year deal with Atlanta. But neither Bird nor Walsh forgot Jackson's passionate interest in their team. In July 2004, they acquired him from the Hawks for Al Harrington and brought him aboard believing he could be the final piece to a team that might vie for the Eastern Conference title, and maybe even the championship.

But now, four months later, Jackson was in the middle of an escalating skirmish in the stands, the last place any NBA player should ever be.

Conner gasped as the fists flew. His father groaned and put his head in his hands.

Earvin Johnson, watching from his study in Beverly Hills, was dumbfounded. He had made a special effort to watch the game, a rematch of the 2004 Eastern Conference Finals, because he knew Bird's team was playing. Magic's habit of keeping tabs on his old rival hadn't subsided even after they stopped competing.

"Cookie, come here, you won't believe this," Magic called to his wife. "These crazy fools are fighting with the fans!"

Detroit forward Rasheed Wallace, attempting to act as a peacemaker, ventured into the stands, but the Palace was in a state of panic, with players and fans exchanging blows. Pacers reserve Fred Jones, attempting to pull his teammates out of the fray, was sucker-punched from behind. A metal chair was tossed into the loge section, striking innocent bystanders.

Soon the melee spilled onto the floor. Pistons coach Larry Brown, his face drained of color, snatched the public-address microphone to appeal to the angry crowd to stop, but they could not hear him. Brown, dodging objects hurled onto the Palace court by his own fans, threw the microphone down in disgust.

As he watched the brawl unfold, Magic began calculating the damage it would inflict on the NBA. The league had been enormously successful, riding the momentum that he and Bird and Michael generated. Their exploits transformed the NBA into must-see TV, and in 2002 the league signed a network contract valued at $4.6 billion, a significant upgrade over the four-year, $74 million pact the NBA inked in Magic and Larry's rookie season.

Michael Jordan had seized the baton and led the league to spectacular new heights with his high-flying, jaw-dropping play. In that time, Jordan cashed in on a portfolio of endorsements that included Gatorade, McDonald's, Coca-Cola, Chevrolet, Hanes, Wheaties, and Rayovac and that was valued at hundreds of millions of dollars at its peak.

But Magic, Larry, and Michael were retired, and in 2004 the league was at a crossroads. The Lakers won three straight championships from 2000 to 2002, but were reeling from allegations of rape by a Colorado woman against their shining star, Kobe Bryant, and from a bitter feud that erupted between Bryant and superstar teammate Shaquille O'Neal.

LeBron James had just completed his rookie season and served notice he would figure prominently in the NBA's future, but he had not yet been ordained "King James." Though his time was surely coming, LeBron's accomplishments, like those of his NBA peers, were about to be dwarfed by the bedlam in Auburn Hills.

"It was the worst thing I'd ever seen," Magic said. "Like watching a car wreck. We're supposed to cherish the fans — no matter what. They say bad things all the time. They throw things and you deal with it and you go home, and it's a new day."

Not this time. The line had been crossed, and the results were teetering on catastrophic. In an unprecedented decision, the referees canceled the final 45.9 seconds of the game. As the Indiana players tried to leave the court, they were pelted with cups, popcorn, batteries, and beer. The Indiana Pacers and the Detroit Pistons, by Magic's calculations, had just set the NBA back ten years.

"Poor Larry," Magic said to Cookie. "This has got to be his worst nightmare."

Within minutes, Bird was on the line with Rick Carlisle, his friend and former teammate who was now the head coach of the Pacers.

"There's cops everywhere," Carlisle told Bird. "It's chaos here."

"Do you have someone with Ronny?" Bird asked.

"Yes, he's surrounded by security," Carlisle reported. "We're getting on the bus and getting the hell out of here. I think we'll be all right."

As Bird hung up the phone and dialed Walsh, who was attending a wedding in New York, he knew the Pacers would not be all right. He recognized a bona-fide disaster when he saw one.

Bill Walton, who was in Auburn Hills to broadcast the game, somberly informed his audience, "This is the lowest moment in my 30 years of the NBA."

While Bird understood the magnitude of what had just occurred, even he couldn't have forecasted how devastating it would be to his franchise.

Commissioner David Stern was out to eat with friends when he was interrupted by a flurry of urgent phone calls. He found the nearest television set and returned to his table, grim-faced. Dinner was over.

So were the championship hopes of Larry Bird and the Indiana Pacers.

Reggie Miller had been injured and wearing street clothes the night Artest whacked Ben Wallace and ignited the worst brawl in NBA history. One of the many things Bird revisited in the wake of the incident was how it might have been different had Miller been in uniform and able to convince Artest to come off the scorer's table.

The morning after the fight, the condemnations began in earnest. This was not just a *SportsCenter* topic; *World News Tonight*, CNN, and the *Wall Street Journal* weighed in. In interviews, Magic Johnson, his voice stern, called for lengthy suspensions of Artest, Jackson, and O'Neal.

"Thanks, buddy," said Bird, as Johnson declared that the Indiana players had "destroyed all the goodwill that Larry and Michael and myself have built up through the years."

Commissioner David Stern handed down sanctions that were unprecedented: Artest was suspended for the remainder of the season, which amounted to 86 games — 76 regular season and 10 postseason. Jackson was suspended for 30 games and O'Neal for 25 games, although his punishment was later reduced to 15 games. Detroit instigator Ben Wallace received a 6-game suspension, which left Artest and his teammates crying foul.

Bird didn't care what penalties were levied against the Pistons. His only concern was how he could salvage his team's season.

"I thought Artest deserved at least 30 games," Bird conceded. "I could have even understood the rest of the regular season. But then to hold him out of the playoffs after our guys worked so hard to keep it all together . . . I thought that really was unfair.

"Jack's mistake was he should have gone into the stands as a peacemaker and instead he ended up fighting. You can't do that.

"One thing I learned throughout my career in the NBA was players cannot go in the stands for any reason."

Even though Bird was aware that he and Walsh needed to make some major changes, it wasn't without regret. He had grown to appreciate his Pacers players, warts and all. He had seen a side of Jackson and Artest he knew the public would never see. "There is a lot of good in those guys," Bird said.

Bird's private stance on Artest was at odds with the public stance he felt obligated to take. Bird was genuinely fond of Artest and identified with his uncommon intensity, but by stubbornly standing by him, he knew his own legacy would lose some of its luster.

"I knew all along it was a major gamble," Bird said. "But I felt sorry for the guy. Some days he'd come in, and he just wasn't prepared to practice. It was so sad, because he just didn't know how to help himself.

"I knew I was going to take some major hits, but I felt it was my responsibility to stand up for him and all the other guys involved. I did it because I cared about them, even when they messed up. When you spend as much time as we did, day in and day out with these guys, you feel a connection with them. I'm not excusing what they did. But I couldn't see turning my back on them either."

In the fall of 2005, after Artest had served his full suspension, public relations director David Benner came to Bird and told him *Sports Illustrated* wanted Artest and Bird to pose together on the cover.

"I don't think so," Bird said. "Hey, I love Ronny, but that is not a good idea."

"Larry," Benner persisted, "think of the organization. We're hurting. We need some positive publicity. You are one of the only guys that can give us that kind of credibility."

"I knew my reputation was on the line," Bird said. "In my heart I knew, if Ronny had another incident, what it would mean for me, but I did what I had to do."

Larry knew Benner was receiving pressure from above to make the photograph happen, so he relented. The October 24, 2005, issue of *Sports Illustrated* featured a seated Artest on the cover with Bird standing behind him, his arms folded. The headline, "The Odd Couple," was accompanied by a caption that read, "You may not love Ron Artest but Larry Bird does."

In the accompanying article, Bird claimed Artest's work ethic made him a guy he would "pay money to watch." Artest professed his love for Indianapolis, the Pacers, and Bird and asked for a Polaroid copy of his cover shoot with his Hall of Fame boss.

Yet, when asked by *Sports Illustrated* reporter L. Jon Wertheim what he learned from the brawl, Artest answered, "People want to be like, Ron Artest is changed. He's a new man. Wait. I never said I changed. I'm pretty much the same guy. I got a better understanding of things, but it wasn't like I was provoking all that stuff that happened. So what's to learn? Nothing. Only thing to learn is that David Stern was trying to kick me out of the league."

Magic winced when he saw the "Odd Couple" cover. He wondered why Bird would align himself with Artest, and he became even more perplexed when he read the player's comments.

"What's Larry doing with that knucklehead?" Magic said to his brother. "Probably trying to save the franchise. Only Larry Bird could put a positive spin on this. He's taking one for the team, I guess."

Despite Artest's assertions that he wanted to finish his career with the Pacers and owed the fans and management a championship for standing behind him, it took all of 15 games for him to renege on his promise.

Artest announced that he needed a one-month sabbatical from basketball to work on and promote his new rap CD. It was a stunning act of selfishness that immediately put the franchise in a tailspin — again.

"Ronny, what are you doing? I put myself on the line for you," Bird said to Artest.

"I know," Artest said. "That was cool."

One afternoon Artest timidly knocked on Bird's office door and slumped into the seat opposite his desk. He apologized profusely for letting his boss down and promised to be at practice, focused and ready.

Forty-eight hours later, he told coach Rick Carlisle he had changed his mind and was going to record the CD.

"I can always play basketball," Artest told Carlisle. "I can play basketball until I'm 50. But I've got to do this CD thing because I'm hot right now."

"Ronny," Bird said. "You are under contract to us."

Artest shrugged.

The conversation was over. There would be a dozen more just like it, but Bird had already made up his mind that the Pacers had to cut ties with their forward.

"Ron had no idea how badly he was hurting us," Bird said. "He couldn't see it."

Artest was placed on the inactive list and eventually shipped to the Sacramento Kings for shooter Peja Stojakovic. He was traded again in July 2008 to the Houston Rockets. A month before that swap, Artest came through Indianapolis to work out and ran into Bird on the practice court. He apologized for all the trouble he had caused and asked Larry to bring him back to the Pacers.

"Ron, how do you expect me to bring you back here after everything that's happened?" Bird said.

By then, Indiana had already traded Stephen Jackson to Golden State and was in the process of dealing Jermaine O'Neal to Toronto. They were going to have to start over, with a fresh approach and new faces.

Larry understood that he was dealing with a new breed of athlete. They were a different generation that wanted to carve out their own course, just as Bird did when he came to the NBA.

"But sometimes it was hard," Bird conceded. "You could see they were heading in the wrong direction, no matter how much you tried to help them."

Indiana began rebuilding around young swingman Danny Granger, who in his fifth season with the team in 2008–2009 was selected to play in the All-Star Game.

"We're on our way back," Granger said during All-Star weekend. "It's all about looking forward now."

While Bird's Pacers pointed to the future, Magic's Lakers were poised to make some noise in the here and now. Johnson took his role as the Lakers vice president seriously. He spent time talking with his players and sharing his experiences with superstar Kobe Bryant, who submitted an MVP year in 2007–2008 and quickly established the Lakers as the favorite to win the NBA crown.

The Celtics, meanwhile, had undergone some changes. After a wretched 24-win season in 2006–2007, Celtics boss Danny Ainge acquired veteran sniper Ray Allen. Then Ainge pried away former MVP Kevin Garnett from his friend, Minnesota general manager Kevin McHale, in a blockbuster deal that transformed Boston's prospects virtually overnight.

Bird (who earned the final say over personnel decisions when Walsh left the Pacers in 2007) inquired about Garnett's availability a week before the Timberwolves made the deal with the Celtics. At the time, McHale told Bird he didn't want to trade Garnett and the face of their franchise was content to stay put.

"So I called him back after the trade," Bird said. "I asked him, 'What changed?' He talked around and around it. Then it finally hit me. Kevin wasn't really making the final decision. I know he didn't want to part with Garnett. He was smart enough to know they'd never get enough in return. It probably came from up above."

With Garnett setting the tone in 2007–2008, the Celtics played lockdown defense, the best Bird had seen in a long time. He liked their rotation and applauded the maturation of Paul Pierce, who seemed liberated by the new personnel. Allen was the perimeter spoke of the new Big Three. Their bench players James Posey, Eddie House, P. J. Brown, and Leon Powe thrived in their specific roles.

Magic eyed the Boston roster warily, but was optimistic that when the Lakers added forward Pau Gasol they'd have enough strength up front to offset the loss of center Andrew Bynum, their young and rapidly improving big man whose knee injury ruled him out of playoff contention.

LA's world revolved around Kobe, the most prolific scorer in the league. Before the Finals started, Bryant assumed the unofficial role of the team's spokesman and predicted his team would be united and prepared against Boston.

Magic believed it — until he looked out of the window of Boston's Four Seasons Hotel just hours before Game 2 and saw Lamar Odom loaded up with shopping bags less than three hours before game time. Johnson was fond of Odom, but couldn't believe his eyes.

"What is he doing?" Magic said. "It's 95 degrees outside. He should be resting! Does he know there's a game today?"

Johnson rode down the elevator with the Lakers coaches and informed them of what he'd seen.

"They don't grasp the magnitude of this moment," said veteran assistant Frank Hamblen. "They don't understand they might never have this chance again."

Before the Finals started, the league asked Bird and Magic to conduct a conference call for the legions of journalists who wanted to revisit the great rivalry of the eighties. Bird was hesitant. He called Magic to discuss how they should handle it.

"This shouldn't be about us," Bird said. "These young guys deserve their turn. Let's do this one thing and get out of the way."

"Agreed," said Magic, who knew Kobe chafed at comparisons to the Showtime days. "We'll keep the 'Magic and Larry Show' to one hour."

The two icons conducted the conference call, then agreed to pose for a split-screen advertisement promoting the Finals.

"After that," Bird said, "I disappeared."

As the Boston-LA series got under way, Magic sat down in front of a TV and popped in eighties footage of the epic battle between his Lakers and Bird's Celtics. He watched in silence, admiring the ball movement and the speed of the game. He marveled at the passing skills of his teammates and how the ball rarely touched the floor.

"I wish they still played the game like this," he told his son E.J.

Bird placed a phone call to one player before the Finals: Lakers forward Luke Walton, son of Bill Walton. Bird, who had known Luke since he was a young hellion riding his tricycle through Larry's kitchen, left him a message wishing him luck and reminded him to savor every moment.

Magic also placed a call to one player: Celtics star Paul Pierce, who grew up in the shadows of the Forum in Inglewood, California, worshiping Magic and the Lakers. Pierce had played summer ball with Magic, who counseled him on everything from the proper dribbling drills to the knack of staying humble amid his sudden change in fortune. He also cautioned Pierce "to leave the street behind" as he made his climb to the NBA elite.

"You can't be hanging on that corner anymore," he told Pierce. "You can see your guys, say hello, but then you've got to keep on moving. You have different responsibilities now. They just can't be a central part of your life anymore. You can see them once in a while, help 'em out if you want, but there's too much at stake to find yourself in a position that just doesn't make sense."

In their final conversation before the Finals, Bird and Magic talked briefly about Pierce's personal growth. Bird said he was happy the kid would finally have some of his own Finals highlights. For years Pierce had looked up at his own Jumbotron and seen clips of Russell, Havlicek, and Bird. His franchise had been stuck in the past, and now, finally, with Garnett and Allen alongside him, the future was now.

"Lakers in six," Magic told Bird, before he signed off.

"Your boys are going down," Bird shot back.

Bird didn't believe the Lakers could match Boston's defensive intensity. He felt that Lamar Odom was the key to the series and was stunned by how easily the Celtics negated him.

"I thought the Lakers were the softer team," Bird said. "And as great as Kobe is, everything has to run through him. He dominates the ball a lot. If he has any inkling things aren't going the team's way, then it's up to him to take over the game the way Michael [Jordan] used to. But even Michael will tell you, it's hard to win that way.

"The Lakers are at their best when Kobe comes down, gives the ball up, cuts through, and they swing it back around to him. That's when he's most deadly. I always felt the same way about Michael."

As Danny Ainge sat court-side in the third quarter of Game 6, with his Celtics up 3–1 in games and bulldozing their way to an insurmountable 31-point advantage that would clinch the championship, he looked down at his cell phone and saw a new text message in the inbox.

"Congratulations," Bird wrote. "You, your players, and [coach] Doc [Rivers] deserve it."

When the Celtics secured their 17th championship on the fabled parquet, neither Bird nor Magic was in the building to witness it. Bird was home in Indianapolis, keeping his promise to stay away from the limelight of the current players. Although Johnson was on the Lakers' masthead, his interaction with the 2008 team was minimal because so few of the players seemed interested in his input.

"I love the Lakers," Magic said. "I've been through it all. In our day you went up to the old players and asked them how it was. You learned from them.

"It bothers me the young guys don't have enough respect to do that today. They feel they know it already. And the second part is, they think we're 'old school,' like they are playing a different game than we did. They don't realize basketball is basketball. The only player that's ever asked me anything is [point guard] Derek Fisher."

Magic noted that Kobe Bryant appeared to be more invested in his teammates during the 2008 Finals than in other seasons. He witnessed some leadership from the gifted guard that he hadn't seen before.

"I wanted Kobe to enjoy it, because the work it takes to get to the Finals is too hard to be joyless," Magic said. "You need to be able to share it with the guys.

"You don't want your teammates to be walking down the street someday and have their son or daughter say to them, 'Daddy, what kind of teammate was Kobe Bryant?' and have him say, 'I didn't know him. He never let me in,' or worse, 'He's not my kind of guy.' I thought Kobe made great strides in the [2008] Finals. He's always been a tremendous player, and now he's figuring out how to add the leadership component to that."

Kobe and the Lakers were again among the best in 2008–2009. Boston also contended until Garnett suffered a knee injury in February. The Lakers beat Orlando for the title, and the revised LA-Boston rivalry came full circle.

The only missing component was Magic and Larry. Their rivalry was one for the ages, a timeless bridge to a day when the shorts were shorter, the game was simpler, and the two best players dominated by setting someone else up to succeed. While Jordan became widely recognized as the best player of his generation, the absent piece of his résumé was the consistent foil to measure himself against. There were a number of challengers, among them Clyde Drexler, Charles Barkley, John Stockton, and Karl Malone, yet none could match Michael's intensity or his abilities. He was a singular sensation, while his predecessors were a tandem of brilliance.

"Larry and Magic are still the only two guys I know who could take ten or eleven shots and still dominate the game," said Kevin McHale. "That was the major difference between them and Jordan. If you got Michael to take eleven shots, you had dominated *him*."

Knicks executive Donnie Walsh warmed to Bird and Magic because they shattered the myth that you didn't have to come to an NBA game until the fourth quarter because nobody played hard until then.

"Larry and Magic played hard from the first possession to the last," Walsh said. "They didn't take a single play off, and they forced their teammates to match their intensity.

"Great players are difficult. They're different, driven. They operate on a different plane. Everyone says, 'I don't want to lose.' Magic and Larry said, 'I'll kill you if I lose.'"

Kurt Rambis, an assistant coach with the Lakers, has never forgotten that Magic's championship performance in 1980 was on tape delay. (He occasionally utilizes that snippet of information to illustrate the growth of the league for today's players.) The role Johnson and Bird played in the rejuvenation of the NBA, he said, has cemented their legacy.

"Their college rivalry pulled an audience toward the NBA that might not ever have come otherwise," Rambis said. "The characteristic that set them apart was their willingness to let someone else hit the winning shot. They didn't need to do it themselves. They were happy to make the pass.

"That was a huge thing. You didn't see much of it then, and you don't see much of that now."

Danny Ainge was one of those fair-weather NBA fans Rambis referred to. Although he was an accomplished college basketball player, Ainge also excelled in baseball and was a draft pick of the Toronto Blue Jays. At the time, he had only a passing interest in professional basketball.

"But then I started following the Celtics and the Lakers and Larry and Magic," Ainge said. "They piqued my interest. I started thinking, 'Maybe I should try the NBA.'"

Together, Magic and Larry amassed 39,498 career points, 15,836 assists, 15,533 rebounds, and 3,280 steals. Yet the numbers don't begin to explain their impact on the game. When Bird and Johnson called it quits, the NBA emitted a collective sigh.

"You will never see anyone like them again," declared Bill Walton. "When Larry and Magic retired, the lost art of passing — that elusive team game — went with them."

They are occupied with their growing families now. After Barcelona, the Johnsons adopted a baby girl, Elisa, to join E.J. and Andre, Magic's adult son from a previous relationship. When the family seeks privacy, they sneak off to their elegant oceanfront home in Dana Point, California.

After Barcelona, the Birds also adopted a baby girl, Mariah. She has matched her father's competitive spirit, competing in track and field with the same intensity her father brought to the hardwood.

When the Birds want to escape, they retreat to their ranch in Indiana, with trails for four-wheeling, lakes for fishing, and 100 acres just waiting to be mowed.

Although their children are similar in age, the families do not vacation together. They do not exchange obligatory Christmas cards. When Magic and Larry see each other during the NBA season, the greetings are warm and genuine, but their interaction is fleeting.

It does not matter. As the years roll on, the connection remains unbroken. When the game belonged to them, Magic and Larry shared a bond predicated on fierce competition. Now, with their legacies intact — and forever linked — none of the animosity lingers.

Only respect remains.

CAREER STATISTICS

Larry Bird
....

HIGH SCHOOL: Springs Valley, French Lick, Indiana

COLLEGE: Indiana State University

DRAFTED BY: Boston Celtics, 1978 (sixth overall)

CAREER ACCOMPLISHMENTS: NBA champion (1981, 1984, 1986);
NBA Finals MVP (1984, 1986); NBA MVP (1984, 1985, 1986);
nine-time All-NBA First Team (1980–88); All-NBA Second Team
(1990); All-Defensive Second Team (1982, 1983, 1984); 12-time
All-Star; All-Star MVP (1982); NBA Rookie of the Year (1980);
Olympic gold medalist (1992); co-captain (with Magic Johnson) of
U.S. Olympic Team; elected to Naismith Memorial Basketball Hall
of Fame (1998).

ABBREVIATIONS

APG	Assists Per Game	MIN	Total Minutes
AST	Total Assists	MPG	Minutes Per Game
BLK	Total Blocks	PF	Personal Fouls
BPG	Blocks Per Game	PPG	Points Per Game
FG	Field Goals	RPG	Rebounds Per Game
FGM-A	Field Goals Made–Field Goals Attempted	SPG	Steals Per Game
		STL	Total Steals
FT	Free Throws	3PM-A	Three-Pointers Made–Three-Pointers Attempted
FTM-A	Free Throws Made–Free Throws Attempted		
		TO	Turnovers
G	Games		

CAREER STATISTICS

YEAR	G	MPG	FG%	3P%	FT%	REBOUNDS			APG	SPG	BPG	TO	PF	PPG
						OFF	DEF	RPG						
79-80	82	36.0	0.474	0.406	0.836	2.6	7.8	10.4	4.5	1.74	0.65	3.21	3.4	21.3
80-81	82	39.5	0.478	0.270	0.863	2.3	8.6	10.9	5.5	1.96	0.77	3.52	2.9	21.2
81-82	77	38.0	0.503	0.212	0.863	2.6	8.3	10.9	5.8	1.86	0.86	3.30	3.2	22.9
82-83	79	37.7	0.504	0.286	0.840	2.4	8.6	11.0	5.8	1.87	0.90	3.04	2.5	23.6
83-84	79	38.3	0.492	0.247	0.888	2.3	7.8	10.1	6.6	1.82	0.87	3.00	2.5	24.2
84-85	80	39.5	0.522	0.427	0.882	2.1	8.5	10.5	6.6	1.61	1.23	3.10	2.6	28.7
85-86	82	38.0	0.496	0.423	0.896	2.3	7.5	9.8	6.8	2.02	0.62	3.24	2.2	25.8
86-87	74	40.6	0.525	0.400	0.910	1.7	7.5	9.2	7.6	1.82	0.95	3.24	2.5	28.1
87-88	76	39.0	0.527	0.414	0.916	1.4	7.8	9.3	6.1	1.64	0.75	2.80	2.1	29.9
88-89	6	31.5	0.471	0.000	0.947	0.2	6.0	6.2	4.8	1.00	0.83	1.83	3.0	19.3
89-90	75	39.3	0.473	0.333	0.930	1.2	8.3	9.5	7.5	1.41	0.81	3.24	2.3	24.3
90-91	60	38.0	0.454	0.389	0.891	0.9	7.6	8.5	7.2	1.80	0.97	3.12	2.0	19.4
91-92	45	36.9	0.466	0.406	0.926	1.0	8.6	9.6	6.8	0.93	0.73	2.78	1.8	20.2
Career	897	38.4	0.496	0.376	0.886	2.0	8.0	10.0	6.3	1.73	0.84	3.14	2.5	24.3
Playoff	164	42.0	0.472	0.321	0.890	2.2	8.1	10.3	6.5	1.80	0.88	3.09	2.8	23.8
All-Star	10	28.7	0.423	0.231	0.844	1.9	6.0	7.9	4.1	2.30	0.30	3.10	2.8	13.4

CAREER TOTALS

YEAR	MIN	FGM-A	3PM-A	FTM-A	REBOUNDS			AST	STL	BLK	TO	PF	PTS
					OFF	DEF	TOT						
79–80	2,955	693–1,463	58–143	301–360	216	636	852	370	143	53	263	279	1,745
80–81	3,239	719–1,503	20–74	283–328	191	704	895	451	161	63	289	239	1,741
81–82	2,923	711–1,414	11–52	328–380	200	637	837	447	143	66	254	244	1,761
82–83	2,982	747–1,481	22–77	351–418	193	677	870	458	148	71	240	197	1,867
83–84	3,028	758–1,542	18–73	374–421	181	615	796	520	144	69	237	197	1,908
84–85	3,161	918–1,760	56–131	403–457	164	678	842	531	129	98	248	208	2,295
85–86	3,113	796–1,606	82–194	441–492	190	615	805	557	166	51	266	182	2,115
86–87	3,005	786–1,497	90–225	414–455	124	558	682	566	135	70	240	185	2,076
87–88	2,965	881–1,672	98–237	415–453	108	595	703	467	125	57	213	157	2,275
88–89	189	49–104	0–0	18–19	1	36	37	29	6	5	11	18	116
89–90	2,944	718–1,517	65–195	319–343	90	622	712	562	106	61	243	173	1,820
90–91	2,277	462–1,017	77–198	163–183	53	456	509	431	108	58	187	118	1,164
91–92	1,662	353–758	52–128	150–162	46	388	434	306	42	33	125	82	908
Career	34,443	8,591–17,334	649–1,727	3,960–4,471	1,757	7,217	8,974	5,695	1,556	755	2,816	2,279	21,791
Playoff	6,886	1,458–3,090	80–249	901–1,012	360	1,323	1,683	1,062	296	145	506	466	3,897
All-Star	287	52–123	3–13	27–32	19	60	79	41	23	3	31	28	134

CAREER STATISTICS

Earvin "Magic" Johnson

....

HIGH SCHOOL: Everett, Lansing, Michigan

COLLEGE: Michigan State University

DRAFTED BY: Los Angeles Lakers, 1979 (first overall)

CAREER ACCOMPLISHMENTS: NBA champion (1980, 1982, 1985, 1987, 1988); NBA Finals MVP (1980, 1982, 1987); NBA MVP (1987, 1989, 1990); nine-time All-NBA First Team (1983–91); All-NBA Second Team (1982); 12-time All-Star; All-Star MVP (1990, 1992); Olympic gold medalist (1992); co-captain (with Larry Bird) of U.S. Olympic Team; elected to Naismith Memorial Basketball Hall of Fame (2002).

ABBREVIATIONS

APG	Assists Per Game	MIN	Total Minutes
AST	Total Assists	MPG	Minutes Per Game
BLK	Total Blocks	PF	Personal Fouls
BPG	Blocks Per Game	PPG	Points Per Game
FG	Field Goals	RPG	Rebounds Per Game
FGM–A	Field Goals Made–	SPG	Steals Per Game
	Field Goals Attempted	STL	Total Steals
FT	Free Throws	3PM–A	Three-Pointers Made–
FTM–A	Free Throws Made–		Three-Pointers Attempted
	Free Throws Attempted	TO	Turnovers
G	Games		

CAREER STATISTICS

Magic Johnson, Los Angeles Lakers

YEAR	G	MPG	FG%	3P%	FT%	REBOUNDS OFF	DEF	RPG	APG	SPG	BPG	TO	PF	PPG
79–80	77	36.3	0.530	0.226	0.810	2.1	5.6	7.7	7.3	2.43	0.53	3.96	2.8	18.0
80–81	37	37.1	0.532	0.176	0.760	2.7	5.9	8.6	8.6	3.43	0.73	3.86	2.7	21.6
81–82	78	38.3	0.537	0.207	0.760	3.2	6.4	9.6	9.5	2.67	0.44	3.67	2.8	18.6
82–83	79	36.8	0.548	0.000	0.800	2.7	5.9	8.6	10.5	2.23	0.59	3.81	2.5	16.8
83–84	67	38.3	0.565	0.207	0.810	1.5	5.8	7.3	13.1	2.24	0.73	4.57	2.5	17.6
84–85	77	36.1	0.561	0.189	0.843	1.2	5.0	6.2	12.6	1.47	0.32	3.96	2.0	18.3
85–86	72	35.8	0.526	0.233	0.871	1.2	4.7	5.9	12.6	1.57	0.22	3.79	1.8	18.8
86–87	80	36.3	0.522	0.205	0.848	1.5	4.8	6.3	12.2	1.73	0.45	3.75	2.1	23.9
87–88	72	36.6	0.492	0.190	0.853	1.2	5.0	6.2	12	1.58	0.18	3.74	2.0	19.6
88–89	77	37.5	0.509	0.310	0.911	1.4	6.4	7.8	12.8	1.79	0.29	4.05	2.2	22.5
89–90	79	37.2	0.480	0.384	0.890	1.6	5.0	6.6	11.5	1.67	0.43	3.66	2.1	22.3
90–91	79	37.1	0.477	0.320	0.906	1.3	5.7	7.0	12.5	1.29	0.22	3.97	1.9	19.4
91–95						Did not play — retired								
95–96	32	30	0.466	0.379	0.856	1.2	4.5	5.7	6.9	0.81	0.41	3.21	1.5	14.6
Career	906	38.4	0.496	0.303	0.848	1.7	5.5	7.2	11.2	1.73	0.41	3.87	2.3	19.5
Playoff	190	39.7	0.506	0.241	0.838	1.8	5.9	7.7	12.3	1.88	0.34	3.66	2.8	19.5
All-Star	11	30.1	0.489	0.476	0.905	1.9	3.3	5.2	11.5	1.90	0.64	4.36	2.3	16.0

CAREER TOTALS

Magic Johnson, Los Angeles Lakers

YEAR	MIN	FGM-A	3PM-A	FTM-A	REBOUNDS OFF	DEF	TOT	AST	STL	BLK	TO	PF	PTS
79–80	2,795	503-949	7-31	374-462	166	430	596	563	187	41	305	218	1,387
80–81	1,371	312-587	3-17	171-225	101	219	320	317	127	27	143	100	798
81–82	2,991	556-1,036	6-29	329-433	252	499	751	743	208	34	286	223	1,447
82–83	2,907	511-933	0-21	304-380	214	469	683	829	176	47	301	200	1,326
83–84	2,567	441-780	6-29	290-358	99	392	491	875	150	49	306	169	1,178
84–85	2,781	504-899	7-37	391-464	90	386	476	968	113	25	305	155	1,406
85–86	2,578	483-918	10-43	378-434	85	341	426	907	113	16	273	133	1,354
86–87	2,904	683-1,308	8-39	535-631	122	382	504	977	138	36	300	168	1,909
87–88	2,637	490-996	11-56	417-489	88	361	449	858	114	13	269	147	1,408
88–89	2,886	579-1,137	59-188	513-563	111	496	607	988	138	22	312	172	1,730
89–90	2,937	546-1,138	106-276	567-637	128	394	522	907	132	34	289	167	1,765
90–91	2,933	466-976	80-250	519-573	105	446	551	989	102	17	314	150	1,531
91–95					Did not play — retired								
95–96	958	137-294	22-58	172-201	40	143	183	220	26	13	103	48	468
Career	34,443	6,211-11,951	325-1,074	4,960-5,850	1,601	4,958	6,559	10,141	1,724	374	3,506	2,050	17,707
Playoff	7,538	1,291-2,552	51-212	1,068-1,274	349	1,116	1,465	2,346	358	64	696	525	3,701
All-Star	331	64-131	10-21	38-42	21	36	57	127	21	7	48	25	176

ACKNOWLEDGMENTS

I'd like to thank my editor, Susan Canavan, whose guidance and support during this project were invaluable. There's no doubt — you made this a better book. Thanks to Jill Leone, Lon Rosen, and Jay Mandel for keeping all of us on course, which was no small task. Many people assisted me in researching this book, among them Jeff Twiss, Brian Olive, and Heather Walker of the Celtics; John Black of the Lakers; Craig Miller of USA Basketball; former Converse executives Gib Ford and Lou Nagy; and the unparalleled NBA duo of Brian McIntyre and Tim Frank. My gratitude to Ed Kleven for dotting the *i*'s and crossing the *t*'s. Thanks to Ian Thomsen, Leigh Montville, Steve Fainaru, Don Skwar, and Todd Balf; I value your journalistic insight and, more important, your friendship. Thanks to the Westford moms for getting my kids where they needed to be, especially Eileen Barrett and Monet Ewing. A shout out to the Ya Yas — where would I be without you? Lifelong thanks to Janice McKeown and Jane Cavanaugh Smith, who have been there since the beginning. Stephanie Baird and Liz Douglas have been excellent sounding boards and cherished friends. Thanks to the Sunday morning basketball crew for all the Good Things they provide. To my parents, Margarethe and Fred MacMullan, to Sue, Vinny, Julia and Christopher Titone, and all the Boyles, far and near, much love and thanks. To Michael Boyle, an incredible husband and father, I can never thank you enough for your love and support and patience. My children, Alyson and Douglas, find a new way each day to fill my life with joy. Thanks, kids. I love you. And finally I'd like to offer my gratitude to Earvin Johnson and Larry Bird. I'm honored to have helped you tell your story.

JACKIE MacMULLAN

INDEX